Issue

The Debate on the French Revolution

MANCHESTER
1824

Manchester University Press

Issues in Historiography
General editor
R. C. RICHARDSON
University of Winchester

Already published

The Debate on the Norman Conquest
Marjorie Chibnall

The Debate on the English Revolution
R. C. Richardson

The Debate on the American Civil War Era
H. A. Tulloch

The Debate on Black Civil Rights in America
Kevern Verney

The Debate on the Rise of the British Empire
Anthony Webster

Issues in Historiography

The Debate
on the French Revolution

PETER DAVIES

MANCHESTER
UNIVERSITY PRESS

MANCHESTER AND NEW YORK

distributed exclusively in the USA by Palgrave

The right of Peter Davies to be identified as the author of this work has been
asserted by him in accordance with the Copyright, Designs and Patents Act 1988.

Published by Manchester University Press
Oxford Road, Manchester M13 9NR, UK
and Room 400, 175 Fifth Avenue, New York, NY 10010, USA
www.manchesteruniversitypress.co.uk

Distributed exclusively in the USA by
Palgrave, 175 Fifth Avenue, New York,
NY 10010, USA

Distributed exclusively in Canada by
UBC Press, University of British Columbia, 2029 West Mall,
Vancouver, BC, Canada V6T 1Z2

British Library Cataloguing-in-Publication Data
A catalogue record for this book is available from the British Library

Library of Congress Cataloging-in-Publication Data applied for

ISBN 0 7190 7176 3 *hardback*
EAN 978 0 7190 7176 8

ISBN 0 7190 7177 1 *paperback*
EAN 978 0 7190 7177 5

First published 2006

15 14 13 12 11 10 09 08 07 06   10 9 8 7 6 5 4 3 2 1

Typeset by Action Publishing Technology Ltd, Gloucester
Printed in Great Britain by Bell & Bain Ltd, Glasgow

I noticed tonight

That the world has been turning

Keane, *Can't Stop Now* ('Hopes and Fears', 2004)

To my wonderful, amazing Grandma who passed
away just before this book was published

CONTENTS

General editor's foreword   *page* ix
Preface   xiii

Introduction: competing interpretations   1

1   Immediate responses: for and against   9

Part I Nineteenth century

2   The liberal perspective   35

3   Idealist and romantic views   51

4   Tocqueville   73

5   Third Republic historians   90

Part II Twentieth century

6   Marxist 'orthodoxy'   111

7   'Soft revisionism'   134

8   'Hard revisionism'   151

9   Bicentenary re-evaluations   169

Postscript   192
Further reading   199
Index   201

GENERAL EDITOR'S FOREWORD

History without historiography is a contradiction in terms. No historian writes in isolation from the work of his or her predecessors nor can the writer – however clinically objective in intention – stand aloof from the insistent pressures, priorities and demands of the ever-changing present. Though historians address the past as their subject they always do so in ways that are shaped – consciously or unconsciously as the case may be – by the society and systems of their own day, and they communicate their findings in ways which are specifically intelligible and relevant to a reading public consisting of their own contemporaries. For these reasons the study of history is concerned most fundamentally not with dead facts and sterile, permanent verdicts but with highly charged dialogues, disagreements and controversies among its presenters, and with the changing methodologies and discourse of the subject over time. *Issues in Historiography* is a series designed to explore such matters by means of case studies of key moments in world history and the interpretations and reinterpretations they have engendered.

Few upheavals in any country's history have been more momentous, dislodging and controversial than the French Revolution of the late eighteenth century. It divided France and Europe at the time and has gone on divisively reverberating ever since. The bicentennial in 1989 showed how very topical this subject still was; it positively refuses to be consigned to a past that is 'over'. The Revolution's impact on France is indelible; it permanently changed the country. This critical stage of France's past is still very much part of France's present. (That the conservative Vendée region stood aloof from the 1989 celebrations is no less eloquent testimony to some of the still unhealed wounds of a Revolution that was also a bitter, brutal civil war). Peter Davies's book vividly brings the subject of the French Revolution to life, highlighting in a very clear and accessible way the successive phases of the historiography of this densely structured subject, the key players in the ongoing debate, the different 'schools' to which they belonged, the changing political and ideological context which surrounded and impinged on them, and the passionate subjectivity with which so many of them wrote. Liberals, romantics, conservatives, Marxists, revisionists and post-revisionists are all systematically examined here. Key individual figures in the historiography such as Madame de Staël, Thiers, Guizot, Michelet, Taine, Jaurès, Aulard, Lefebvre, Soboul and Furet are properly positioned and assessed; Tocqueville, author of the seminal *L'Ancien Régime et la Révolution Française* (1856), appropriately, gets a whole chapter to himself. Different depictions of the role of the 'people' as well as the leaders come out clearly and, in the handling of more recent treatments of the Revolution, the increasing attention given to Counter Revolution, to regional variations in revolutionary experience, and to women's histories are all foregrounded. The coverage is principally French, but by no means wholly so. The different interventions of British historians such as Carlyle, Macaulay, Acton, Cobban (the most influential modern revisionist), Hampson, Rudé and Cobb are insightfully discussed. So are those of American historians Palmer, Taylor, Baker, Lynn Hunt and Joan Landes. (As Davies makes clear, the work of the last two writers, along with that of Olwen Hufton in Britain, provides a welcome indicator that the historiography of this subject is belatedly becoming less male dominated).

This is a book which, quite demonstrably, fills a major gap and will help students make sense of the complex events and trends of the French Revolution and the different ways in which they have been interpreted and judged. It also, by extension, links with other volumes in this same series. The English Revolution of the mid-seventeenth century (already represented in the *Issues* series) and the French Revolution of the late eighteenth century have historiographies which in so many ways are intertwined. Some of the writers discussed in Davies's book – Guizot, Marx and Macaulay – also wrote about seventeenth-century England; Guizot, indeed, coined the label 'English Revolution'. George Lefebvre's *Quatre Vingt Neuf* (1939) – published in German-occupied France at the start of the Second World War and commemorating the 150th anniversary of the outbreak of the French Revolution – easily invites comparison with Christopher Hill's *The English Revolution* (1940) – which appeared in Battle of Britain year and marked the 300th anniversary of England's great upheavals. (No less significant in a completely different way was Margaret Thatcher's attempt in 1989 both to downplay the significance of the French Revolution and to ignore the English Revolution). Future volumes in this series on the American and Russian Revolutions now being prepared will open up other points of contact in revolutionary ideology and experience and in the historiography of revolution. The 'anatomy of revolution', as Crane Brinton's trail-blazing comparative study of that name (1938) long since taught us to recognise, can be a rewarding subject.

R. C. Richardson

PREFACE

When I was officially invited to write this volume, I passed on the news to one of my colleagues at the University of Huddersfield, who specialises in a completely different historical period. He was visibly impressed. 'I'd certainly be flattered if I had been asked to write an *Issues in Historiography* book for MUP.' Clearly, the reputation of the series is extremely high.

Writing this book has been an enjoyable and fascinating experience and I have learnt a lot. I would like to thank Professor Roger Richardson, the Series Editor, for his support, and everyone at Manchester University Press for their help and assistance. Thanks too to all the students at the University of Huddersfield who have taken the Year 3 module, The French Revolution. I have thoroughly enjoyed the seminar discussions, and they have really helped me to clarify my own thoughts about the history and historiography of the event.

The story of the Revolution is an endlessly stimulating subject, and over recent years I have come to appreciate the fact that the historiography of the Revolution is also a highly stimulating topic.

INTRODUCTION: COMPETING INTERPRETATIONS

Much of the problem with studying the French revolution involves sorting through what others have said about it.[1]

It is an oft-quoted tale but when, in the middle of the twentieth century, Chinese revolutionary leader Zhou Enlai was asked to judge the significance of the French Revolution, he replied: 'It's too early to say.'

This is a hackneyed story, but so far as this book is concerned, it reveals an essential truth. In many contexts, the significance of the Revolution has been immeasurable. Without even mentioning the arguments that historians have involved themselves in since, it is clear that 1789 was à watershed. The political map of France changed forever, and there are regions that, in 2006, would still define themselves as being 'anti-Revolution' – the Vendée for one. Likewise, mention of the Revolution is never far away when rival politicians get together, whether in private or in the media. Ever since the *Alternance* of 1981, the Socialist Party has made great show of its allegiance to the 'rights of man' as a concept and as the basis for practical political action. Equally, those on the right, most notably the Front National of Jean-Marie Le Pen, have used the Revolution as a reference point: an event, an era, an idea that has been blackened and demonised to such an extent that many on the right and far right would like editors of school text-books to reappraise the way in which it is presented to children.

Lest we forget, it was the Revolution, and the National Assembly it established, that gave birth to the terms 'left' and 'right' – the terms denoted the location of (radical) Jacobin and (moderate) Girondin deputies when they gathered to debate the issues of the day in the Assembly building.

One school of thought says that the written word was a fundamental cause of the Revolution. The *philosophes* of the eighteenth century had developed their enlightened and reformist ideas in an array of important publications, including pamphlets,

1

tracts, treatises and encyclopedias and, at the other end of the spectrum, the hacks who plied their trade on Grub Street also put their ideas down on paper, albeit in a less sophisticated way.

In the days leading up to the Revolution, as well as during its early years, more and more ideas were articulated on paper. Sieyès led the way with his provocative treatise, *What is the Third Estate?*, an army of pamphleteers sought to influence events with their rough-and-ready scribblings, and serious writers like Arthur Young also joined in. By 1795 three constitutions had been published, to add to the *Declaration of the Rights of Man and of the Citizen* which had been published hastily by the revolutionaries in the autumn of 1789. It would not be long before commentators and essayists entered the fray, with weighty, polemically-charged works. Edmund Burke, Joseph de Maistre and Madame de Staël were three of the most famous 'early' observers. But neither the Irishman, the Savoyard, nor the Frenchwoman would have said that they were 'historians' in the traditional sense, or that they were actually trying to write 'history'. How could they when the dust had hardly settled on the Revolution and when all three were 'involved', to some degree at least, in the events of the revolutionary era? In addition, none had access to orthodox historical sources, and what is more, none actually wanted this! Instead, they each wrote extremely partisan commentaries on the Revolution, published in 1790, 1796 and 1818 respectively.

So, if revolutionary historiography has an 'embryonic stage' it is the period in which Burke, de Maistre and de Staël were delivering their near contemporary verdicts. It was impossible in practical terms for the Revolution to have its historians while it was still deciding on its own resting place, and if we are to believe the modern line on these things, it would have been impossible, anyway, for the Revolution to acquire its own *genuine* historians in the three decades following 1789.[2] Thus, the first chapter of this book deals with the 'pre-historiography' of the Revolution, the immediate responses, with Burke, de Maistre and de Staël the focus.

Thereafter, two 'family lines' start to emerge. The 'Great Tradition', or 'classical' tradition (as historians of the republican school preferred), denotes that group of historians who viewed the Revolution as a positive, pioneering and patriotic phenomenon.[3] It was a 'good thing', something to be lauded and upheld, something unique and path-breaking, something that was as radical and revolutionary as its most fervent supporters would have us believe. There was nothing monolithic about this way of thinking – there was room for Marxists and non-Marxists – but in time, another 'family' started to emerge, enveloping historians like Tocqueville, who were slightly ambiguous in their interpretation, and Taine, who was downright hostile. Throw in the 'soft' and 'hard' revisionists of the late-twentieth century (Cobban, Furet *et al.*) and you have a genuine alternative to the established tradition.

The legacy of 1789 was given further, irreversible momentum when the first sources and archives were made available and the first *trained* historians turned their attention to its meaning and significance. This book deals with the various types of revolutionary history and the various schools of historical thought on the Revolution. The structure of the book is similar to the other books in the *Issues in Historiography* series. The survey of writings is, at the same time, both 'chronological' and 'thematic' – essentially, a vertical cross-section of historians from the centuries containing the original events to the present day. Occasionally there may be some (necessary) overlap between chapters, but this has been kept to a minimum.

The first two chapters examine the earliest theorising on the subject: by non-historians who were chiefly interested in scoring political points (Chapter 1) and the 'grandparents' of revolutionary historiography, the liberal writers, Mignet and Thiers (Chapter 2). We will then deal with a tranche of nineteenth-century historians: those who put forward epic, idealist and romantic interpretations (Chapter 3) and those who responded to the dawn of the Third Republic by revisiting the events of 1789 and the revolutionary decade (Chapter 5). Sandwiched in between is an in-depth examination of the work of Alexis de Tocqueville, possibly the most celebrated French historian of modern times (Chapter 4).

In the early and middle decades of the twentieth century, the 'Great Tradition' of revolutionary historiography was hijacked by a cohort of leftist writers including Jean Jaurès, Albert Mathiez, Georges Lefebvre and Albert Soboul. The way in which they delineated a 'bourgeois revolution' occurring in 1790s France was a defining moment in the history of revolutionary studies. What is more, they put their case in such a concerted and convincing manner that the left-wing, Marxist interpretation of the Revolution gradually came to be regarded as the historical orthodoxy. For decades the monolith that was 'Marxist orthodoxy' remained untouched and untouchable. Until, that is, the British historian Alfred Cobban sought to revise the main tenets of the Jaurès-Mathiez-Lefebvre-Soboul school. His 'non-Marxist social' interpretation opened up what had, until then, been something of a barren, no-go area. Cobban's 'soft revisionism' – he had dared to challenge the Marxist view, but had not strayed from socioeconomic theorising – was complemented, later, by a body of work known as 'hard revisionism'. Here François Furet and others had gone even further and moved into the very un-Marxist arena of politics and political history.

By 1989 and the all-embracing Bicentenary celebrations, the historiographical field had been opened up so much that it was impossible to speak with any certainty about any kind of new 'orthodoxy' at all. The fact that the decade and a half following the Bicentenary offered up its own hotch-potch of theorising merely confirmed this.

It would be difficult to disagree with the view which says that the French Revolution is one of the most *complex*, and also one of the most *analysed*, historical events. From his standpoint as a revisionist, Cobban says that, over the decades, interpretations have tended to fall into two main categories – either 'conspiracy' or 'destiny'.[4] Those hostile to the Revolution do tend to view it as some kind of 'plot' or 'punishment' meted out on France, while those more favourable can sometimes get carried away by the inevitability and wonder of 1789. But the real question is this: why has the Revolution provoked so many widely differing interpretations? Before we begin our era-by-era examination of revolutionary historiography, it is probably worth grappling with this fundamentally important question. There are a number of angles we could take on this issue.

First, the rich tapestry of revolutionary historiography reflects, and almost imitates, the kaleidoscopic nature of France's history of revolutions. Over the last two centuries the French political landscape has been ever-changing. There have been absolute monarchies, constitutional monarchies, republics and empires – and this has meant that, on occasions, historians attached to a specific regime have considered the period 1789–99 from a partisan point of view, with the intention of scoring political points. Thus, we have to treat the views of historians with more caution and scepticism than is perhaps usual. As Norman Hampson, another revisionist, wrote in the mid-1980s:

> In 1989 historians throughout the world will be celebrating the bicentenary of the French Revolution. The Revolution itself was an immensely divisive experience, splitting Frenchmen into royalists and republicans, Catholics and anticlericals, in ways that have survived until the present day. It was the legacy of these revolutionary conflicts, more than the consequences of industrialization and urbanization, that made France a very difficult country to govern in the nineteenth century. Naturally enough, the history of a revolution that left such deep fissures in French society has reflected the divisions that it set out to explain. French historians saw themselves as crusaders for political causes in their own times that perpetuated the conflicts of the revolutionary period. Defending a particular point of view about the French Revolution was one way of legitimising the monarchy before 1848, or the Republic in 1848 and again after 1870, or the Empire from 1851 to 1870.[5]

In this sense, the Revolution, and its interpretations, cannot be detached from France's post-revolutionary history.

Second, there is the event itself. It was not just radical – putting an end to centuries of arbitrary, absolutist rule – but also complex.[6] In essence, the 'Revolution' comprised three 'mini-revolutions': the liberal revolt (1789–91), the illiberal interlude (1792–94), and the reversion to moderation (1794–99). So, when historians come to examine the event, they can either become fascinated by its evolving trajectory or blinkered by one particular phase with which they seek to identify themselves. Either way, there is a compulsion to discover more.

There has also been a range of complicating factors. 'When did the French Revolution end?' This question has dogged historians throughout the nineteenth and twentieth centuries, and has not made it easy for them to interpret the period with clarity. If the French Revolution was a 'continual process', and if its 'outcome' was still in doubt throughout the nineteenth century (as many contemporaries believed), it was surely inevitable that the job of the historian would take on a new dimension.

One conclusion that we can arrive at straight away – before we have even begun – is that historians have been, and still are, key players in the French political drama. The French Revolution, perhaps more than any other historical event, has provoked and challenged historians. Noel Parker, for one, talks about the advancing 'status' of historians in nineteenth-century France, and perhaps this is no coincidence.[6] The Revolution and its aftermath almost *forced* France to grapple with, and analyse, its past.

Sometimes it is dangerous to attach 'labels' to historians, but as we reflect on two hundred years of historical writings it is possible to delineate some general positions. 'Liberal' historians emphasised the progressive gains of 1789 and sought to rescue these from the wreckage of the Terror. 'Conservative' historians played on the 'extreme' and 'anarchical' nature of the Revolution, and argued that, in breaking with 'tradition', it brought terrible consequences to France. Meanwhile, 'radical', 'left-wing' historians upheld 1793 as a significant achievement; moreover, those with Marxist sympathies argued that the Revolution was fundamentally 'bourgeois' in nature, and thus fits in neatly with Marx's 'scientific' interpretation of history. In and amongst there have been 'republican' and 'counter-revolutionary' historians; historians interested in 'regional' perspectives on the Revolution, in the 'ideological' and 'philosophical' background, and in interpretations 'from above' and 'from below'. And, as we have already noted, there have also been 'revisionist' historians – those who sought to throw cold water on the Marxist 'orthodoxy' that began to emerge in the middle of the twentieth century. And that is not forgetting the many and various historians on whom it has been almost impossible to affix a label.

There is another way in which we can classify historians. Do they interpret the Revolution as a battle between bourgeoisie and aristocracy or between 'ordered society' and 'mob rule'? Or between other forces? Was there one revolution or several? Was the revolutionary decade primarily about politics or economics? Or something else? Do they focus on the origins of the

Revolution, its meaning and significance, or its legacy? Further, we should be aware that many non-historians have contributed to our understanding of the Revolution (for example, Burke, de Maistre, Chateaubriand, Hugo, Scott, Macaulay, Dickens, Herder, Condorcet, Comte, de Tracy and St Simon). Also, even though most historians of the Revolution have been French, there has been something quite distinctive about the contribution of Anglo-American writers to the debate. We deal with both of these issues in the course of the book.

Finally, there are two stories that make important points. On a recent trip to Paris I met up with a group of French friends. We sat down for dinner and started chatting. I was expecting a conversation about football or music, but instead one chap said to another: 'Jean, let me ask you a hypothetical question: If we were transported back in time two hundred years, and you were alive in Paris during the 1790s, which political grouping would you have been loyal to? Would you have been a Girondin or Jacobin? A Feuillant or Hébertist?' I was astonished, and also fascinated, by what I was hearing. In contemporary France, the Revolution is still a live topic for debate, even among young twenty-somethings who have only had personal experience of the modern Fifth Republic. Amazing!

It is also possible for us to adapt a tale that is told about professionals involved in another academic discipline. For surely, if you placed a hundred historians of the Revolution in a room together, and asked for opinions about the event, you would probably be hard pushed to find more than one advancing the same interpretation. This is more than likely true, but even so it will not distract us from the task in hand – to detect patterns and connections in two centuries of historiography, and to trace the emergence of individual schools of historical research across this period.

This book takes its place in the *Issues in Historiography* series published by Manchester University Press. Like other titles – *The Debate on the English Revolution* (Prof. R.C. Richardson), *The Debate on the Norman Conquest* (Dr Marjorie Chibnall) and *The Debate on the American Civil War Era* (Dr Hugh Tulloch) – *The Debate on the French Revolution* explores all aspects of the Revolution's historiography. It aims to identify and explore the main areas of debate, link them to the context in which the debate took place, and examine some of the principal tendencies in research and writing on the subject.

This book is not an anthology or reader, or a history of the Revolution. Rather, it is a history of histories. It focuses on those individuals who are generally perceived to be the 'major' or 'pre-eminent' figures within revolutionary historiography. There is a surprising degree of consensus on this matter. But the book delves into some obscure areas, and considers some of the 'minor' figures as well. In each chapter the aim is the same: to unpack the ideas of the key historians, to discover what they said about the Revolution and how they said it. We quote extensively from each writer in an attempt to understand and comprehend their specific perspective on 1789. We are also interested in the reaction to their ideas – at the time and later.

The series as a whole is aimed at undergraduate students, and *The Debate on the French Revolution* is crafted likewise. For those students studying the French Revolution as part of a survey module on modern French history or world revolutions, or for those students studying the French Revolution as a special subject, this book is an ideal starting point. In a rigorous but concise style, this book considers the main eras and phases of historiography. The main objective is to capture the essence of the 'Great Tradition', to explore the controversy surrounding it, and to illuminate the state of the debate in the early years of the twenty-first century.

Notes

1 G. Kates (ed.), *The French Revolution* (London, 1998), p. 1.
2 Convention and the 'Thirty Year Rule' in Britain seem to dictate that this is the 'rule of thumb'.
3 Note on definitions: The 'Great Tradition' is the term used generally to describe the set of pro-Revolution interpretations that have emerged over the last two centuries. There is some overlap with the 'classical' tradition which normally covers historians from the 'republican' school.
4 A. Cobban, *Aspects of the French Revolution* (London, 1971), p. 36.
5 www.nybooks.com/articles/article-preview?article_id=4405.
6 N. Parker, *Portrayals of Revolution* (Hemel Hempstead, 1990), p. 115.

1

Immediate responses: for and against

France, by the perfidy of her leaders, has utterly disgraced the tone of lenient council in the cabinets of princes, and disarmed it of its most potent topics.[1]

Our first task is to spotlight the earliest interpretations of the Revolution; these emanated from intellectuals, politicians and writers who, literally, found themselves caught up in events. They all felt the need to 'understand' what was going on around them.

Arguably the two famous treatises were Edmund Burke, *Reflections on the Revolution in France* (1790) and Joseph de Maistre, *Considerations on France* (1796). Burke and de Maistre were giants among early writers, and interestingly, perhaps significantly, neither was French. Burke was Irish and de Maistre a Savoyard. This gave them a unique perspective on French affairs. They were close to events, but also detached. They were interested in France, but they were not French, neither did they reside in France. They did not have to wrestle with French patriotism or national loyalty in their writings, and their work is probably all the better – and all the better to analyse – for this.

Perhaps it was also significant that the titles of the two works were quite similar. As words, *reflections* and *considerations* are quite 'neutral' and do not give much away, but in the case of the two volumes mentioned above, they hide the fact that both Burke and de Maistre had serious and substantive criticisms of the Revolution and the revolutionaries. All writers and intellectuals were to some extent *involved* in the Revolution; they *had* to be, it was impossible for them not to be. For conservatives like Burke and de Maistre, the situation was stark. The world was changing before their very eyes and it would have been very strange if they had ignored French events and their implications.

Predictably, most of the early commentators approached the Revolution from the right. They had been provoked into writing by the 'evils' of 1789 and the 'disaster' it had brought upon France. Almost without exception, these early writers – people like Bonald, Chateaubriand, Lamennais, Mallet du Pan, Rivarol and Barruél – regarded the Revolution as a 'bad' thing, as an 'abomination', and as something to be opposed and countered at every opportunity. But there were also writers like Thomas Paine, a passionate liberal, and Arthur Young, a travelling economist, who observed the Revolution from a different vantage point. They were English too, and this could not help but affect the tone of their observations.

It should be pointed out that, as events progressed through the 1790s, it would have been absurd, and also technically impossible, for any writer – French or otherwise – to set to work on any kind of history of the Revolution. That is not to say that these early writers were historians or indeed *saw themselves* as historians in any sense. They were not and they did not. They were writers, often polemicists, with a partisan point to make. They did not base themselves in archives, or consult an array of sources. They just wrote spontaneously. Little daylight separated them from the events they were writing about. They were the equivalent, in modern-day terms, of the pundits and serious commentators who pop up in the media, with a considered take on the events of the day. They wanted to understand, comprehend, and also to opine. And of course they set a fashion, being the first of many writers to be dominated by the Revolution. In time, 'historians' would displace 'writers', though that is not to say that the early historians of the Revolution resembled later historians in their attitude to sources, for many confined themselves to gossip, innuendo and hearsay and placed very little premium on the sources. For the record, it is generally agreed that the first conventional history of the Revolution was Madame de Staël's *Considerations on the Main Events of the French Revolution*, published in 1818.

This chapter considers a number of issues: How did the first commentators view the Revolution? What motivated them in their writings? And what kind of impact did they have?

Edmund Burke was born on 12 January 1729. He spent his formative years in the city of his birth, Dublin, but moved to London in 1750 to pursue a legal career. Burke is variously described as political thinker, statesman and parliamentarian but significantly *not* as a historian. In political terms, Burke had liberal tendencies, but is widely viewed as one of the founding fathers of conservatism as an ideology or school of thought. That is not to say that his ideas were either politically coherent or systemised, but they did have a profound influence.

His attitude to the English Revolution is symptomatic of his broader political outlook. He applauds the way in which this revolution took great care to preserve, conserve and consolidate key elements of the past rather than dramatically break with them. When he comes to examine the French Revolution, he cannot but compare and contrast. He finds it impossible to tolerate or condone what he sees as the violence and barbarism of the 1790s, particularly when the revolutionaries take such obvious delight in expunging, rather than building on, the past (by 'abolishing' feudalism and executing the King, for example). Like many historians of the nineteenth century, Burke found it useful to refer to the English example, if only to view the state of affairs in France with greater clarity.

Burke's *Reflections on the Revolution in France* was written in 1790. It alienated a number of his fellow Whigs, most notably Fox, and stamped him as a conservative, whereas prior to 1790 he had displayed some liberal inclinations. The book was read all over Europe and on the back of it he gained great notoriety and fame. As Burke explains at the start of the book,

> It may not be unnecessary to inform the reader that the following Reflections had their origin in a correspondence between the Author and a very young gentleman at Paris, who did him the honour of desiring his opinion upon the important transactions, which then, and ever since, have so much occupied the attention of all men. An answer was written some time in the month of October, 1789; but it was kept back upon prudential considerations.[2]

Thus, he depicts his work as a 'response', as if somehow he had a *reason* and a *justification* for writing, rather than just self-indulgence. He was asked for his 'opinion' on developments in France, and he gave it, notwithstanding a short time delay. This is significant. Burke is being honest and nowhere does he imply that *Reflections* was any kind of history. How could it be, when it was published only twelve months after the Fall of the Bastille? Having said this, it is interesting to note that many people who read the book assumed that it had been written much later than 1790 – maybe because he so accurately prophesied the future (the Terror and the ascendancy of a military dictator, for example).[3] This is a compliment to Burke, and highlights his ability to read history intelligently. He goes on to say:

> I have little to recommend my opinions but long observation and much impartiality. They come from one who has been no tool of power, no flatterer of greatness; and who in his last acts does not wish to belie the tenor of his life. They come from one, almost the whole of whose public exertion has been a struggle for the liberty of others; from one in whose breast no anger durable or vehement has ever been kindled, but by what he considered as tyranny; and who snatches from his share in the endeavours which are used by good men to discredit opulent oppression, the hours he has employed on your affairs; and who in so doing persuades himself he has not departed from his usual office: they come from one who desires honours, distinctions, and emoluments, but little; and who expects them not at all; who has no contempt for fame, and no fear of obloquy; who shuns contention, though he will hazard an opinion: from one who wishes to preserve consistency, but who would preserve consistency by varying his means to secure the unity of his end; and, when the equipoise of the vessel in which he sails may be endangered by overloading it upon one side, is desirous of carrying the small weight of his reasons to that which may preserve its equipoise.[4]

Here Burke presents himself as experienced and wise, as someone whose only motivation is the preservation of 'liberty' and the hatred of 'tyranny' and 'oppression'.

Like many later writers, Burke is also keen to emphasise his 'impartiality', but as with almost every other historian he is prey to a certain set of conditions, factors and biases. He cannot escape them. He was sceptical about the initial gains of the Revolution precisely because of his traditional, conservative background. He implied that it was a dangerous experiment, and declared:

> When I see the spirit of liberty in action, I see a strong principle at work; and this, for a while, is all I can possibly know of it. The wild *gas,* the fixed air, is plainly broke loose: but we ought to suspend our judgment until the first effervescence is a little subsided, till the liquor is cleared, and until we see something deeper than the agitation of a troubled and frothy surface. I must be tolerably sure, before I venture publicly to congratulate men upon a blessing, that they have really received one. Flattery corrupts both the receiver and the giver; and adulation is not of more service to the people than to kings. I should therefore suspend my congratulations on the new liberty of France, until I was informed how it had been combined with government; with public force; with the discipline and obedience of armies; with the collection of an effective and well-distributed revenue; with morality and religion; with the solidity of property; with peace and order; with civil and social manners. All these (in their way) are good things too; and, without them, liberty is not a benefit whilst it lasts, and is not likely to continue long.[5]

Burke is a firm believer in liberty, but he argues that liberty cannot be 'untrammelled' and actually requires 'discipline and obedience', and other counterweights, to keep it in check. This is a theme he returns to:

> The effect of liberty to individuals is that they may do what they please: we ought to see what it will please them to do, before we risk congratulations, which may be soon turned into complaints. Prudence would dictate this in the case of separate, insulated, private men; but liberty, when men act in bodies, is power. Considerate people, before they declare themselves, will observe the use which is made of power; and particularly of so trying a thing as new power in new persons, of whose principles, tempers, and dispositions they have little or no experience, and in situations, where those who appear the most stirring in the scene may possibly not be the real movers.[6]

Burke, a man of the upper classes, a parliamentarian and a man of letters, is offended by the 'popular' dimension to 1789. He attacks both the National Assembly and the Third Estate – he seems to group the middle classes and the town dwellers into one amorphous mass. He talks about the 'arbitrary Assembly of France' and its plans to commence their schemes of reform with abolition and total destruction. But is it in destroying and pulling down that skill is displayed? Your mob can do this as well at least as your assemblies. The shallowest understanding, the rudest hand, is more than equal to that task. Rage and phrensy will pull down more in half an hour, than prudence, deliberation, and foresight can build up in a hundred years. The errors and defects of old establishments are visible and palpable. It calls for little ability to point them out.

Here he is lamenting the negative rationale of the revolutionaries and their *destructive* rather than *constructive* attitude. He then develops the point further:

The assembly, their organ, acts before them the farce of deliberation with as little decency as liberty. They act like the comedians of a fair before a riotous audience; they act amidst the tumultuous cries of a mixed mob of ferocious men, and of women lost to shame, who, according to their insolent fancies, direct, control, applaud, explode them; and sometimes mix and take their seats amongst them; domineering over them with a strange mixture of servile petulance and proud, presumptuous authority. As they have inverted order in all things, the gallery is in the place of the house. This assembly, which overthrows kings and kingdoms, has not even the physiognomy and aspect of a grave legislative body – *nec color imperii, nec frons ulla senatûs*. They have a power given to them, like that of the evil principle, to subvert and destroy; but none to construct, except such machines as may be fitted for further subversion and further destruction.[7]

He also argues that the makers of the Revolution have acted illegally:

She [France] has sanctified the dark, suspicious maxims of tyrannous distrust; and taught kings to tremble at (what will hereafter be called) the delusive plausibilities of moral politicians. Sovereigns will consider those, who advise them to place an unlimited confidence in their people, as subverters of their thrones; as traitors who aim at their destruction, by leading their easy good-nature, under specious pretences, to admit combinations of bold and faithless men into a participation of their power. This alone (if there were nothing else) is an irreparable calamity to you and to mankind.[8]

The vocabulary is so vivid: 'perfidy', 'tyrannous distrust', 'delusive plausibilities', 'subverters', 'traitors', 'specious pretences', 'irreparable calamity'. Burke has little time for the abstract nature of the revolutionaries' demands and the disrespectful attitude they display towards the authorities. He continues:

> Remember that your parliament of Paris told your king, that, in calling the states together, he had nothing to fear but the prodigal excess of their zeal in providing for the support of the throne. It is right that these men should hide their heads. It is right that they should bear their part in the ruin which their counsel has brought on their sovereign and their country. Such sanguine declarations tend to lull authority asleep; to encourage it rashly to engage in perilous adventures of untried policy; to neglect those provisions, preparations, and precautions, which distinguish benevolence from imbecility; and without which no man can answer for the salutary effect of any abstract plan of government or of freedom. For want of these, they have seen the medicine of the state corrupted into its poison. They have seen the French rebel against a mild and lawful monarch, with more fury, outrage, and insult, than ever any people has been known to rise against the most illegal usurper, or the most sanguinary tyrant. Their resistance was made to concession; their revolt was from protection; their blow was aimed at a hand holding out graces, favours, and immunities.[9]

The corollary of this is extreme sympathy for France's 'legitimate' institutions. Take this piece of homage to the *parlements* of the *Ancien Régime*:

> [They] had furnished, not the best certainly, but some considerable corrective to the excesses and vices of the monarchy. Such an independent judicature was ten times more necessary when a democracy became the absolute power of the country. In that constitution, elective, temporary, local judges, such as you have contrived, exercising their dependent functions in a narrow society, must be the worst of all tribunals. In them it will be vain to look for any appearance of justice towards strangers, towards the obnoxious rich, towards the minority of routed parties, towards all those who in the election have supported unsuccessful candidates. It will be impossible to keep the new tribunals clear of the worst spirit of faction. All contrivances by ballot we know experimentally to be vain and childish to prevent a discovery of inclinations. Where they may the best answer the purposes of concealment, they answer to produce suspicion, and this is a still more mischievous cause of partiality. If the parliaments had been preserved, instead of being dissolved at so ruinous a change to

the nation, they might have served in this new commonwealth, perhaps not precisely the same (I do not mean an exact parallel), but nearly the same, purposes as the court and senate of Areopagus did in Athens; that is, as one of the balances and correctives to the evils of a light and unjust democracy.[10]

On a similar theme, Burke is saddened by what had happened to Louis XVI. In 1790, when *Reflections on the Revolution in France* was published, he was still king in name, but his powers were gradually being diminished. He was a constitutional monarch, King of the *French* rather than *France*. He was still popular, still viewed as a 'father figure' by the population at large, but the noose was tightening, and a year later he made the fateful error of trying to escape. This was the moment he 'died' in the eyes of ordinary French people. Eighteen months later he was executed. Back in 1790, Burke was disenchanted with the role and powers assigned to Louis:

> Let us now turn our eyes to what they have done towards the formation of an executive power. For this they have chosen a degraded king. This their first executive officer is to be a machine, without any sort of deliberative discretion in any one act of his function. At best he is but a channel to convey to the National Assembly such matter as it may import that body to know. If he had been made the exclusive channel, the power would not have been without its importance; though infinitely perilous to those who would choose to exercise it. But public intelligence and statement of facts may pass to the Assembly with equal authenticity, through any other conveyance. As to the means, therefore, of giving a direction to measures by the statement of an authorized reporter, this office of intelligence is as nothing.[11]

And also, putting his own ideas into context:

> All these considerations leave no doubt on my mind, that if this monster of a constitution can continue, France will be wholly governed by the agitators in corporations, by societies in the towns formed of directors of assignats, and trustees for the sale of church lands, attornies, agents, money-jobbers, speculators, and adventurers, composing an ignoble oligarchy, founded on the destruction of the crown, the church, the nobility, and the people. Here end all the deceitful dreams and visions of the equality and rights of men. In 'the Serbonian bog' of this base oligarchy they are all absorbed, sunk, and lost for ever.[12]

He encourages France and French people to resist in whatever way they can. What is more, he worries that the unity and integrity of the country has been placed in jeopardy:

> You see I only consider this constitution as electoral, and leading by steps to the National Assembly. I do not enter into the internal government of the departments, and their genealogy through the communes and cantons. These local governments are, in the original plan, to be as nearly as possible composed in the same manner and on the same principles with the elective assemblies. They are each of them bodies perfectly compact and rounded in themselves. You cannot but perceive in this scheme, that it has a direct and immediate tendency to sever France into a variety of republics, and to render them totally independent of each other without any direct constitutional means of coherence, connexion, or subordination, except what may be derived from their acquiescence in the determinations of the general congress of the ambassadors from each independent republic. Such in reality is the National Assembly, and such governments I admit do exist in the world, though in forms infinitely more suitable to the local and habitual circumstances of their people. But such associations, rather than bodies politic, have generally been the effect of necessity, not choice; and I believe the present French power is the very first body of citizens, who, having obtained full authority to do with their country what they pleased, have chosen to dissever it in this barbarous manner.[13]

Overall, it could be argued that Burke was something of a prophet, ahead of his time and so convincing and persuasive in his observations that he provoked a backlash in the form of Mary Wollstonecraft's *A Vindication of the Rights of Men* and Thomas Paine's *Rights of Man*. He could not help but contrast the 'moderation' and 'gradualism' of British political leaders with the 'radicalism' and 'violence' of the revolutionaries in France. Hence the illiberal plea he made to his masters in London to curtail freedom of speech in an attempt to forestall revolution in Britain.

Mary Wollstonecraft's *A Vindication of the Rights of Men*, published in 1790, was a highly controversial offering. Not only because it was authored by a woman, but also because it was so vehement in its attack on Burke. That is why she had to publish the first edition of the book anonymously. She was a member of a group known as the English Jacobins, and a pre-eminent early feminist, so she was a confirmed radical and her criticism of Burke was concerted:

> It is not necessary, with courtly insincerity, to apologise to you for thus intruding on your precious time, nor to profess that I think it an honour to discuss an important subject with a man whose literary abilities have raised him to notice in the state ... Reverencing the rights of humanity, I shall dare to assert them; not intimidated by the horse laugh that you have raised, or waiting till time has wiped away the compassionate tears which you have elaborately laboured to excite ... Liberty ... is a fair idea that has never yet received a form in the various governments that have been established on our beauteous globe ... I perceive, from the whole tenor of your reflections, that you have a mortal antipathy to reason.[14]

Wollstonecraft visited Paris in 1792 to gather more information about the Revolution. There she associated with Thomas Paine, a fellow radical whom she knew well.

We have mentioned Paine in passing, but he and his work are now worthy of much more attention. In a sense, he is better known for his role in encouraging the American Revolution, but as an intellectual interested in political ideas, he could not help but be fascinated by events in France during the 1780s and 1790s. Needless to say, Paine was a great supporter of the French Revolution and his liberal, progressive ideas, already articulated in the American context, juxtaposed neatly with those that came to dominate in France in the period 1789–91.

As the first lines of *Rights of Man* indicate, Paine disagreed wholeheartedly with Burke's stance on the Revolution:

> Among the incivilities by which nations or individuals provoke and irritate each other, Mr. Burke's pamphlet on the French Revolution is an extraordinary instance. Neither the People of France, nor the National Assembly, were troubling themselves about the affairs of England, or the English Parliament; and that Mr. Burke should commence an unprovoked attack upon them, both in Parliament and in public, is a conduct that cannot be pardoned on the score of manners, nor justified on that of policy. There is scarcely an epithet of abuse to be found in the English language, with which Mr. Burke has not loaded the French Nation and the National Assembly. Everything which rancour, prejudice, ignorance or knowledge could suggest, is poured forth in the copious fury of near four hundred

pages. In the strain and on the plan Mr. Burke was writing, he might have written on to as many thousands. When the tongue or the pen is let loose in a frenzy of passion, it is the man, and not the subject, that becomes exhausted.[15]

Paine left for Paris soon after submitting the manuscript of *Rights of Man*. He took an active interest in the politics of the National Convention, and was actually elected to it (representing the Pas de Calais area). Although he was passionate about the founding ideas of the Revolution, and voted for the Republic in 1792, he did not agree with the execution of the King. That said, he was extremely critical of the institution of the monarchy:

> The natural moderation of Louis XVI contributed nothing to alter the hereditary despotism of the monarchy. All the tyrannies of former reigns, acted under that hereditary despotism, were still liable to be revived in the hands of a successor. It was not the respite of a reign that would satisfy France, enlightened as she was then become. A casual discontinuance of the practice of despotism, is not a discontinuance of its principles: the former depends on the virtue of the individual who is in immediate possession of the power; the latter, on the virtue and fortitude of the nation.[16]

In many ways, Paine's intellectual duel with Burke symbolised the way in which the Revolution had forced writers and commentators on both sides of the (new) political fence to state their position.

When Wollstonecraft returned to England she married the writer and philosopher William Godwin (ironic given that both had grave misgivings about the institution). Godwin, like his wife, was an admirer of Paine and, together, these three intellectuals were the embodiment of the English radical movement during the 1790s.

Some commentators view Godwin as the founder of modern anarchism. This is mainly because *Enquiry Concerning Political Justice and its Influence on Morals and Happiness*, written in 1793, formed a rounded critique of illiberal government. George Woodcock points out that Godwin was inspired by 'the problems of government illuminated by the French Revolution and the conservative reaction to it in England.'[17] Events in France through the 1780s and into the 1790s certainly gave Godwin plenty of ammunition. He writes: 'The real enemies of liberty in any country are not the people, but those higher orders who profit by a contrary system. Infuse just views of society into a certain number of the liberally educated and reflecting members; give to the people guides and instructors, and the business is done.'[18]

Later, he makes a number of comments that mark him out as a libertarian, as a writer and thinker who, whether consciously or subconsciously, was developing proto-anarchist ideas. For example:

> 'as government is a transaction in the name and for the benefit of the whole, every member of the community ought to have some share in its administration'.[19]

> 'there is no criterion perspicuously designating any one man or set of men to preside over the rest.'[20]

> 'Government is a contrivance instituted for the security of individuals; and it seems both reasonable that each man should have a share in providing for his own security.'[21]

> 'no measure is to be resisted on account of the irregularity of its derivation.'[22]

There are certainly clues here as to the uses to which Godwin's work might one day be put.

Burke, Wollstonecraft, Paine and Godwin have relatively little in common with another celebrated 'Anglo' writer on the Revolution, Arthur Young. Whereas Burke and Paine were polemically motivated, and interested in issues of politics and philosophy, Young was an economist who just happened to be in France, collecting data on French agriculture, when the Revolution commenced.

Young's writings cover the years 1787, 1788 and 1789. He also updates the reader with news of events in 1792, 'which I draw from the correspondence of some friends, on whose accuracy I can rely'.[23] The undoubted strength of Young's main writings is his proximity to events. He is an eye-witness – something which cannot be said of many commentators on the Revolution. In September 1788 he writes about his visit to Britanny:

> To Combourg. The country has a savage aspect; husbandry not

much further advanced, at least in skill, than among the Hurons, which appears incredible amidst inclosures. The people almost as wild as their country, and their town of Combourg one of the most brutal, filthy places that can be seen; mud houses, no windows, and a pavement so broken as to impede all passengers, but ease none. Yet here is a château, and inhabited. Who is this Monsieur de Châteaubriant, the owner, that has nerves strung for a residence amidst such filth and poverty? ...

To Montauban. The poor people seem poor indeed; the children terribly ragged, – if possible, worse clad than if with no clothes at all; as to shoes and stockings, they are luxuries. A beautiful girl of six or seven years playing with a stick, and smiling under such a bundle of rags as made my heart ache to see her. They did not beg, and when I gave them anything seemed more surprised than obliged. One third of what I have seen of this province seems uncultivated, and nearly all of it in misery. What have kings, and ministers, and parliaments, and states to answer for their prejudices, seeing millions of hands that would be industrious idle and starving through the execrable maxims of despotism, or the equally detestable prejudices of a feudal nobility. Sleep at the Lion d'Or, at Montauban, an abominable hole.[24]

These vivid word-pictures help us to understand the state of France 'on the eve of Revolution' – to use that well-worn phrase beloved of students and historians.

Ten months later, and only two days before the storming of the Bastille, Young found himself in the east of France:

[July 12.] Walking up a long hill to ease my mare, I was joined by a poor woman, who complained of the times, and that it was a sad country. Demanding her reasons, she said her husband had but a morsel of land, one cow, and a poor little horse, yet they had a franchar (forty-two pounds) of wheat and three chickens to pay as a quitrent to one seigneur; and four franchar of oats, one chicken, and one franc, to pay to another, besides very heavy tailles and other taxes. She had seven children, and the cow's milk helped to make the soup. 'But why, instead of a horse, do not you not keep another cow?' Oh, her husband could not carry his produce so well without a horse; and asses are little used in the country. It was said, at present, that something was to be done by some great folks for such poor ones, but she did not know who nor how.[25]

Not only does Young write about what he sees, but he does so, apparently, without any specific or consistent political motivation. After all, he was not a politician or polemicist, but an economist, interested in raw observation and statistical data rather than anything else.

In France the Revolution met with an array of negative reactions. Hughes Felicité Robert de Lamennais, Ultramontane priest and philosopher, was shocked by events and dismayed by the attack on the Catholic church, and *Réflexions sur l'état de l'église en France pendant le 18ième siècle et sur sa situation actuelle* (1808), was his response. Meanwhile, Antoine Rivarol, the famed satirist, fought for his beliefs but ended up making his name as the royalists' chief propagandist.[26] Rivarol was different from Lamennais and others in the way that he viewed religion. For him, it was a useful 'instrument' of social control and it did not really matter whether the main tenets of religion were true or false.[27]

The French writers of most substance to emerge in this early period were Mallet du Pan, Bonald and Chateaubriand. Jacques Mallet du Pan was another journalist and propagandist, who also served as a royalist emissary. He wrote for *Mercure de France* and also started producing his own pamphlets. Lord Acton praises him for his wisdom and objectivity: 'Mallet du Pan was neither a brilliant writer like Burke and De Maistre … nor an original and constructive thinker like Sieyès; but he was the most sagacious of all the politicians who watched the course of the Revolution. As a Genevese republican he approached the study of French affairs with no prejudice towards monarchy, aristocracy, or Catholicism.'[28] According to Reedy, Louis-Gabriel-Ambroise, Viscount de Bonald, 'was a major ideologist of the French counterrevolution, a "prophet of the past" who diagnosed and even anticipated many of modernity's social problems. He was also a considerable figure in the parliamentary life of the Bourbon restoration.'[29] If Bonald is famous for one position, it is his anti-secularism and his belief that religion could be used for social purposes – in short, 'political catholicism'.[30] In many ways, Bonald shared almost identical political and philosophical beliefs with de Maistre,[31] so much so that one commentator inserts a hyphen between their surnames to indicate a common outlook and purpose.[32]

Like Bonald, François-Auguste-René, Vicomte de Chateaubriand, became a major figure during the Restoration years. He was the epitome of reaction, but this betrayed the fact that in the early years of the Revolution (1789–91) he had seen the merits of sensible liberal reform.[33] But the violence of the Terror and the general dislocation of war turned him into an *émigré* and a focus for conservative opposition. Chateaubriand's first work, *Essai sur les révolutions* (1797), poured scorn on the Jacobins. 'These infuriated men alone could have devised the means, and what is still more incredible, partly have succeeded in the execution of their project. The means were doubtless execrable, but it must be acknowledged that they were of gigantic conception.' He goes on:

> The Jacobins possessed minds rarefied by the fire of republican enthusiasm, and they may be said to have been reduced, by their purifying scrutinies … to the quintessence of infamy. Hence they displayed, at the same time, a degree of energy which was completely without example, and an extent of crimes, which all those of history, put together, can scarcely equal. They saw that to obtain the end which they had in view, the received systems of justice, the common axioms of humanity, and the whole range of principles, adopted by Lycurgus, would not be of use, and that they must arrive at the same object by another road. To wait till death took away the great proprietors of estates, or till they consented to their own spoliation; to wait till years rooted out fanaticism, and effected a change in customs and manners; to wait till recruits, raised in the ordinary way, could be sent to the armies: all this appeared doubtful and tedious. As if, therefore, the establishment of a republic and the defense of France, taken separately, afforded too little employment for their genius, they resolved on attempting both at the same time. Agents having been placed at their posts in every corner of the republic, and the word communicated to affiliated societies, the monsters … gave the fearful signal which was to recall Sparta from its ruins. It resounded though France like the trump of the exterminating angel – the monuments of the sons of men crumbled away, and the graves opened. At the same moment a thousand sanguinary guillotines were erected in all the towns and villages of France. The citizen was suddenly awoke in the night by the report of cannon and roll of the drum, to receive an order for his immediate departure to the army. He was thunderstruck, and knew not whether he was awake.

However, in trying to understand and comprehend 1789 and its aftermath, Chateaubriand tried to balance out royalist and revolutionary claims, and ended up alienating many people close to him who had suffered at the hands of the radicals. Thereafter, he made a pronounced shift to the right. In fact, it has been argued that, 'the political concept of "conservative" was coined after the revolution when Chateaubriand gave the name *Le conservateur* to a journal he issued.'[34]

Probably the most notorious of all early writers on the Revolution was Augustin Barruel. He was a dogmatic Jesuit priest who spent most of his career advancing the view that the Revolution was an intricate plot (*complot*). In his writings on the right, Michael Billig situates Barruel at the start of a long and varied line of conspiracy theorists (that also includes Nazis and neo-Nazis) and summarises his argument thus: 'The conspirators had succeeded in poisoning the minds of the masses so that they turned from their natural allegiances to the monarchy to espouse the alien and internationalist ideas of republicanism.'[35] In effect, the masses had been 'duped'.[36]

In *Mémoires pour servir a l'histoire du Jacobinisme*, Barruel blamed the Revolution on Voltaire, for his anti-Christian teachings, and Rousseau and Montesquieu for their anti-monarchical writings. Also implicated in the 'plot' were the Knights Templar, the Illuminati, Freemasons and Jews – not forgetting the Jacobins as well. Barruel was one of many conspiracy theorists, but probably the most celebrated on account of the complexity of his theses and the concerted nature of his campaign to have the origins of the Revolution re-evaluated. Winock has argued that he was the most successful of all those writers who claimed that the Revolution was the product of a 'plot' and 'total subversion'.[37]

Joseph de Maistre's fame rests not only on the fact that he offered a powerful critique of the Revolution, but that he is now viewed as the founding father of the counter-revolutionary right in France. Alan Forrest states: 'Just as the Revolution had its theorists and intellectual defenders, so did the counter-revolution.'[38] De Maistre was a lawyer from Savoy who, at first, had displayed some warmth towards the Revolution. However, when the Reign of Terror began, and when the revolutionaries' European war caused him personal dislocation, he knew that he could not tolerate it any more. He was not a historian, nor did he ever pretend to be so. He was simply an individual caught up in a momentous historical event – someone whose instinctive reaction, because of his training and outlook, was to put his ideas down in writing.

Considerations on France, de Maistre's key work, was published in 1796. Noel Parker interprets de Maistre's treatise as 'a mystical, God-fearing response to the upheaval of the Revolution'. Paul Beik argues that the book crystallised ideas for the French right (and thus, by extension, for the extreme right). And Roger Soltau says that 'the world has never been without people who thought the clock of time could be put back, who saw in the rejected past the true goal of mankind'.[39] Whatever the verdict, it is clear that de Maistre viewed the Revolution as a seminal event, a turning point, a 'chance for regeneration'. As a piece of literature, *Considerations* was of profound significance.

There is no doubt that de Maistre's influence was long-lasting. His immediate impact in the late-1790s was marked, but it was during the Restoration that his writings assumed pivotal importance. The Ultras of the 1820s might have 'distorted' the essence of his doctrine – de Maistre would not have agreed with everything that was done in his name – but writers like Murray view him as the unofficial theorist of the Restoration and, moreover, as some kind of 'spokesman' for the Bourbon reaction.[40] Others argue that his influence stretched into the second half of the nineteenth century.

De Maistre was born in 1753 and came from Savoy, an Italian province later to be incorporated into France. It is ironic that the founding father of the extreme-right tradition in France should hail from outside its borders, but it is easy to empathise with his situation. The French invasion of Savoy in 1792 forced him into exile and meant he had to 'take sides' on the Revolution. Other aspects of de Maistre's early life are also interesting. He was born the son of a recently ennobled father and a devout mother, and as a young man pursued legal studies. Aristocracy, Catholicism, law – these were to become central values in his thought system. Phillips says the circumstances of de Maistre's life had a 'profound' resonance in his thinking.[41]

Interestingly, de Maistre's attitude to the Revolution evolved over time and was not always negative. During the period

1789–91 he could accept much of what the revolutionaries projected. As a lawyer he was always going to understand the aspirations of the upper Third Estate; indeed, as a young man de Maistre was a liberal conservative, and was actually disciplined for his radicalism by the King of Sardinia. But war and terror – the bywords of 1792–4 – were totally alien to his temperament and put in jeopardy the peaceful society for which he yearned. Greifer suggests that he evolved from conservative to reactionary in quick time.[42]

De Maistre felt that Providence had punished France for her 'sins' in 1789 and, even though he himself came to personify counter-revolutionary thinking, he was sensible enough to acknowledge the weaknesses and failings of the Ancien Régime. As Murray states, 'de Maistre's apparently impossible request for the re-establishment of the monarchy was not a request for the monarchy which immediately preceded 1789'.[43] This is a good indicator of the Savoyard's realism. But, at the same time, de Maistre puts unquenchable faith in Providence, believing that the Counter-Revolution will come and triumph, just like the Revolution came and triumphed. He never puts a date on it, but he is confident he will be proved right. As such, it is extremely difficult to argue against de Maistre.

So what were the main themes in de Maistre's work? Michel Winock suggests that *Considerations on France* should have been renamed *Religious Considerations on France*. The first line of the book sets the tone: 'We are all bound to the throne of the Supreme Being by a flexible chain which restrains without enslaving us. The most wonderful aspect of the universal scheme of things is the action of free beings under divine guidance.'[44] De Maistre is in awe of God and constantly invokes religious imagery. The Revolution is likened to 'evil' and 'original sin', order is viewed as 'angelic' and chaos as 'diabolic', and he is aghast at the dechristianisation policy pursued by the revolutionaries. In essence what de Maistre offers is a theological interpretation of events.

At the apex of de Maistre's 'new society' is the Papacy – an institution that unifies earthly and spiritual power. He argues that French society is in desperate need of 'Pope and Executioner'; in other words, more religious devotion (order) and more 'policing' (less disorder). There is a constant emphasis on discipline and control, and it is in this sense that de Maistre and the Theocrats are viewed as 'anti-Revolution authoritarians'.[45] Muret says they based their doctrine on religious authority rather than compromise.[46] De Maistre displays an 'unflagging' belief in Providence. In his mind, Providence, and nothing else, caused the French Revolution: 'Every nation, like every individual, has a mission which it must fulfil ... (France) was at the head of the religious system, and it was not without reason that her king was called most Christian ... However, as she has used her influence to pervert her vocation and to demoralise Europe, it is not surprising that terrible means must be used to set her on her true course again.'[47] He uses coded language – the phrase 'terrible means' equates to 'revolution' – but he is sure that Counter-Revolution will follow Revolution, just as night follows day. Again, God will be responsible. Steiner says that 'Maistre takes it as self-evident that divine providence commands the lives of nations and of individuals.'[48]

The author of Considerations believes in the 'natural' social and political order. He argues for inequality, privilege and hierarchy, and also acknowledges the role of 'intermediate' social bodies such as family, commune and province. In this sense his doctrine is anti-individualistic. He believes that man has 'duties' rather than 'rights' a position that marks him out as an arch-exponent of the traditionalist, counter-revolutionary right and signals his profound opposition to 1789 (and the 'rights of man'). Moreover de Maistre puts a special premium on the restoration of hereditary kings. He views the monarchy as a kind of social cement, but is realistic enough to know that it must become less corrupt and more religious. Reform was always going to be a problematic idea for him to embrace but he knew that in the aftermath of 1789 limited and measured change was essential. On the one hand, he wanted to make the monarchy less arbitrary; on the other, he wished to establish a new theocratic regime. Either way, de Maistre knew the Ancien Régime was finished. But he still believed the monarch had God-given power and that within certain parameters he, or she, had absolute authority. He remained convinced that monarchy was 'natural' for France.

The corollary of de Maistre's belief in 'divine' monarchy was his contempt for 'man-made' constitutions, abstract ideas and *'philosophisme'*. Murray says that de Maistre wanted 'stability, unity, and continuity' – three things the *philosophes* put in doubt. The Savoyard believed that constitutions were 'natural' and 'organic' and thus, by implication, condemned the revolutionary charters of 1791, 1793 and 1795. In one of the most compelling parts of the book, he states:

> What a prodigious number of laws has resulted from the labours of three French National Assemblies! From July 1st to October, 1791, the National Assembly passed 2,557. The Legislative Assembly passed, in eleven and a half months 1,712. The National Convention, from the first day of the Republic until 4 Brumaire year IV (October 26, 1795), passed in 57 months 11,210. Total 15,479 ... Astonishment must quickly change to pity when the futility of these laws is recalled ... Why are there so many laws? Because there is no legislator.[49]

In the light of this, de Maistre demanded that Assemblies and Conventions give way to God and King. He poured ridicule on the individuals at the vanguard of the Revolution: 'It has been said with good reason that the French Revolution leads men more than men lead it ... The very villains who appear to guide the Revolution take part in it only as simple instruments; and as soon as they aspire to dominate it, they fall ingloriously.'[50] It does not need stating, but he had very little faith in human beings. More fundamentally, de Maistre attacked intellectuals, reason, and the very notion of universal rights. He viewed the Enlightenment as a dangerous and foolhardy enterprise and the Revolution as 'the political manifestation of this Satanic revolt'. But de Maistre was convinced that in the end Christianity would triumph over Philosophy.

In its own terms, de Maistre's thought system is coherent, but weaknesses abound: for example, the over-reliance on Providence – what Steiner calls 'theological fatalism'[51] – and the paradox inherent in an intellectual criticising intellectualism and other intellectuals. There are other criticisms too. De Maistre exaggerates key aspects of the Revolution in order to legitimise his own ideas, and similarly it is clear that he pays scant attention to the Revolution's social and economic dimensions – a serious flaw. And, overall, the author of *Considerations* pedals a fairly simplified interpretation of history: one in which the monarchy can do very little wrong. Winock says that de Maistre was impotent – a 'spectator' with 'no programme', a man happy just to 'wait' for things to happen. Soltau says he 'destroys better than he builds'. Lebrun, summing up, states: 'Joseph de Maistre's status as a symbol of reactionary opposition to the spirit of modern civilisation is possibly beyond revision.'[52]

Only individuals of calibre and political and intellectual merit could make themselves known, and their ideas heard, during the Revolution. Burke and de Maistre certainly fitted the bill. Both had the ability to produce cogent, passionate prose with a strident political message. Not many writers can claim to have 'founded' either political or intellectual traditions, but these two men can. Burke is generally regarded as the 'father' of modern conservatism; de Maistre the thinker who first espoused 'right-wing' or 'extreme right-wing' ideas in France.

It is curious that neither was actually French, or living in France during the period of revolution. Some may argue that this was a handicap and a problem. Others claim that this 'detachment' was invaluable, and gave them powers of observation and insight that others – blinkered by loyalty or patriotism – could not match. Either way, it is clear that any examination of revolutionary historiography must begin with Burke and de Maistre, not because they were the first historians of the Revolution – they were not – but because they articulated a point of view that was not so much influential as taken seriously (quite an achievement in a period of violent political change).

However, as we have seen, many voices were raised, and viewpoints articulated, in the years that followed the storming of the Bastille. The Revolution had been a catalyst: it had inspired the ultra-liberal ideas of Paine and also the strange and sinister Jesuit-inspired theories of Barruel, and a kaleidoscope of opinions in between. Burke the founder of conservatism? Godwin the father of anarchism? Wollstonecraft the first feminist? Could any other political upheaval have produced so many significant contributions to the history of political thought?

But we should not be surprised. The Revolution was a landmark event, a political earthquake in a genuine sense. In time, these statements and testimonies would become crucial reference points for historians of the future, not least the liberal writers of the early nineteenth century.

Notes

1 E. Burke, *Reflections on the Revolution in France* (Harmondsworth, 1986), p. 125.
2 Ibid., p. 84.
3 See C. Cruise O'Brien's introduction to *Reflections* in the Penguin edition.
4 Burke, *Reflections*, pp. 376–7.
5 Ibid., pp. 90–1.
6 Ibid., p. 91.
7 Ibid., p. 161.
8 Ibid., p. 125.
9 Ibid., pp. 125–6.
10 Ibid., pp. 326–7.
11 Ibid., p. 316.
12 Ibid., p. 313.
13 Ibid., p. 297.
14 Cited in I. Hampsher-Monk (ed.), *The Impact of the French Revolution* (London, 2005), pp. 106–7.
15 See www.ushistory.org/paine/rights/c1–010.htm.
16 Ibid.
17 G. Woodcock (ed.), *The Anarchist Reader* (Glasgow, 1980), p. 374.
18 Hampsher-Monk, *Impact of the Revolution*, p. 217.
19 Ibid., p. 228.
20 Ibid., p. 228.
21 Ibid., p. 229.
22 Ibid., p. 229.
23 http://oll.libertyfund.org/ToC/0455.php, p. 345.
24 http://history.hanover.edu/texts/young.html._
25 Ibid.
26 A newspaper on the counter-revolutionary right today in France is called *Rivarol* in homage to his life and work.
27 M. Winock, *Histoire de l'extrême droite en France* (Paris, 1994), p. 29.
28 http://oll.libertyfund.org/Texts/Acton0003/FrenchRevolution/HTMLs/0001_Pt03_Part3.html_XIII.
29 Taken from *The Canadian Journal of History*, Aug 1997.
30 J. Hayward, *After the French Revolution* (Hemel Hempstead, 1991), p. 45.
31 See pp. 24–9.
32 Hayward, *After the Revolution*, p. 71.
33 Like de Maistre in fact.
34 R. Eatwell, 'The Nature of the Right, 2: The Right as a Variety of "Styles of Thought"' in R. Eatwell & N. O'Sullivan (eds), *The Nature of the Right: American and European Politics and Political Thought since 1789* (London, 1989), p. 63.
35 M. Billig, 'The Extreme Right: Continuities in Anti-Semitic Conspiracy

Theory in Post-War Europe' in Eatwell & O'Sullivan, *The Nature of the Right*, p. 156.

36 Ibid.

37 Winock, *Histoire*, pp. 44–5.

38 A. Forrest, *The French Revolution* (Oxford, 1993), p. 134.

39 See N. Parker, *Portrayals of Revolution* (Hemel Hempstead, 1990), p. 163; P. Beik, *The French Revolution seen from the Right* (Philadephia, 1956), and R.H. Soltau, *French Political Thought in the Nineteenth Century* (London, 1931), p. 15.

40 J. Murray, 'The Political Thought of Joseph de Maistre', *Review of Politics*, 1949.

41 C.S. Phillips, *The Church in France* (London, 1966), p. 209.

42 E. Greifer, 'Joseph de Maistre and the Reaction against the Eighteenth Century', *American Political Science Review*, Vol 15 (Sep 1961), pp. 591–8.

43 Murray, 'Joseph de Maistre', pp. 63–86.

44 J. de Maistre, 'Considerations on France', taken from J. Lively, *The Works of Joseph de Maistre* (London, 1965), p. 47.

45 Ibid., p. 81.

46 C. Muret, *French Royalist Doctrines since the Revolution* (New York, 1933), p. 11.

47 De Maistre, 'Considerations', p. 50.

48 G. Steiner, 'Aspects of Counter-Revolution' in G. Best (ed.), *The Permanent Revolution: The French Revolution and its Legacy 1789–1989* (London, 1989), p. 144.

49 De Maistre, 'Considerations', p. 81.

50 Ibid., p. 49.

51 Steiner, 'Aspects', p. 145.

52 R. Lebrun, 'Joseph de Maistre, Cassandra of Science', *French Historical Studies*, 1969 (Fall), pp. 214–31. The point is made in the context of science but it has a more general application.

Part 1

Nineteenth century

2

The liberal perspective

After twenty years ... we must combine our acute contemporary indignation with an enlightened examination that may serve as a guide for the future.[1]

With hindsight it is possible to argue that the first real 'school' of revolutionary historiography emerged in the first half of the nineteenth century. Germaine de Staël, Adolphe Thiers and François Mignet all shared a liberal, bourgeois view of revolutionary events. Furthermore, two important political figures under Napoleon – Benjamin Constant and Pierre Louis Roederer – also put forward interpretations that were considered liberal in tone, and thus could be considered for membership of this school.

The importance of de Staël, Thiers and Mignet lies in the fact that, essentially, they were the first genuine historians of the Revolution. Of course, as Chapter 1 demonstrated, many contemporaries wrote about the Revolution, opining and offering polemical interpretations – with Burke and de Maistre prime examples. Alfred Cobban, who would become embroiled in historiographical controversy during the 1960s, sums up the situation thus: 'As the Revolution receded into the past it became possible for historians to envisage it with a degree of cautious sympathy, and to begin to assess its causes more objectively. But the first two notable historians to tackle the problem, Thiers and Mignet, both wrote their histories of the Revolution partly as contributions to the political campaign against the Bourbons.'[2]

The point that Cobban makes here is an important one. In nineteenth-century France, 'writing history' was not just an occupation. It was a 'cause' rather than a profession. And given the political instability that beset France during this period, precisely as a result of 1789 and its reverberations, there was always going to be a premium on history and the writing, or production, of history. Statements could be made and political points could be scored. And that is why, in the hands of a Thiers or a Mignet, history, and the manufacture of history, could be employed as a weapon against the ruling elite – the Bourbons, for example.

The advantage that the early liberal writers had was that they had access to bona fide sources. When they sat down to write, close on three decades had elapsed since 1789 and archive material was now becoming available. We should not assume that they utilised the sources well – or even at all in some cases – but we are entitled to label them 'historians' without fear of contradiction. As such, we can say that the *real* historiography of the Revolution commenced in this period. It was the beginning of a long and fascinating tradition, with other, later historians building on, or actually trying to knock away at, this platform. Thus, for all later historians, the liberal writers of the early nineteenth century would have been a key reference point.

The liberal interpretation of the Revolution incorporated a range of inter-linked themes and ideas. The growth of the middle classes was acknowledged and accepted as a progressive thing; the trauma and anarchy of the Terror was viewed as 'unprecedented' and 'unexplainable'; but at the same time the view was that liberty – true liberty – would triumph in the end. This chapter weighs up the significance of the liberal view. In what sense were the liberal historians self-consciously 'liberal'? What common ideas and concepts did they put forward? And to what extent was there dissent from this liberal view?

In one sense Germaine de Staël was an eyewitness to, and actively involved in, the French Revolution. ('When the King came into the middle of [the] assembly to take the throne, I felt frightened for the first time. For one thing I could see that the Queen was greatly moved. She came late and the colour of her complexion was altered').[3] In another, though, it could be argued that, courtesy of *Considerations on the Main Events of the French Revolution*, published posthumously in 1818, she was its first proper historian. Consequently, the book she produced can be viewed as part primary source, part secondary source.

Anne-Louise-Germaine Necker, Baroness de Staël-Holstein, was born in 1766 to Jacques and Suzanne Necker. In 1777 her father had been appointed Louis XVI's finance minister, and it could be argued quite plausibly that his sacking indirectly precipitated the first revolutionary outburst of 1789. In terms of her work, she is impossible to pigeon-hole. She wrote novels, serious social and literary studies, politics and philosophy, and autobiographical work. It is also difficult to 'categorise' de Staël politically and philosophically. She was moderate and idealistic, and illustrated this by championing the cause of women's rights. She probably felt most at home during the early, liberal phase of the Revolution (1789–91), when 'sensible' constitutional monarchy was the order of the day. But she was also the daughter of Necker, a man of the *Ancien Régime* (albeit a minister with significant reforming inclinations), and had absolutely no truck with radicalism or despotism of any kind. As she once said: 'In monarchies, women have ridicule to fear; in republics, hatred.'[4]

We are interested mainly in *Considérations sur les principaux événements de la Révolution française* (1818), her study of the Revolution which – to put things into context – was published twenty-nine years after the Fall of the Bastille and nineteen years after Napoleon's coup. Her analysis of the causes of the Revolution was straightforward. The clergy had been inefficient, too political, and 'had lost a certain amount of public respect'. Also, France had lost the taste for 'military glory' and this had impacted on the amount of respect that the population at large had for the nobility, the country's 'warrior' class. They had 'fallen from splendour', and the estates system in France, more generally, was riddled by 'unfair privilege'.[5] In her writings, de Staël is preoccupied with the phase of the Revolution known as the 'Reign of Terror':

> Although England, like France, is stained by the murder of Charles I and the despotism of Cromwell, the Reign of Terror is a horrible and unique phenomenon whose weight must be borne throughout history by France alone ... Where did the disorderly tendencies of the early years of the Revolution come from, after all, if not from a hundred years of superstition and arbitrary rule? In 1793 it seemed as if France had no

room for any more revolutions. Everything had already been over-thrown – Crown, nobility, clergy – and the success of the Revolutionary armies made peace throughout Europe something to hope for. This is just when popular tyrannies do arise, though: as soon as the danger is past. The worst of men control themselves as long as there are obstacles and fears; after they have won, their repressed passions know no bounds. After the death of the King, the Girondins tried vainly to put some sort of laws into effect – any laws. But they could not force people to accept any social organization whatsoever; an instinct for savagery rejected them all.[6]

She portrays the period in vivid terms. Her natural sympathies seem to lie with the 'moderate' Girondins, for elsewhere she talks about their 'intrepid eloquence', 'their admirable presence of mind', and the fact that they were the only group of people, 'still worthy of taking their place in history'.[7] She comes across as being slightly condescending in her attitude towards the ordinary people, with talk of 'popular tyrannies', 'the worst of men', 'repressed passions' and 'an instinct for savagery'.[8] There is also a very personal dimension to her history:

I hardly know how to approach the fourteen months after May 31, 1793, when the Gironde was condemned. It is like Dante's Hell – one keeps on going down and down, from circle to circle. The relentless attack on nobles and priests becomes an inflamed anger at the existence of landowners; then at talent of any kind; then even at beauty: in the end, at anything great or generous still in the possession of human nature. The facts about this period tend to merge into each other, and I am afraid it is impossible to begin such a story without staining one's imagination ineradicably in blood ... Once the people were freed from their harness there is no doubt that they were in a position to commit any kind of crime. But how can we explain their depravity?[9]

De Staël seems genuinely perplexed by the violence of 1792–94. At the time, and also afterwards, this was the natural liberal reaction. She was so disturbed that she left France in 1792, and only returned from her self-imposed exile when the Directory, and moderate bourgeois politics, gained the ascendancy after 1795. She places the blame for the Terror, fairly and squarely, on the shoulders of political extremists:

Let us look carefully, however, at the principle underlying these monstrous phenomena: political fanaticism. Worldly passions have always played some part in religious fanaticism, and a genuine belief in abstract ideas is often food for political fanaticism...The political fanaticism we have witnessed in France must be attributed to this state of things, more or less pronounced in individual cases, more or less softened by manners and education. A sort of fury took hold of the poor in the presence of the rich; as the jealousy inspired by property was reinforced by aristocratic distinctions, the people grew proud of their own numbers. Everything constituting the power and brilliance of the minority seemed to them simple usurpation. The seeds of this sentiment have always been there, but we have felt human society shaken to its foundation only during the French Reign of Terror. We should not be surprised at the deep scars this abominable Scourge has left on people's minds. The only reflection we can allow ourselves to make – confirmed, hope, by the rest of this work – is that the remedy for popular passion lies in the rule of law rather than in despotism.[10]

The last line articulates an archetypal liberal position: only the law – the law that was so precious to the bourgeois revolutionaries of 1789[11] – could serve as an antidote to terror. She reinforces the point elsewhere: 'Political fanaticism ... can be calmed only by liberty.'[12] Predictably, given this tirade against extremism and fanaticism, de Staël has no time for the 'men at the top' in 1793–94:

The three great resources of the Committee of Public Safety were the scarcity of basic foods, the abundance of worthless assignats, and the enthusiasm aroused by the war. The Committee frightened the people, or paid them, or made them march to the border, all at its own convenience. 'We must continue the war,' as one of the deputies of the Convention said, 'so that the convulsions of liberty will be stronger.' No one can tell whether or not these twelve members of the Committee of Public Safety had the slightest notion in their minds of any kind of government at all. Except for the war, the direction of national concerns was nothing but a melange of coarseness and savagery in which the only apparent plan was to make one-half the nation massacre the other half. The Jacobins included people among the condemned aristocracy with such facility that half the inhabitants of France were running the risk of suspicion, and suspicion was enough to lead anyone to his death.[13]

And again:

> The Jacobin party wanted to wield despotic power – it is completely inaccurate to call their form of government anarchy. Authority stronger than theirs has never ruled in France. Theirs was a peculiar sort of power, however; derived from popular fanaticism, it inspired terror even in the men who ruled in its name, who all lived in constant fear of being condemned in turn by others who might take the audacity of persecution one step further. At this time the only man who lived fearless was Marat. Marat's face was so coarse, his emotions so frantic, his opinions so bloodthirsty that he was convinced no-one could plunge deeper than he into the abyss of crime. Robespierre himself did not achieve this hellish sense of security.[14]

Here she plays on an important and much discussed theme: the curious ability of the Revolution to 'eat itself'. Almost *everyone* became a 'suspect' in time, even Robespierre himself – hence his execution in 1794.

Tess Lewis sums up de Staël's significance: 'When it became clear that the Revolutionary ideals were irredeemably betrayed by the Jacobins, she tirelessly advocated a constitutional monarchy. She defended the rights of women, and, to her peril, cosmopolitanism and intellectual freedom.'[15] It is clear that the Terror was the key issue for de Staël. It was the event, or series of events, that undid all the good work of the liberal revolutionaries in 1789, 1790, 1791 and 1792.

De Staël was arguably the first genuine historian of the Revolution, but it would not be diminishing or belittling her significance as a writer to assert that the 'liberal' school owed its existence primarily to two historians who were contemporaries as young men and who had a shared personal history of political agitation. From his vantage point, Norman Hampson labels them the 'first serious historians of the Revolution ... Thiers and Mignet began what was to become a Great Tradition, developed by most of their successors over the next century'.[16] It is difficult to argue with this view.

During the early years of Napoleon's rule, Louis Adolphe Thiers and François Auguste Marie Mignet studied law together in the southern town of Aix-en-Provence, and also developed an interest in literature. Thereafter, their careers as writers, political activists and historians followed a similar path. Along with Armand Carrel, they founded the powerful liberal daily newspaper, *Le National*, in January 1830. As journalists – Thiers took on the editorship of the new paper and Mignet acted as one of his assistants – they campaigned vociferously against the restored Bourbon monarchy. It was perfectly natural for Thiers and Mignet to combine political agitation with the writing of history. History was part of their ammunition. As liberals they could argue that the gains of the Revolution had been placed in jeopardy by the arrival of the Bourbons in power. Writing history was a means of putting the issue in perspective, of adding depth and (they hoped) legitimacy to their argumentation. This line of thinking was understandable.

But the well-advertised political affiliations of Thiers and Mignet could also be viewed as a problem, as their Achilles heel. How could any reader trust the observations and analyses of two such 'involved' individuals? After all, the pair participated in the 'protest of the journalists' in 1830 and thus played an active role in deposing Charles X. As bourgeois liberals, they were then ideally placed to serve under the July Monarchy, and they did this, with their political careers lasting as long as the regime.

It is important to make this point. But at the same time, we need to acknowledge the role of Thiers and Mignet as pioneers, for they are viewed, not without reason, as the founding fathers of the liberal interpretation. Hampson helps us here. Writing in 1989, he states: 'They saw the Revolution as both political and social: Mignet contrasted it with the revolution in England that had merely changed the government. Thiers claimed that 1789 had put an end to a "feudal constitution".'[17] In passing, Hampson identifies what was unique about the Revolution. For their part, both Mignet and Thiers viewed it as 'the inevitable product of circumstances' and also as a 'beneficent' event.[18] This was their liberal perspective: the Revolution had the potential to change the course of French history for the better.

Thiers was born in Marseilles in 1797, the third year of Directorial rule in France. After studying, and then plying his trade as a campaigning journalist, he was elected deputy for Aix; and in this role he emerged as one of France's most talented parliamentarians. As a historian, Thiers was prolific. He wrote his epic *Histoire de la Révolution française* (10 volumes) between 1823 and 1827, and the even more voluminous *L'Histoire du consulat et de l'empire* between 1845 and 1862 (20 volumes). His method has caused much comment. It should be pointed out, first, that in his adult life Thiers came to know many individuals who had been actively involved in the Revolution.[19] As such, he used 'records and recollections' to piece together the history of the period. Most onlookers agree that Thiers revealed himself to be far more interested in the nature and course of political events than in key analytical issues, like the matter of origins, for example. Cobban, who in the late twentieth century would challenge the 'Great Tradition' (of which Thiers was a part), was cutting in his verdict: 'Thiers began by taking over the work of a hack writer employed by a bookseller to turn out historical textbooks, so the early pages are not the best. Apart from this, an historian who keeps as persistently to the surface of events as Thiers is not likely to have much of interest to say on the causes of anything.'[20] This is harsh, but there is some truth in what Cobban says. The reason why Thiers fits so comfortably into this chapter is that he puts a premium on liberty, tolerance and progress. Curiously, he is not too disheartened by the descent into terror and violence. He doesn't approve – obviously – but he does try to understand and comprehend the years 1793–4. Hampson, a 'soft' revisionist like Cobban, comments: 'Thiers thought it utopian to imagine that the transition from a "feudal" to a liberal society could be accomplished peacefully'.[21] He also exhibits an amazing trust and faith in progress. Parker puts it well: 'For Thiers, the long-term movement of history is towards liberty ... Liberty is excluded from the empirical content of the Revolution and saved for the future.'[22]

In some ways, Thiers is a curious case. He was a politician of note, a productive writer, and also popular. But as a historian of the Revolution he has never been showered with praise. Perhaps this is because, as an individual, he was notoriously pragmatic and opportunistic. Or maybe it is because, as both historian and politician, Thiers displayed a lack of real concern for ordinary people. He served the notoriously 'bourgeois' regime of Louis Philippe in the early 1830s. This was a sure sign of his political affiliations. It was no surprise, therefore, that in 1848 he found it difficult to come to terms with the February Revolution. His time came again in 1870 when, after France's disastrous defeat in the war against Prussia, he was named head of the provisional government, and then elected President of France in August. His deep-seated hatred of radicalism meant that he brought enthusiasm to the task of suppressing the Paris Commune. To reiterate: Thiers showed little empathy for the masses.

Parker's perspective on Thiers helps to link the early part of this chapter with the later part: 'As in the views of de Staël and Mignet, the Revolution is located in an inevitable long-term progress. In that chronology, it has yet to realize its purpose.'[23]

From the perspective of the late 1960s, Cobban views Mignet as a 'greater name' than Thiers in the annals of revolutionary historiography, a contention with which it is difficult to disagree.[24] Mignet was born in Aix a year before Thiers in Year IV, as it was known in the revolutionaries' new calendar. After studying law in his home town, he travelled to Paris where he made a living teaching history and working as a journalist on the *Courrier français*. So far as we are concerned, Mignet's most important work was *Histoire de la Révolution française* (1824).

Mignet's general position was that the Revolution had occurred because of the prevailing social and economic conditions in France. In many ways he was willing, and also happy, to defend it, but as a moderate, and a liberal, he was totally alienated by the Terror of 1793–4. The very first lines of his book set the scene:

> I am about to take a rapid review of the history of the French revolution, which began the era of new societies in Europe, as the English revolution had begun the era of new governments. This revolution not only modified the political power, but it entirely changed the internal existence of the nation. The forms of the society of the middle ages still remained. The land was divided into hostile provinces, the population into rival classes. The nobility had lost all their powers, but still retained all their distinctions: the people had no rights, royalty no limits; France was in an utter confusion of arbitrary administration of class legislation and special privileges to special bodies. For these abuses the revolution substituted a system more conformable with justice, and better suited to our times. It substituted law in the place of arbitrary will, equality in that of privilege; delivered men from the distinctions of classes, the land

from the barriers of provinces, trade from the shackles of corporations and fellowships, agriculture from feudal subjection and the oppression of tithes, property from the impediment of entails, and brought everything to the condition of one state, one system of law, one people.[25]

Here, in the space of one paragraph, we see the liberal credo writ large. There is talk of 'justice', 'law' and 'equality', and of 'barriers', 'shackles', 'subjection' and 'oppression' becoming things of the past. This is textbook stuff, and in among it all there is a hope, perhaps a belief, that liberal values *will* ultimately triumph. There is also something very idealistic about Mignet's position. To contend that 'equality' triumphed over 'privilege' is to generalise and to misinterpret the course of the Revolution and the motives of the middle classes.[26] Be that as it may. What *is* clear is that Mignet's liberal instincts are strong. His critique of the *Ancien Régime* is damning:

> The government of France, from Louis XIV to the revolution, was still more arbitrary than despotic; for the monarchs had much more power than they exercised. The barriers that opposed the encroachments of this immense authority were exceedingly feeble. The crown disposed of persons by *lettres de cachet*, of property by confiscation, of the public revenue by imposts. Certain bodies, it is true, possessed means of defence, which were termed privileges, but these privileges were rarely respected. The parliament had that of ratifying or of refusing an impost, but the king could compel its assent, by a *lit de justice*, and punish its members by exile. The nobility were exempt from taxation; the clergy were entitled to the privilege of taxing themselves, in the form of free gifts; some provinces enjoyed the right of compounding the taxes, and others made the assessment themselves. Such were the trifling liberties of France, and even these all turned to the benefit of the privileged classes, and to the detriment of the people. And this France, so enslaved, was moreover miserably organised; the excesses of power were still less endurable than their unjust distribution. The nation, divided into three orders, which subdivided themselves into several classes, was a prey to all the attacks of despotism, and all the evils of inequality.[27]

Passages such as this leave the observer in no doubt that Mignet was a firm supporter of early, liberal phase of the Revolution (1789–91). In addition, it helps us to understand his perspective on the issue of origins.

Mignet's thoughts on causation are a mixed bag. On the one

hand, he highlights traditional political factors such as the actions of the Estates General. On the other, he focuses on 'long-term' trends. He also throws light on subsidiary factors such as 'irrational passions'.[28] But what did he make of the years of the Terror, the ascendancy of the Jacobins and the Committee of Public Safety? A writer with liberal sensibilities could only be horrified by the beginnings of organised state violence. Robespierre is described as a man 'who played so terrible a part in our revolution', as someone who had the 'qualifications for tyranny', and a political operator who 'had the support of an immense and fanatical sect'.[29] Mignet portrays Danton in slightly more amenable terms, but claims nevertheless that 'The welfare of his party was, in his eyes, superior to law and even to humanity.'[30] Moving on from personalities, Mignet opined:

> During this war [the foreign war], the committee of public safety gave way to the most terrible excesses ... The usage of all governments being to make their own preservation a matter of right, they regard those who attack them as enemies so long as they fight, as conspirators when they are defeated; and thus destroy them alike by means of war and of law. All these views at once guided the policy of the committee of public safety, a policy of vengeance, of terror, and of self-preservation. This was the maxim upon which it proceeded in reference to insurgent towns: 'The name of Lyons,' said Barrère, 'must no longer exist.'[31]

Mignet talks of the 'dictatorial government', the 'extreme Mountain', and the Commune's attachment to 'political anarchy and religious symbolism',[32] but elsewhere he chronicles the work of the Terror in fairly neutral and matter-of-fact terms. For instance, when he comes to explaining the Religious Terror in action, and in particular the initiative to create a new calendar, he describes the Jacobin leaders as 'innovators' (and with no obvious sense of irony or dismay).[33]

It is interesting to observe his depiction of St Just and the mechanics of dictatorship-building. It is one of the curiosities of the revolutionary era that the word 'liberty' is defined in so many different ways by so many different people. Mignet quotes St Just as stating, 'Liberty must triumph at any cost. In the present circumstances of the republic, the constitution cannot be established; it would guarantee impunity to attacks on our liberty, because it would be deficient in the violence necessary to restrain them.'[34] Here St Just introduces his own definition of 'liberty'. Through violence and near-totalitarian government, he and his colleagues will create a situation in which France is free of 'enemies' and 'suspects' intent on destabilising the Revolution. To his way of thinking, such a campaign of 'illiberal' measures will reap a truly 'liberal' reward in the end. But Mignet, offering a more balanced and less skewed vision of 1793–94, has a different view: 'The committee [of public safety] did everything in the name of the convention, which it used as an instrument ... By means of the law touching suspected persons, it disposed of men's liberties; by the revolutionary tribunal of men's lives; by levies and the *maximum*, of property; by decrees of accusation in the terrified convention, of its own members.'[35] He put a premium on liberty and liberties, and thus felt totally alienated by the Terror.

Mignet's is a mainly political narrative, and he rarely delves into the social and economic history of the period. Nonetheless, in the language that he uses he reveals interesting things about his position and perspective as an individual. Most of the time he refers to the lower classes as the 'people' but occasionally he talks of the 'mob' and the 'multitude'. Does this indicate a lack of genuine affinity with the majority element of the Third Estate?[36] Perhaps the fact that Mignet, like Thiers, held office under the ultra-bourgeois July Monarchy suggests this was the case.[37]

By contrast, when he makes reference to the leaders of the Revolution, he does so without using pejorative terms. Thus, on the morrow of the Tennis Court Oath: 'The national assembly, composed of the elite of the nation, was full of intelligence, pure intentions, and projects for the public good.'[38] Perhaps the National Assembly in the aftermath of a liberal revolution is where Mignet – a moderate man of the middle class – would have liked to have been himself if he had been transported back into the Revolution. Moreover, Mignet does not ignore the question of class. He recognises the increasing size and influence of the French middle class, and their identification with the idea of liberty. But he also claims that the middle classes were slightly underdeveloped.[39] It is profoundly significant that Mignet identified a 'social' dimension to the Revolution. He contrasted 1789 in France with 1688 in England, and could see that in France society had been changed, not just the government.[40] But before those on the left get too excited, it should be pointed out that Mignet was fairly oblivious to the notion of collective action.

Finally, it is interesting that Mignet's history goes right through to 1814. While other histories stop at 1799, or 1795, he includes chapters on the Consulate and Empire. And he justifies this decision in an extremely matter-of-fact way, seemingly disregarding the fact that Napoleon was noticeably illiberal, and authoritarian in many of his utterances and policies. He writes:

> The 18th Brumaire had immense popularity. People did not perceive in this event the elevation of a single man above the councils of the nation; they did not see in it the end of the great movement of the 14th of July, which had commenced the national existence. The 18th Brumaire assumed an aspect of hope and restoration ... All felt the need of being restored by a skilful hand, and Bonaparte, as a great man and a victorious general, seemed suited for the task.[41]

Mignet had grown up during the Empire – he would have been eighteen when the Emperor was deposed in 1814 – and when he started to research and write his *History of the French Revolution* during the early and middle years of the Restoration, he may well have been influenced, on the one hand, by nostalgia for Napoleon – his modernity, efficiency and liberal concessions (especially in individual European states that he had conquered) – and, on the other, by his loathing for the increasingly illiberal attitudes displayed by Louis XVIII and Charles X. In consequence, Mignet sounds naively enthusiastic about 1799, and also at times realistic and pragmatic:

> Almost every one, except the dictatorial republicans, declared in favour of the events of that day. Violation of the laws and *coups-d'état* had occurred so frequently during the Revolution, that people had become accustomed no longer to judge them by their legality, but by their consequences. From the party of Sieyès down to the royalists of 1788, every one congratulated himself on the 18th Brumaire, and attributed to himself the future political advantages of this change. The moderate constitutionalists believed that definitive liberty would be established; the royalists fed themselves with hope by inappropriately comparing this epoch of our revolution with the epoch of 1660 in the English Revolution, with the hope

that Bonaparte was assuming the part of Monk, and that he would soon restore the monarchy of the Bourbons; the mass, possessing little intelligence, and desirous of repose, relied on the return of order under a powerful protector; the proscribed classes and ambitious men expected from him their amnesty or elevation.[42]

Or perhaps this is what people, Mignet in particular, wished to believe?

Benjamin Constant, the French-Swiss writer, is an interesting case. He served Napoleon, was elected as a parliamentary deputy under the Restoration but always remained loyal to the idea of constitutional monarchy. For this reason he was very much in favour of the Revolution of 1830. In many ways, Constant is a classical liberal. In *De la liberté des anciens comparée à celle des modernes* (1819) and *De l'esprit de conquête et de l'usurpation* (1814), he meditates on the meaning of freedom and the relationship between public and private domains. In the aftermath of the French Revolution, he puts the case for modern representative government as a panacea for the nation's ills.

Pierre Louis Roederer falls into the same kind of category as Constant. He pamphleteered on behalf of the Third Estate in the 1780s and was appointed recorder of the Paris department in the early-1790s. Like Constant, he held office under Napoleon, as minister of finance at Naples (1806), administrator of the Grand Duchy of Berg (1810), and imperial commissary in the south of France. During the Hundred Days he was created a peer of France. As a writer, his most celebrated works were *L'Esprit de la Révolution de 1789* (1831) and *Chronique des cinquante jours, an account of the events of the 10th of August 1792* (1832). He was interested in matters of religious and economic freedom, and not unnaturally he was totally alienated by the rise of Robespierre and the beginnings of the Terror.

Much later (1895–99), Lord Acton delivered his *Lectures on the French Revolution*.[43] Acton was one of the great liberal historians of the Victorian era. His main concern was freedom: protecting it and allowing it to flourish. He saw enormous danger in the accumulation of political power, and for this reason, later in his life, he turned his attention to the French Revolution. In his analysis of the period 1793–94, Acton emphasises the authoritarianism of Robespierre and the Committee of Public Safety. The press and key political factions were denied the freedom and liberty they required to exist and make a contribution to political debate.[44] As Acton explains: 'The liberal and constitutional wave with which the Revolution began ended with the Girondins; and the cause of freedom against authority, of right against force was lost.'[45]

Together with de Staël, Thiers and Mignet, Constant, Roederer and Acton form, arguably, the first genuine school of revolutionary history. They were reacting to a momentous political event only a generation or so after the event took place. Acton apart, they were all French, and so had patriotic as well as philosophical reasons for wanting to validate the Revolution. The 'Great Tradition', or 'classical' tradition, had been born, even though these writers themselves would have been unaware of the fact.

De Staël, Thiers, Mignet and company were liberals in the sense that they supported and empathised with the early period of the Revolution, when the talk was of individual liberty, rights and duties, tolerance and constitutionality. The Terror, obviously, was a watershed. The officials of the Committee of Public Safety and Committee of General Security had their own definition of 'liberty', but it was a warped one, and not one that most of the French population as a whole shared. The liberal historians of the early nineteenth century certainly could not align themselves with this kind of thinking. They were frustrated and annoyed with the descent of the Revolution into terror, but what is most noticeable about their writings is the in-built confidence they have in the future. Liberty, they argue, *will* eventually win through.

Notes

1 Germaine de Staël quoted in V. Folkenflik (ed.), *Major Writings of Germaine de Staël* (Oxford, 1987), p. 366.
2 A. Cobban, *Aspects of the French Revolution* (London, 1968), pp. 34–5.
3 Folkenflik, *Major Writings*, p. 361.
4 www.kirjasto.sci.fi/stael.htm.
5 Folkenflik, *Major Writings*, pp. 359–60.
6 Ibid., p. 366.
7 Ibid., p. 367.
8 Ibid., pp. 359–73.

9 Ibid., p. 365.

10 Ibid., p. 363.

11 *The Declaration of the Rights of Man and of the Citizen*, published in 1789, is littered with references to the 'law '... and was written mainly by lawyers.

12 Folkenflik, *Major Writings*, p. 364.

13 Ibid., p. 368.

14 Ibid., p. 367.

15 T. Lewis, 'Madame de Staël: The Inveterate Idealist', *The Hudson Review*, Autumn 2001.

16 N. Hampson, 'The French Revolution and its Historians', in G. Best (ed.), *The Permanent Revolution* (London, 1989), p. 214.

17 Ibid., p. 214.

18 Ibid., p. 215.

19 Cobban, *Aspects*, p. 102.

20 Ibid., p. 35.

21 Hampson, 'Revolution', p. 215.

22 N. Parker, *Portrayals of Revolution* (Hemel Hempstead, 1990), pp. 126–7.

23 Ibid., p. 124.

24 Cobban, Aspects, p. 35.

25 F. Mignet, *History of the French Revolution* (London, 1913), p. 1.

26 See Hampson, 'Revolution', p. 215.

27 Mignet, *History*, pp. 4–5.

28 Cobban, *Aspects*, pp. 35–6; Parker, *Portrayals*, p. 123.

29 Mignet, *Aspects*, pp. 190–1.

30 Ibid., p. 177.

31 Ibid., p. 254.

32 Ibid., pp. 254–6.

33 Ibid., p. 258.

34 Ibid., p. 257.

35 Ibid., p. 257.

36 Ibid., pp. 46–7, 257–8.

37 Mignet was appointed to the position of senior archivist at the Foreign Office.

38 Ibid., p. 62.

39 Parker, *Portrayals*, p. 121.

40 Hampson, 'Revolution', p. 214.

41 Mignet, *Aspects*, p. 399.

42 Ibid., pp. 399–400.

43 They were originally published in 1910.

44 Lord Acton, *Lectures on the French Revolution* (Liberty Fund online: http://oll.libertyfund.org/Home3/Book.php?recordID=0001, 2000), pp. 272, 280.

45 Ibid., p. 269.

3

Idealist and romantic views

> Nobody can behold that marvellous unanimity, in which the self-
> same heart beat together in the breasts of twenty millions of men,
> without returning thanks to God.[1]

This chapter considers the middle years of the nineteenth century, when there was a discernible shift in focus. Historians and writers started to emphasise the 'idealistic' and 'romantic' nature of the Revolution. 'Romanticism', thus, was not simply a literary genre. It impacted upon the way that historians wrote history, in the sense that, more often than not, they could be seen to be hankering after an ideal or trying to bring to life a vision. They were not realists or pragmatists, but individuals with grand ambitions and unlimited horizons.

Thomas Carlyle described the Revolution in colourful, dramatic terms while Jules Michelet highlighted the dynamic role of *le peuple*. François Guizot talked about 1789 in terms of the 'growth of civilisation', and Edgar Quinet was interested in the relationship between republicanism and Christianity. Alphonse de Lamartine described the birth of the French Republic in epic terms, Louis Blanc saw the Revolution as a glorious, wonderful event, and Auguste Comte viewed it through a positivist lens. Several of these writers revealed an interest in medieval France and the course of French history in the Middle Ages (this fascination with the Middle Ages was a key feature of later romanticism). It was all part of their ambitious and grandiose strategy, to see 1789 as a key staging-post in France's historical journey and her quest for a future.

Furthermore, Carlyle and Guizot both studied, and wrote about, the English Revolution of 1640. Carlyle was interested in a number of issues that were crystallised by the event – the meaning of authority and hierarchy, and the role of religion, for example. Meanwhile, for Guizot, 1640 was a helpful reference point as he evaluated the significance of 1789 and 1830. Thus, for both men, curious and fascinated by the idea of revolution as they were, it was instinctive to look back to the Middle Ages and to England in the seventeenth century. This was vital if they were to contextualise 1789 and comprehend its meaning more accurately.

So, in this chapter, the main questions we need to address are these: Why did historians seek to romanticise the people and the Revolution? How did these 'romantic' writers view the 'liberal' position? How did the 1830 and 1848 revolutions colour the judgement of these mid-century historians?

In one sense, Thomas Carlyle was an ally of Thiers and Mignet. He had liberal inclinations and shared many of their main concerns. But, in reality, he had little regard for their work. As Cobban, a more sophisticated twentieth-century scholar, puts it: 'The more recent historians, Thiers and Mignet, make no appearance among his references. He had read Thiers, but dismissed him with "Dig where you will you come to water"; his work was superficial and full of errors; Mignet was more honest, but his history lacked life and colour and its ideas were mere logical abstractions.'[2] Of course, it is relatively easy for a historian of the late twentieth century, like Cobban, to criticise those of the early nineteenth century, but in truth there was something rather slapdash and unorthodox about Carlyle in particular.

One of the few non-French historians to gain acclaim for their work on the Revolution, Carlyle was born in Ecclefechan, Dumfriesshire in 1795, the year in which the constitution of the Directory was proclaimed. He finished *The French Revolution* in 1837, but only after a freak accident had put his work in jeopardy. Carlyle's friend John Stuart Mill had offered to have a look at the manuscript before it went to press. This is what happened, but Mill's maidservant inadvertently used the script to light a fire! Given the catastrophe that had occurred, Carlyle stayed remarkably calm. Apparently, when they were left alone, the first words he uttered to his wife were: 'Well, Mill, poor fellow, is terribly cut up; we must endeavour to hide from him how very serious the business is to us.'[3] We are told that Carlyle had 'kept no notes and could not recall a sentence that he had written'.[4] So, when we study Carlyle's book we are in fact studying the second version of it. As the author stated after he had completed his re-write: 'You have not had for a hundred years any book that comes more direct and flamingly from the heart of a living man.'[5]

Carlyle's historical method was an unusual one. The general style is epic, literary and grandiose, almost biblical in tone, and as such, very much in keeping with Carlyle's life as a writer and essayist. To the modern reader, The French Revolution reads more like a historical thriller than a piece of reflection and considered analysis. There is a helter-skelter of anecdote and vivid, colourful picture-painting. As Cobban says, 'He is the word-painter of a society in shipwreck'[6] – a description that Carlyle, a man who liked a colourful phrase, would surely have approved of. The book is based primarily on memoirs, newspaper reports, minutes of official proceedings and already-published histories of the Revolution. It is highly eccentric and individualistic but it is 'history' in a way that the writings of a Burke or a de Maistre are probably not. Moreover, it is a kind of 'history from below', not particularly in the sense that it focuses on the lives of the 'lower classes', but in the way that it tells the story of the Revolution through grandiose tittle-tattle and the everyday lives of key individuals. This is demonstrated best in the way that Carlyle organises and arranges his book. His 'section' titles are predictable enough ('The Bastille', 'The Constitution', 'The Guillotine') but some of his chapters have odd, abstract and sometimes humorous titles. Thus, we have 'Windbags' (Section 1, Book II, Chapter VI), 'Not a Revolt' (Section 1, Book V, Chapter VII), 'No Sugar' (Section 2, Book V, Chapter IV), 'Stretching of Formulas' (Section 3, Book II, Chapter V). Self evidently this is an eccentric and rather idiosyncratic way of structuring a book.

One way to understand and explain the nature of Carlyle 'as historian' is to examine his commentaries on some of the key phases of the Revolution. On the convening of the Estates General, Carlyle writes:

The universal prayer, therefore, is to be fulfilled! Always in days of national perplexity, when wrong abounded and help was not, this remedy of States-General was called for; by a Malesherbes, nay by a Fenelon; even Parlements calling for it were 'escorted with blessings.' And now behold it is vouchsafed us; States-General shall verily be! To say, let States-General be, was easy; to say in what manner they shall be, is not so easy. Since the year of 1614, there have no States-General met in France, all trace of them has vanished from the living habits of men. Their structure, powers, methods of procedure, which were never in any measure fixed, have now become wholly a vague possibility. Clay which the potter may shape, this way or that: – say rather, the twenty-five millions of potters; for so many have now, more or less, a vote in it! How to shape the States-General? There is a problem. Each Body-corporate, each privileged, each organised Class has secret hopes of its own in that matter; and also secret misgivings of its own, – for, behold, this monstrous twenty-million Class, hitherto the dumb sheep which these others had to agree about the manner of shearing, is now also arising with hopes! It has ceased or is ceasing to be dumb; it speaks through Pamphlets, or at least brays and growls behind them, in unison, - increasing wonderfully their volume of sound.[7]

Two aspects of this passage stand out, in addition to its old-fashioned tone, its semi-religious flavour, and its hyperbole (four exclamation marks!). First, there is the way in which the Third Estate is depicted. Carlyle talks about a 'monstrous' class of 'dumb sheep', but, as a liberal and radical, he probably has his tongue in his cheek at this point, or is trying to reflect popular perceptions of the Third Estate at the time. By the end of the excerpt, he has noted their penchant for 'Pamphlets' and their vocal efforts, which are 'increasing wonderfully'. He seems to be indicating that he is on their side. Second, there is the description of the Estates General itself and, in and amongst, he makes several pertinent points about the unpredictability of the whole ritual. Obviously he was speaking with half a century of hindsight, but he quickly gets to the point: 'How to shape the States-General? There is a problem.' A problem, it should be said, that would eventually lead to revolt.

With the fall of the Bastille, we discover Carlyle in 'racy' thriller mode:

For four hours now has the World-Bedlam roared: call it the World-Chimaera, blowing fire! The poor Invalides have sunk under their battlements, or rise only with reversed muskets: they have made a white flag of napkins; go beating the chamade, or seeming to beat, for one can hear nothing. The very Swiss at the Portcullis look weary of firing; disheartened in the fire-deluge: a porthole at the drawbridge is opened, as by one that would speak. See Huissier Maillard, the shifty man! On his plank, swinging over the abyss of that stone-Ditch; plank resting on parapet, balanced by weight of Patriots, – he hovers perilous: such a Dove towards such an Ark! Deftly, thou shifty Usher: one man already fell; and lies smashed, far down there, against the masonry! Usher Maillard falls not: deftly, unerring he walks, with outspread palm. The Swiss holds a paper through his porthole; the shifty Usher snatches it, and returns. Terms of surrender: Pardon, immunity to all! Are they accepted? – 'Foi d'officier, On the word of an officer,' answers half-pay Hulin, – or half-pay Elie, for men do not agree on it, 'they are!' Sinks the drawbridge, – Usher Maillard bolting it when down; rushes-in the living deluge: the Bastille is fallen! Victoire! La Bastille est prise![8]

This is a colourful description. It is as if Carlyle is penning the last paragraph of an epic film score. There is high drama and poignancy. His description of the Swiss guard – 'weary of firing' – conveys the mood of the time. The King had lost his capital city and most of his allies knew also that the battle was over. There was resignation and, almost, defeatism – hence the mention of a 'white flag' and 'terms of surrender'.

Carlyle is equally vivid in his description of the Flight to Varennes:

We are to have a civil war; let us have it then. The King is gone; but National Assembly, but France and we remain. The People also takes a great attitude; the People also is calm; motionless as a couchant lion. With but a few broolings, some waggings of the tail; to show what it will do! Cazales, for instance, was beset by street-groups, and cries of Lanterne; but National Patrols easily delivered him. Likewise all King's effigies and statues, at least stucco ones, get abolished. Even King's names; the word Roi fades suddenly out of all shop-signs; the Royal Bengal Tiger itself, on the Boulevards, becomes the National Bengal one, Tigre National. (Walpoliana.) How great is a calm couchant People! On the morrow, men will say to one another: 'We have no King, yet we slept sound enough.' On the morrow, fervent Achille de

Chatelet, and Thomas Paine the rebellious Needleman, shall have the walls of Paris profusely plastered with their Placard; announcing that there must be a Republic! – Need we add that Lafayette too, though at first menaced by Pikes, has taken a great attitude, or indeed the greatest of all? Scouts and Aides-de-camp fly forth, vague, in quest and pursuit; young Romoeuf towards Valenciennes, though with small hope. Thus Paris; sublimely calmed, in its bereavement. But from the Messageries Royales, in all Mail-bags, radiates forth far-darting the electric news: Our Hereditary Representative is flown. Laugh, black Royalists: yet be it in your sleeve only; lest Patriotism notice, and waxing frantic, lower the Lanterne! In Paris alone is a sublime National Assembly with its calmness; truly, other places must take it as they can: with open mouth and eyes; with panic cackling, with wrath, with conjecture.[9]

Carlyle depicts the King's exit as a 'bereavement' for the people of France, but he also articulates adeptly the fact that nothing really changed, epitomised best perhaps by the image of ordinary people still sleeping 'sound enough'.

Some of the 'word pictures' he creates are superb; others are cryptic and slightly obscure. But some questions and queries do emerge. When he talks about 'we', who exactly is he referring to? And is there significance in the fact that he uses a capital 'P' every time he spells the word 'People'? Does this indicate where his sympathies really lie? Throughout, his use of language is exquisite, interesting and provocative, if also slightly over-the-top. The biggest compliment one can pay to Carlyle is that his narrative style gives the impression that he was actually there, in Paris during the early years of the Revolution, and that his *French Revolution* is a *primary* rather than a *secondary* historical source. While in one sense this is something on which to congratulate the author – the realism, the detail, the graphic description that he is able to bring to his work – it is also a criticism, because the undeniable fact is that Carlyle was *not* there.

There is no doubt that Carlyle, although unsubtle and blustering in his style, had radical and liberal instincts at this stage in his career (later, his views became much more conservative). He was influenced by Saint Simon and the German Romantic movement, and he has virtually no sympathy for the wreckage of the *Ancien Régime*.[10] But the Terror was a watershed for him and affected his view of the Revolution greatly. He became more lukewarm in his attitude, and maybe even a little anti-French. He was fearful of terroristic violence being exported to Britain and came to the conclusion that liberal objectives were not easily achievable in any society.

Jules Michelet romanticised the way in which *le peuple* achieved prominence during the Revolution. He described the people as an 'ideal', and his interpretation moved centre stage during the Second Empire and the early days of the Third Republic. His 'romantic' interpretation of the Revolution attracted both admiration and criticism.

Michelet's humble background – his father was a printer, his mother came from a peasant family – was a significant influence on his early life. For example, he was dismayed when his father's printing works was closed by order of Napoleon, and it has been argued that this instilled in him sympathy for, and an understanding of, ordinary working people. M. Michelet Senior had great ambitions for his son and kept him in school for longer than the required minimum term. This decision paid off. Michelet spent much of his later life in Italy – which maybe explains why he came to be so fascinated by the Renaissance.

Over the decades, Michelet gained accolade after accolade and came to be fêted as France's greatest-ever historian. His most famous works were *Histoire de France* (24 volumes, 1833–67), *Le Peuple* (1846) and *History of the French Revolution* (1847). He also wrote one of the first books about revolutionary women. *Histoire de France* took the form of a long, dramatic narrative, and was particularly strong and detailed on the Middle Ages. *Le Peuple* was a vivid celebration of patriotism and the French working class. It sold around a thousand copies on its first day of publication and was soon translated into English. In his introduction to the book, Lucien Refort talks about Michelet's 'love of the people'; they were an 'inspiration' and also the 'source of his lyricism'. *Amour* is the key word for Refort – Michelet displays a simple but hugely powerful love for *le peuple*.[11] Meanwhile, *History of the French Revolution* was a conventional narrative history. All three works revealed the radical side of Michelet and in particular his love for ordinary people – as individuals and as an embryonic 'social force'.

Michelet's writings are distinctive. He plays with language and gives power to myths and legends. There is also something inescapably emotional and romantic about the history that he writes. Here, the influence of the Italian philosopher Vico is evident. Michelet studied Vico and was obviously influenced by his anti-rationalist approach – so much so that Michelet has been criticised variously for having *too much* of an imagination and for putting a premium on this rather than reasoned analysis.

Michelet's *History of the French Revolution* is a wonderful book to read because the author is so open and disarming in his prejudices, both positive and negative. As the revisionist Hampson put it: 'With Michelet the Great Tradition found its most eloquent and extreme spokesman. To present the bare outline of his argument is like paraphrasing one of Shakespeare's tragedies: one can convey a general impression of what it was all about but the real meaning is inseparable from the hypnotic language that is an essential part of it.'[12] It is predictable that Michelet's history scores so highly with fellow historians of the Revolution. There was a graceful quality to his writings and an authentic and attractive sense of idealism.

But, when Michelet wrote his history, in 1847, there was still some naivety about what the job of the historian entailed. We are still almost half a century away from Aulard and the 'profession-alising' of the historian's trade via the Chair in Revolutionary History at the Sorbonne. Thus, when Michelet talks about his technique as a historian, he reveals that he establishes and verifies his findings, 'either by written testimony, or by such as I have gathered from the lips of old men'.[13] Contrast this with Aulard's later strictures against the use of memoirs as a historical source.[14]

Michelet is unfailingly honest in the way he says that studying and writing about the Revolution affected him. For him it was a personal joy to be able to recount such a heroic period:

> I am endeavouring to describe to-day that epoch of unanimity, that holy period, when a whole nation, free from all party distinction, as yet a comparative stranger to the opposition of classes, marched together under a flag of brotherly love ... These are the sacred days of the world – thrice happy days for history. For my part, I have had my reward, in the mere narration of them. Never, since the compo-sition of my Maid of Orleans, have I received such a ray from above,

such a vivid inspiration from Heaven.[15]

However, Michelet's openness is also his Achilles heel. Whereas twenty-first century historians try to conduct their business dispassionately, he almost admits to being swept along by the events he is describing. He implies that he is flattered to be acting as a historian of the Revolution and, whatever the innate strengths of his historical work, perhaps this is its undoing. It is too obvious that Michelet is emotionally involved in a set of events that he did not witness, but that he is attempting to chronicle decades later. This comes through most powerfully when Michelet refers to 'the people'. His self-identification with *le peuple* is so strong and formidable that as one turns the pages of the book, one could be forgiven for thinking that they are not an amorphous collection of individuals, but rather a solid 'block'. There is an enormous amount of love in Michelet's depiction of 'the people'. It is as if they are 'warm' and 'glowing', as if somehow, in one particular decade (1789–99), they acquired supernatural strength and influence, and had it in them to take on the world.

It is interesting that 'the people' remains quite a nebulous and ambiguous phrase in Michelet's writings. As an indication of this, take the following: 'A thing to be told to everybody, and which it is but too easy to prove, is, that the humane and benevolent period of our Revolution had for its actors the very people, the whole people – everybody. And the period of violence, the period of sanguinary deeds, into which danger afterwards thrust it, had for actors but an inconsiderable, an extremely small number of men.'[16] The general meaning of these sentences is clear, but Michelet is not particularly helpful or incisive when it comes to defining his terms. The 'people' – he probably means the totality of the Third Estate, bar those who took on a leadership role in the Girondin or Jacobin factions – obviously account for the vast majority of the population. But it would not have done Michelet any harm to have been more specific in this area and to use a few more socio-economic descriptors. That said, his weakness is also his strength. He writes with feeling and fervour. His narrative is gripping, and it would lose quite a lot if it stopped off at key junctures to offer the reader technical definitions, even as footnotes.

Michelet also characterises the people as being increasingly assured. They switch from being 'spectators' to 'actors' in the historical drama with profound simplicity. Describing how in mid-1789 ordinary Parisians were waiting for the King to leave Versailles, he states: 'That is what the people expected, what they believed and talked of. They said so at the Hôtel-de-Ville, and repeated it in the streets. The king hesitated, consulted, postponed for one day, and all was lost.'[17] Another example makes the point too: 'At Versailles, a man was going to be broken on the wheel as a parricide; he had raised a knife against a woman, and his father, throwing himself between them, had been killed by the blow. The people thought the punishment still more barbarous than the act, prevented the execution, and overthrew the scaffold.'[18] Michelet is demonstrably proud of these individual acts of defiance. It is as if during the Revolution *le peuple* were being encouraged to take on board a new code of behaviour, and fifty years on, he has taken it upon himself to chart this amazing story.

So Michelet's people are confident. They are also together, united. It is but a short step from adulation of the people to love of fraternity. Michelet is direct:

> Fraternity! fraternity! It is not enough to re-echo the word – to attract the world to our cause, as was the case at first. It must acknowledge in us a fraternal heart. It must be gained over by the fraternity of love, and not by the guillotine. Fraternity! Why who, since the creation, has not pronounced that word? Do you imagine it was first coined by Robespierre or Mably? Every state of antiquity talked of fraternity; but the word was addressed only to citizens – to men; the slave was but a thing. And in this case fraternity was exclusive and inhuman ... Liberty alone, as founded in the last century, has rendered fraternity possible.[19]

His emphasis on 'the people' and 'fraternity' has led many commentators to pigeon-hole him on the patriotic left. Kamenka highlights his populism and likens him to 'a Mazzini or a Mickiewicz', while O'Brien labels him a 'fiery nationalist historian'.[20]

And confident, united, the people are committed to peaceful means: 'What will astonish those who are acquainted with the history of other revolutions is, that in this miserable and famished state of Paris, denuded of all authority, there were on the whole but very few serious acts of violence. One word, one reasonable observation, occasionally a jest, was sufficient to check them.'[21] Again, it does not feel right to puncture Michelet's enthusiasm, or to nit-pick when his adoration for the events of the 1789 is so genuine and passionate, but he may well be viewing the year of several revolutions with rose-tinted spectacles. We are told elsewhere that the people who ransacked the Bastille felt inclined to place the head of the prison's governor on a pike as an act of vengeance and triumph. How would he have viewed this piece of theatre?

It is clear that Michelet cannot tolerate the Reign of Terror, 1793–94. This is where, for him, the Revolution takes a wrong turning, where individuals like Robespierre and small factions like the Jacobins upstage the mass of the people. The point we made above is valid again. Michelet does not want to believe that his beloved people were in any way involved in the period of 'Revolutionary Government', except as victims. Historians like Gwynne Lewis have picked up on this: 'For Michelet, "the People" – this undifferentiated mass of the French nation – are, in many ways, the driving-force of the Revolution. When they are told to "go home" in 1793 by the Jacobins, the Revolution, according to Michelet, is already on the road to Terror and military dictatorship.'[22]

At times, Michelet's love letter to *le peuple* takes on a mystical, semi-religious quality. He internalises the Revolution just as Christians sometimes internalise the presence of God:

> I commune with my own mind. I interrogate myself as to my teaching, my history, and its all-powerful interpreter – the spirit of the Revolution. It possesses a knowledge of which others are ignorant. It contains the secret of all bygone times. In it alone France was conscious of herself. When, in a moment of weakness, we may appear forgetful of our own worth, it is to this point we should recur in order to seek and recover ourselves again. Here, the inextinguishable spark, the profound mystery of life, is ever glowing within us. The Revolution lives in ourselves – in our souls; it has no outward monument. Living spirit of France, where shall I seize thee, but within myself?[23]

He goes on: 'Genius utterly humane! I love to follow and watch its progress, in those admirable fetes wherein a whole people, at once the actors and spectators, gave and received the impulse of moral enthusiasm; wherein every heart expanded with all the sublimity of France – of a country which, for its law, proclaimed the rights of humanity.'[24] The image is of men and women – totally *ordinary* men and women – coming together, rising up, as if caught up in an epic biblical tale.

Michelet's attitude towards the *Ancien Régime* is based on a devastating critique of traditional religion. As if anticipating later, more explicitly secular histories of the Revolution, he was cutting:

> What bears an overwhelming testimony against the Church in '89 is the state of utter neglect in which she had left the people. For two thousand years she alone had the duty of instructing them; and how had she performed it? What was the end and aim of the pious foundations in the middle ages? What duties did they impose on the clergy? The salvation of souls, their religious improvement, the softening of manners, the humanising of the people. They were your disciples, and given to you alone. Masters, what have you taught them? Ever since the twelfth century, you have continued to speak to them a language no longer theirs, and the form of worship has ceased to be a mode of instructing them. The deficiency was supplied by preaching; but gradually it became silent, or spoke for the rich alone. You have neglected the poor, disdained the coarse mob. Coarse? Yes, through you.[25]

And in even more vindictive terms, he declares: 'Those who know by history, by the study of the middle ages, the prodigious tenacity of the clergy in defending their least interest, may easily judge what efforts they would now make to save their possessions, and their most precious possession, their cherished intolerance.'[26]

What provoked Michelet into this rage against the Church? Obviously, he had lived through the Restoration and witnessed the extremes and absurdities of near-theocratic government. And, writing and researching in the 1840s, he could not but be influenced by the lukewarm relationship that developed between the July Monarchy and the Church. Given these factors, it would have been unimaginable for any historian in the 1840s, let alone Michelet, to have written a history of the Revolution that was not anti-clerical to some degree. He explores other causes of the Revolution – the Enlightenment and social deprivation, for instance – but in the end he returns to the *Ancien Régime* and its innate failings.[27]

Michelet's history of the Revolution should not be viewed in isolation. It should be placed in context, and we need to be aware of his reference points at the time, as well as bringing in our own. In the 1840s, when Michelet was preparing his work, the Orleanists were in power, with Louis Philippe as their monarch. Guizot – whose work as a historian we will examine in due course[28] – was acting as the King's chief minister and his philosophy was clear: the July Monarchy stood for the upper middle classes. As a result, its franchise was narrow, and its credo, 'Get rich!', was a fairly blunt challenge to the lower middle classes and ordinary working people, as if encouraging them to aspire to 'membership' of the governing party.

So when, in 1847, Michelet lauds 'the people' and congratulates them on their inspiring, pivotal role in 1789, he is doing so against the backdrop of hardline middle-class rule. Was he gently provoked into this stance by the harsh realities of Orleanist rule? And was he, consciously or subconsciously, speaking to 'the people' of France in 1847 when he poured adulation on 'the people' who made a revolution happen in 1789? It is certainly not irrelevant to point out that twelve months after Michelet's history was published, France erupted into revolution once more. He had been hoping for, and also encouraging, revolt against the July Monarchy; and naturally, the outpouring of radical ideas in France – and throughout Europe – in 1848 was of immense interest to him. It was also a source of encouragement. He did not take on any official role in the Second Republic, but he did refuse to swear the oath of allegiance to Louis Napoleon once the latter had overturned this regime. This demonstrates an in-built attachment to the idea of republicanism on Michelet's part. Predictably, he was forced to keep a low profile during the period of the Second Empire – the Emperor, it seems, distrusted Michelet on account of his 'radical' inclinations. Michelet was momentarily inspired by the Franco-Prussian War and the dawn of the Third Republic, but he died in Hyères on 9 February 1874.

In the same way that it is impossible to disconnect Michelet from the political events of his lifetime, so it is problematic to view his *History of the French Revolution* in a void. For the truth is that, to some extent, he was influenced by writers who had gone before, and also, he and his work had a significant impact on later historical writings. Here the natural starting point is the relationship between Michelet and Carlyle. Both wrote their history as if they were writing novels, or thrillers, and their style is less reasoned analysis than powerful, evocative description. It is easy to understand the comparison. Consider this passage, as Michelet describes the manoeuvrings at Court in the early months of 1789:

> The conspiracy of the court, aggravated with a thousand popular accounts, both strange and horrible, had seized upon every imagination, and rendered them incurably suspicious and distrustful. Versailles, excited as least as much as Paris, watched the castle night and day as the centre of treason. That immense palace seemed a desert. Many durst no longer enter it. The north wing, appropriated to the Condés, was almost empty; the south wing, that of the Count d'Artois, and the seven vast apartments of the ladies Polignac were shut up for ever. Several of the king's servants would have liked to forsake their master. They were beginning to entertain strange ideas about him.[29]

Both writers, too, harboured liberal, sometimes radical, political instincts. This led Taine to describe Carlyle as '*un Michelet anglais*'. Aulard also spoke of them in the same breath, and saw genuine similarities in their 'style', 'lyricism' and 'evocative prose'. However, there seems to have been little love lost between the two men themselves. Michelet labelled Carlyle a 'fantasist' and described his main work on the Revolution as an '*ouvrage pitoyable*'.[30]

In a totally different sense, perhaps Michelet saw a soulmate in the Abbé Sieyès, the radical cleric whose *What is the Third Estate?* was a landmark in progressive, pre-revolutionary statements. On more than one occasion, Michelet mentions the Abbé, on the issue of revolutionary 'subalterns' and that of tithes.[31] Fifty-eight years separated the publication of their respective works, but both writers put a premium on the vastness of the Third Estate and the heroic tenacity of ordinary French people. O'Brien also sees the link: 'Sieyès, at the beginning of the French Revolution, speaks for the new nationalism: "the nation before all" … And Michelet, heir and historian of the Revolution, gives thanks to the country for having filled "the immeasurable abyss" which the Enlightenment had left within him'.[32]

Many later writers demonstrated an allegiance of some kind to Michelet and his work on the Revolution. Jaurès, for example, says that Michelet, along with Marx and Plutarch, was the inspiration behind his own work, *Histoire Socialiste de la Révolution française*.[33] Palmer, who made his name as a 'soft' revisionist a century and more after Michelet, calls him a 'rhapsodist of democracy' and 'the soaring eulogist of the people'.[34] But not everyone is in agreement. Weber claims that Michelet's description of the Revolution was, in places, 'simply silly', while Hampson – a champion of soft revisionism – says there was something 'implausible' about his history.[35] Wayne Northcutt is more balanced in his assessment:

> In many ways, *Le Peuple* and his other historical works expressed the romanticism of his age and reflected the credo of the liberal petite bourgeoisie ... Although the Marxists criticized him because of his faith in the reconciliation of classes and the permanence of the nation state, the twentieth-century historian Lucien Febvre, a founder of the Annales school, viewed his work as an inspiration for a new variety of history.[36]

What is certain is that Michelet's writings were original and provocative. He remains relevant today – a romantic historian whose ideas and opinions were influenced by the political and philosophical climate of the time.

Along with Adolph Thiers,[37] François Guizot is probably the best example of the historian-politician or politician-historian. Of course, in nineteenth-century France there was a significant overlap between the two professions. Guizot stands out as one of the foremost romantic-idealist historians, and also as one of the key political figures of the period. He had a long and distinguished political career, which culminated in his role as first minister to King Louis Philippe during the Orleanist era.

Guizot was born two years prior to the fall of the Bastille. His political career started in earnest on the demise of the Restoration. The general historical consensus is that Guizot moved more and more to the right as the 1830s and 1840s progressed. He came to personify the selfish, narrow-minded philosophy of Orleanism. The July Monarchy was a 'closed shop'. There was an 'in' faction and an 'out' faction, and there was very little social mobility or fluidity. This is how Guizot and his minister colleagues wanted it. Ultimately, this kind of world-view would lead to revolution in 1848. But Guizot was unabashed and unashamed. From the start he openly paraded his ideology. In a speech of 5 October 1831 he declared:

> I have heard equality much spoken of; we have called it the fundamental principle of our political organization. I am afraid there has been a great mistake. Without doubt there are universal rights, equal rights for all, rights inherent in humanity and which no human being can be stripped of without injustice and disorder. It has been the honor of modern civilization to redeem these rights from that mass of violence and force under which they had long been hidden and to bring them back to light. There you have personal rights, universal and equal for all, from which stem equality in civil order and in moral order. But will political rights be of this order? It is through tradition, through heredity that families, peoples, and history subsist; without tradition, without heredity you would have nothing of that. It is through the personal activity of families, peoples, and individuals that produces the perfectibility of the human race. Suppress it, and you will cause the human race to fall to the rank of the animals. I say that aristocracy is the condition of modern societies, a necessary consequence of the nature of modern democracy. Upon this aristocracy two conditions are to be imposed: First, it is to be constantly submitted to the control and examination of democracy; second, it must recruit itself constantly from the people.[38]

There are mixed signals here: the trust in 'aristocracy' and 'tradition', but also the emphasis on 'rights'. In a speech of 15 February 1842 he also showed his hand:

> I am, for my part, a decided enemy of universal suffrage. I look upon it as the ruin of democracy and liberty. If I needed proof I would have it under my very eyes; I will not elucidate. However, I should permit myself to say, with all the respect I have for a great country and a great government, that the inner danger, the social danger by which the United States appears menaced is due especially to universal suffrage; it is that which makes them run the risk of seeing their real liberties, the liberties of everybody, compromised, as well as the inner order of their society.[39]

Guizot, the historian of the Revolution, has a slightly different persona from Guizot the politician (although the two do invariably merge). On one level Guizot the writer displayed many liberal credentials. Under the Restoration he was punished for his radical political instincts: in 1821 he lost his appointments and in 1825 he was forbidden to lecture. In fact, he and his lectures at the Sorbonne played a key role in igniting opposition to the regimes of Louis XVIII and Charles X. As a result there is a case to argue for examining Guizot's ideas on the Revolution in Chapter 2 of this study. On another level, Guizot's writings touch upon many romantic and idealist themes. He sees the Revolution as an important staging post in France's long, evolving history, as a kind of 'revival' or 're-birth'; and like Michelet, he is fascinated by the nature of feudal society and the relationship between modern and medieval France.

But throughout all of this, it is impossible to ignore Guizot the man of action, the practising politician. In this role he was a conservative, someone closed to new ideas. He achieved much as a politician under the July Monarchy. Elected as a *député* in 1830, he served Louis Philippe as minister of the interior and then of public instruction (1832–37), and was appointed premier in 1847. However, in fundamental terms, he reserved power for himself and was loathe to share it with anyone from outside his own social class. In a speech of 20 February 1831 he articulated his ideas about France's recent history, making an implicit connection between the revolutions of 1789 and 1830:

The Revolution destroyed the *ancien régime* but was unable to do more. The Empire arose to re-establish order, order of an exterior, material sort which was the basis of the civil society as the Revolution had founded it. The Empire spread this idea throughout all of Europe; this was its mission and it succeeded at it. It was incapable, however, of establishing a lasting political government; the necessary conditions were lacking. The Empire fell in its turn, to be succeeded by the Restoration. What did the Restoration promise? It promised to resolve the problem, to reconcile order with liberty. It was under this banner that the charter was granted. It had accepted principles of liberty in the charter; it had promised to establish them, but it made this promise under the cloak of the *ancien régime*, on which there had been written for so many centuries: Divine Right. It was unable to solve the problem. It died in the process, overwhelmed by the burden. It is on us, on the Revolution of July, that this job has been imposed; it is our duty and responsibility to establish definitively, not order alone, not liberty alone, but order and liberty at the same time. The general thought, the hope of France, has been order and liberty reuniting under the constitutional monarchy. There is the true promise of the Revolution of July.[40]

It is as if Guizot and the '1830 Generation' have an opportunity to complete the work of 1789, or, to put it another way, rebuild France in line with the principles of 1789 following the blips of Empire and Restoration. Very clearly he says that, 'it is our duty and responsibility to establish definitively, not order alone, not liberty alone, but order and liberty at the same time'. This is why, in 1830, the July Monarchy reverted to the *tricolore*, produced a constitutional charter, and reconnected with the Revolution. Guizot, strong in his belief in the 'progress of civilisation', would have approved.

Throughout his writings, Guizot argued that France was moving forward. For him, 1789 and 1830 were both key milestones on this route. But 1848 and the radicalism that February embodied was a step too far. Thus, it was no surprise when the revolutionaries of 1848 ousted Guizot along with the Orleanist regime he served.

Edgar Quinet was a poet, writer, historian and politician. As such, he moved in many different worlds. In 1830 he was sent on a government mission to Greece; eighteen years later he was present with the revolutionaries on the barricades. Thereafter he was elected to the National Assembly and displayed some sympathy for the radical left. His lectures and literary output were not to everyone's taste: in 1846 the Orleanist regime banned him from public speaking; Later, in 1851, in the aftermath of Louis Napoleon's coup, he fled to Belgium and Switzerland to avoid a confrontation with the new Bonapartist authorities. He returned to Paris during the Franco-Prussian War and sat in the National Assemblies at Bordeaux and Versailles. In this period he became famed for his rousing – and ultra-patriotic – speech-making. *Le Christianisme et la Révolution* (1845) and *La Révolution* (1865) are the two works in which Quinet develops his ideas on 1789, its origins and implications.

There are key indicators in Quinet's career. He took exception to the Terror on the grounds that it 'was a resurgence of absolutism' and 'weakened liberty'.[41] And as a member of the National Assembly he displayed some sympathy towards the radical left. The fact that he was distrusted by *both* the July Monarchy and the Second Empire highlights his loyalty to radical, left-leaning politics and his staunch, if not zealous, republicanism. As the title of his 1845 study indicates, Quinet was fascinated by religion as a force in society and politics. There were two main strands to his thinking. First, he championed the Protestant cause in France. The corollary of this was a fierce hostility to Catholicism. He particularly disliked the Jesuits as a group – something that helped to create a bond and personal friendship with Michelet. Second, he interpreted 1789 as, among other things, a symbol of spiritual revival. On the basis of the above, some commentators have seen in Quinet the epitome of idealism and romanticism. Parker, for example, describes his work as 'romantically personal' and full of 'mystical idealism'. He declares: 'Quinet's romantic idealism is ... more marked than that of earlier historians. It defies the surface events and the temporal sequence of history ... [His] history marks the full expression of idealism and romanticism in defining the character of the Revolution. It is idealist because it views history as the realization of the ideal.'[42]

The school of idealist and romantic historians was buttressed by a quartet of other writers who emphasised the epic and glorious nature of the Revolution. Louis Blanc and Alphonse de Lamartine can be bracketed together. They mixed writing with practical politics, and both men became members of the Provisional Government of 1848. If they were idealistic and utopian in the political ideas they chose to carry round with them – and there is a strong suggestion that they were – they were also two individuals who wanted to experiment with power, with the 'art of the possible'. Hence Blanc's appearance in the administration of 1848 as a representative of the workers and Lamartine's work as minister of foreign affairs.

During his political career, Blanc antagonised both the Orleanist government and the regime of Louis Napoleon. Under the Third Republic, and probably before this time as well, he defined himself as a man of the extreme left and 'of the workers'. In 1848 his most celebrated act was to establish, and then champion, the idea of the 'National Workshops' – very much a socialist project aimed at providing much needed employment for the poverty-stricken masses of the French capital. This idea was ahead of its time and, after a few months, the workshops were scrapped by the moderates and conservatives in the Provisional Government who were insistent on claiming power back for themselves. He spent much of the next two decades in exile, where he wrote the thirteen-volume *Histoire de la Révolution française* (1847–62). Blanc's unconditional, and almost obsessive, admiration for Robespierre, is the most interesting aspect of his historical writings. Robespierre could do no wrong in Blanc's eyes. Even the Terror was somehow viewed as a 'necessity', or at the very least 'justifiable' in the context of what was going on within France and the Revolution in the 1790s. But he also studied the Girondins, and some of his comments – on their policy programme and their mentality as a political faction – were picked up by the great anarchist writer Peter Kropotkin.[43] Like other romantic historians, Blanc interpreted the Revolution as a 'sublime' event that stemmed, ultimately, from France's own history – from the Middle Ages and also from the work of the *philosophes* in the eighteenth century. He was ever-loyal to Robespierre but in the end even Blanc had to admit that the Reign of Terror marked the beginning of the end for the Revolution.

Lamartine shares many of Blanc's characteristics as a political player and historian. They both used epic language to convey their ideas and both made a nuisance of themselves under 'hostile' regimes. But whereas the latter was an agitator and a radical, the former was a poet and a moderate – hence his sympathy for the Girondins. It is also accepted that Lamartine was probably the lesser of the two men when it came to the art and craft of being a historian. Even Auguste Comte and Augustin Thierry, two sociologists with an interest in political ideas, could be slotted into this chapter, for they lived through the aftermath of the Revolution and had their own positivist and liberal views, but this would be stretching the point.

It was not just historians who were imbued with a sense of idealism and romanticism. Charles Dickens, in *A Tale of Two Cities*, empathises with the lot of the poor. He paints a vivid picture of the French lower classes during the reign of Louis XVI and the conditions of life they had to endure. There is no doubt where his social, moral (and anglocentric) sympathies lie.[44]

Carlyle, Michelet, Guizot and Quinet operated on a slightly different plane. They were all taken in by the charm of the Revolution and its high ideals. They shared in its lofty aims and the sense of destiny it seemed to incarnate. Furthermore, all four were literary people who enjoyed the drama and romance of a political event that spanned a decade and gave birth to so many principled and so many flawed political figures. Michelet, Guizot and Quinet were also French. They were proud of what the revolutionaries had achieved in a patriotic sense. As a year of revolution and dramatic change, 1789 stood as a landmark, to be cherished and romanticised by poets, writers and men of letters. The Revolution was a wonderful, colourful story and these men felt it was their duty to idealise it, and even exaggerate its significance and long-term impact.

Michelet, in particular, was a product of his time. The 1840s were a decade of high hopes, visions and expectations, when the people, spurred on by Michelet's confidence and love, felt the time had come, at last, for *them* to achieve and create change. This climate helped to produce the revolution of 1848 and, across Europe, 'The Springtime of the Peoples'. There was optimism about a brighter future. But when the events of February 1848 turned to failure, when the June Days ended in blood and mass murder, the climate was about to change. This new atmosphere was personified by an aristocrat called Alexis de Tocqueville, a man who would write his own eyewitness account of the February Revolution and the butchery of June.

Notes

1 J. Michelet, *History of the French Revolution* (London, 1847), p. 11.
2 A. Cobban, *Aspects of the French Revolution* (London, 1971), p. 246.
3 T. Carlyle, *The French Revolution* (London, 1905), p. vii.
4 Ibid., p. vii.
5 Ibid., p. viii.
6 Cobban, *Aspects*, p. 239.

7 T. Carlyle, *History of the French Revolution* (London, 1900), Vol. 1, p. 90.
8 Carlyle, *History*, Vol. 1, p. 143.
9 Ibid., Vol. 2., pp. 117–18.
10 Cobban, *Aspects*, p. 36.
11 Introduction to Michelet, *History*.
12 N. Hampson, 'The French Revolution and its Historians', in G. Best (ed.), *The Permanent Revolution* (London, 1989), pp. 216–17.
13 Michelet, *History*, p. 10.
14 See Chapter 5.
15 Michelet, *History*, p. 11.
16 Ibid., p. 10.
17 Ibid., p. 170.
18 Ibid., p. 228.
19 Ibid., p. 6.
20 Ibid., pp. 92–93.
21 Ibid., p. 227.
22 G. Lewis, 'The "People" and the French Revolution', http://faculty.goucher.edu/history231/Gwynne_Lewis.htm.
23 Michelet, *History*, p. 1.
24 Ibid., p. 9.
25 Ibid., p. 220.
26 Ibid., p. 224.
27 Cobban, *Aspects*, pp. 50, 62.
28 See later in this chapter, pp. 65–8.
29 Michelet, *History*, p. 175.
30 Cobban, *Aspects*, p. 249.
31 Michelet, *History*, pp. 178, 223.
32 Ibid., p. 19. See also C. C. O'Brien, 'Nationalism and the French Revolution' in G. Best (ed.), *Permanent Revolution*, p. 19.
33 Cobban, *Aspects*, p. 56.
34 R.R. Palmer, *The World of the French Revolution* (London, 1971), p. 262.
35 See E. Weber, 'The Nineteenth-century Fallout' in G. Best (ed.), *Permanent Revolution*, p. 166 and Hampson, 'Revolution', p. 226.
36 www.cats.ohiou.edu/~Chastain/contrib.htm.
37 See Chapter 2.
38 www.fordham.edu/halsall/mod/1848guizot.html.
39 Ibid.
40 Ibid.
41 F. Furet, 'The French Revolution Revisited' in G. Kates (ed.), *The French Revolution* (London, 1998), pp. 75–6.
42 N. Parker, *Portrayals of Revolution* (Hemel Hempstead, 1990), pp. 142–4.
43 See P. Kropotkin, *The Great French Revolution, 1789–1793* (New York, 1927/1909), Book 2, chapter 7.
44 I. Collins, 'Dickens and the French Revolution', *Literature & History*, see 2nd ser.1.1 (1990).

4

Tocqueville

> The French Revolution did not aim merely at a change in an old government; it designed to abolish the old form of society.[1]

There are nine chapters in this book, but only one is devoted exclusively to an individual historian. We have now arrived at this chapter, and for a variety of reasons that will become clear as this section progresses, it is plausible to argue that the writings of Alexis de Tocqueville warrant this attention.

But where does Tocqueville fit in? How should we characterise the relationship between him and those historians we examined in Chapters 2 and 3? There are no easy answers to these questions. Cobban, who like Tocqueville does not fit neatly into the 'Great Tradition', or 'classical' tradition, offers us some help: 'From such historians as Michelet or Louis Blanc, even when they continued their writing well into the second half of the nineteenth century, to Tocqueville, is a far cry, not in the passage of years but because between them lies the great gulf of the Revolution of 1848, which brought disillusionment to so many high democratic hopes in France and elsewhere.'[2] In this statement there is full and clear recognition of the significance of 1848. Michelet, Blanc and others in the 1840s were prophesying liberal and democratic revolution, and thus their writings on 1789 were hugely optimistic. On the other hand, Tocqueville, writing in 1856, had witnessed the reality of 1848 – the chaos and the anarchy – and thus injected a large dose of pessimism into his writings on the Revolution. He was an 'anxious aristocrat', according to Palmer, one who felt that democracy was inevitable but dangerous.[3] It is also possible to make a connection between

Tocqueville and the liberal historians of the early nineteenth century. He shared many of their instincts and inclinations and undeniably placed a premium on the protection of liberty. But he was also a radical and also, at times, extremely conservative in outlook. He is a man who defies neat labels.

Tocqueville's major work was *The Old Régime and the French Revolution* (1856). The middle years of the nineteenth century were not a vintage period for French historical writing, and perhaps this is part of the reason why Tocqueville stands out. But there are other reasons too: his powers of intellect, his interesting historical method, and the unique thesis that emerged from his writings. It would not be too controversial to assert that Tocqueville's study was a landmark in revolutionary historiography, and also a reference point for all future historians interested in the Revolution and the trajectory of revolutionary scholarship.

Alexis Charles Henri Maurice Clérel de Tocqueville was born in 1805. His father was a prefect who became a peer under Charles X. He spent long periods away from home executing his professional duties, and this meant that the young Tocqueville was tutored privately by a local priest, Abbé Lesueur. It is also relevant to note that his mother was a devout Catholic who displayed nostalgia for the *Ancien Régime* and his great-grandfather was a liberal aristocrat who met his death during the Revolution. These early years are significant because they hint at some of the issues that would come to preoccupy Tocqueville in later life. The writings for which he would become famous were a blend of philosophy, law and polemical argument. *The Old Regime and the French Revolution* – his analysis of political change in France – was dominated by his interest in state administration and the legal system. Throughout his writings he would also find it difficult to escape the fact that he had been born into the nobility and all that entailed in terms of ethics and social values. (We are told that even as a youngster he worried about the role of the aristocracy in post-1789 politics.) It is also known that Tocqueville suffered something of a religious crisis in his late teens; thus, we should not be surprised that the 'irreligious' nature of the Revolution became a major issue for him in his work.

On an international level, Tocqueville the writer was probably most famous for his two-volume study, *Democracy in America*, published in 1835. This has gained the reputation as the first classic work on American politics and government by a non-American writer. Tocqueville based this work on observations he gleaned from a visit to America, and it was an extremely positive and optimistic study. He was interested in issues of prison reform and the life-expectancy of the aristocratic class but, more than anything, the key message to emerge was the importance of political democracy and social equality. Through studying the development of another country, Tocqueville hoped that his evaluation of the French body politic would be all the more considered, accurate and thorough. *Democracy in America* was received so enthusiastically that in 1838 he was elected to the Légion d'honneur. Three years later he gained entry to the French Academy and the Academy of Moral and Political Science.

The uniqueness of Tocqueville stems from the fact that he lived through, and actively took part in, a catalogue of defining political events and eras. As a public figure, he also defied neat pigeon-holing. On one level he was a man of the law and a practising politician; on another he was a writer, philosopher and historian. Politically too, he was something of a contradiction, being an aristocrat and a liberal when it was actually quite difficult to be both at the same time. Tocqueville was 25 when the Revolution of 1830 took place. Coming from an aristocratic family, he was always going to be viewed suspiciously by France's new bourgeois, middle-class rulers. With his political loyalty in doubt, he was demoted to a minor judgeship without pay, and his father's peerage was rescinded for good measure. But Tocqueville was not disheartened. In 1839 he put himself up for election to the Chamber of Deputies and won a seat. Two years previously he had also stood for parliament, but failed, again because his noble lineage caused him difficulties in the fairly unforgiving world of post-Restoration politics.

His nine-year stint as a parliamentarian was a fascinating one. He put his not insignificant political weight behind the expansion of French naval power and the role of the Catholic church in education. In 1846 he joined the 'new left' faction within the Chamber, but stayed clear of the 'banqueteers' who – in the most peaceable and civilised manner possible – had begun to campaign against the increasingly narrow and self-interested politics of Orleanism's bourgeois elite. This period also witnessed an important shift in Tocqueville's own political position. He was growing more and more disillusioned with the role of the aristocracy in French politics – a hugely significant position given his own family background. Thus, throughout the 1840s we can see him moving slowly in the direction of liberal, radical and left-wing politics. One landmark came in 1844 when he became co-owner of the radical newspaper *Le Commerce*; another, in early 1848, when he argued that France was on the verge of another revolution, a warning that was fatefully ignored.

Even though his own personal politics were evolving, and radicalising, Tocqueville was staunchly opposed to the 1848 Revolution and to the extreme socialist and republican ideas that came to be disseminated at the same time. *Recollections*, his personal account of the Revolution, demonstrates this more than satisfactorily. Tocqueville displays a curious, paternalistic admiration for the working people of Paris – particularly those who were butchered during the June Days – but underneath he is appalled by the 'mob' chaos and anarchy that Paris and he himself were forced to witness. Nevertheless – or maybe *because* of this – Tocqueville assisted in the task of establishing a new government in the aftermath of the February Revolution. He helped to write the constitution of the Second Republic and was also elected to the Constituent Assembly. In 1849 Tocqueville gained election to the Legislative Assembly and became Vice-President of the Assembly and Foreign Minister. However, his rise to one of the great offices of state was a short-lived affair. Louis-Napoleon Bonaparte, elected to the presidency of the new Republic in December 1848, sacked him after he had spent less than five months in the job.

This episode had both personal and political ramifications for Tocqueville. He suffered a period of ill health, and consequently had to spend time convalescing in Italy. He also had to deal with the return of Bonapartism. To add insult to the injury of being dismissed from office, he was imprisoned briefly by Louis-Napoleon, and then banned from holding public office again because he had refused to swear an oath of loyalty to the new 'Bonapartist' regime. *The Old Régime and the French Revolution* was published in 1856, three years before he died.

At the outset it is important to understand that Tocqueville was writing in a particular kind of climate. 'The Springtime of the Peoples' – the moniker given to the kaleidoscope of liberal-nationalist revolutions in 1848 – had a distinctly French flavour. The initial revolutionary moment had taken place in Paris, and the ideas that had filtered across the continent were stamped 'Made in France'.

For Tocqueville, the Revolution of 1848 was an interesting and curious political event. To some extent, he admired the working-class Parisian agitators who were at the forefront of the Revolution. They had put their lives on the line for a principle they believed in, and Tocqueville, albeit in a somewhat detached and patronising manner, could respect that. But as an aristocrat he knew that 1848 was fundamentally 'bad', and, when push came to shove, he knew he could not, or should not, sympathise with its objectives. The Revolution could not but impact upon Tocqueville's writings: it frightened the middle and upper classes, and as a liberal aristocrat – and someone who was actually present in Paris during the disturbances – Tocqueville was certainly not immune from feelings of fear and unease. 'It was . . . no laughing matter but something sinister and frightening to see the state of Paris when I returned there', he wrote.

> In that city there were a hundred thousand armed workmen formed into regiments, without work and dying of hunger, but with heads full of vain theories and chimerical hopes. Society was cut in two: those who had nothing united in common envy; those who had anything united in common terror. There were no longer ties of sympathy linking these two great classes, and a struggle was every-where assumed to be inevitable soon. There had already been physical clashes with different results between the *bourgeois* and the *people* – for these old names had been revived as battle cries – at Limoges and at Rouen. In Paris hardly a day passed without some attack or threat to the propertied classes' capital or income. Sometimes the demand was that they should provide employment without selling anything; sometimes that they should let their tenants off their rent, when they themselves had no other income to live from. The landlords bent as they could before this tyranny, trying to get at least some advantage from their weakness by publish-ing it.[4]

Given these feelings, it was inevitable that Tocqueville's attitude to 1848 would come to colour his view of 1789.

The longer-term legacy of February (and June) 1848 was that it created a sense of hopelessness and pessimism among the more radical classes. And it was against this background that Tocqueville developed his theses about the *other*, earlier French Revolution. It is clear, therefore, that for a number of reasons, not least the ensuing political climate when he sat down to write, his general perspective on events was always going to be less positive and optimistic than it could have been (although other factors are crucial too, such as his family background and career).

Tocqueville was quite explicit about his aims in the book: 'The especial objects of the work I now present to the public are to explain why the Revolution, which was impending over every country, burst forth in France rather than elsewhere; why it issued spontaneously from the society which it was to destroy; and how the old monarchy contrived to fall so completely and so suddenly.'[5] The stress on 'why' and 'how' questions is significant, for Tocqueville felt more at home analysing issues than simply describing events and regaling stories (although, having said that, his work on 1848, *Recollections*, is full of detail and anecdote).

Tocqueville's method as a historian was very personal. As he stated in the Preface to his book: 'I have endeavoured to make myself acquainted with all the public documents in which the French expressed their opinions and their views at the approach of the Revolution. I have derived much information on this ... from the reports of the States, and, at a later period, from those of the Provincial Assemblies. I have freely used the *cahiers*, which were presented by the three orders in 1789.'[6] He also went to the files of the Department of the Interior and the local prefectures: 'I have found in them, as I anticipated, the actual life of the old régime, its ideas, passions, its prejudices, its practices. I have found men speaking freely their inmost thoughts in their own language. I have thus obtained much information upon the old régime which was unknown even to the men who lived under it, for I had access to sources which were closed to them.'[7] And when he came to examine the nature of feudalism in France, he made himself familiar with the land registers (*terriers*) of the thirteenth and fourteenth centuries.[8]

The style of history developed by Tocqueville has fascinated observers. The revisionist historian Norman Hampson says his aim was to write '"philosophical" history' and that, at the same time, 'he was never much concerned about economic history'.[9] This comes through vividly in *The Old Régime and the French Revolution*. At one point, Tocqueville is happy to state that, 'it was essentially a social and political revolution'.[10] Hence his concerted interest in social history, political change and the relationship between classes, in feudalism and aristocracy, democracy and religion, and the trade-off between equality and liberty. François Furet, a man who knew a thing or two about the different varieties of history, adds to the picture:

> After retiring from politics, Tocqueville returned only to the historical part of his project ... this time he locked himself up in the archives, read the primary sources, took copious notes and for several years practised the hard discipline demanded by the historian's craft. Yet the ultimate purpose of his research remained unchanged: he still wanted to understand, and thus foresee, where France's contemporary history was headed.[11]

Given these tributes it is no surprise to discover that Tocqueville had little time for 'simplistic' theories of 'conspiracy' and 'destiny'. His was a subtle, broad-brush approach. Kamenka puts it well: 'No one was better aware than Tocqueville that the Revolution was a complex phenomenon with a multiplicity of causes. There were long-standing and general causes, specific and recent causes, causes that were part of the special and often accidental history of France and causes that were part of wider European and "Atlantic" developments.'[12] Some historians, like Thiers, have been criticised for ignoring the issue of causation. Tocqueville was quite the opposite; he was almost obsessed with this particular historical controversy. This is probably another reason why it is difficult to categorise or pigeon-hole Tocqueville as a historian.

It is interesting, and perhaps predictable, that he felt he was in no way biased. 'I trust I have written this work without prejudice; but I do not claim to have written dispassionately', he said.

> It would be hardly decent for a Frenchman to be calm when he speaks of his country, and thinks of the times ... My object has been

to draw a perfectly accurate, and, at the same time, an instructive picture ... I have not, I confess, allowed myself to be influenced by fears of either wounding individuals or classes, or shocking opinions or recollections, however respectable they may be. I have often felt regret in pursuing this course, but remorse, never. Those whom I may have offended must forgive me, in consideration of the honesty and disinterestedness of my aim.[13]

Of course this was a genuine claim, but perhaps, at the same time, Tocqueville was underestimating the influence, subconscious or otherwise, of his aristocratic background, legal training and family circumstances. That said, it could be posited that he, more than any other historian of the Revolution perhaps, managed to stay neutral. After all, was not the label 'aristocratic liberal' which he acquired as a result of his book the ultimate accolade for a writer not wishing to be pigeon-holed?

It should also be pointed out that Tocqueville was not a historian of the Revolution, as such, but rather a writer who was fascinated by the relationship between the *Ancien Régime* on the one hand and the Revolution on the other – hence the title of his most famous work. Because of this, he does not exert very much energy, if any at all, on *details* of the revolutionary period, 1789–99. Of course he has his opinions on subjects like the Terror – he views it as pure 'evil' (his father was imprisoned as a result of it)[14] – but he does not go into the minutiae of events.

The major portion of *The Old Régime and the French Revolution* is devoted to an examination of pre-1789 France. As an aristocrat, Tocqueville had natural and obvious sympathies with the *Ancien Régime*, its rationale and *raison d'être*. However, his liberal inclinations, together with the not inconsiderable effect of hindsight (more than sixty years' worth, in fact), meant that he also understood the need for reform in the late eighteenth century.

Tocqueville was critical of French feudalism in the pre-1789 era, but he also attempted to put the system in perspective by engaging in some comparative analysis.[15] He could only conclude that the *cahiers* – the lists of ordinary people's grievances drawn up in the mid-1780s – had a clear message for the French monarchy: namely, that there was disgruntlement in the country at large and that the future of the *Ancien Régime* was uncertain.[16] In fact, on occasions, Tocqueville gives the impression that the Revolution could and should have done more – and this is the base upon which he develops his thesis of 'continuities', whereby he argues that the *Ancien Régime* and the Revolution had key attributes in common when, really, the latter, if it was to live up to its name, should have been significantly different in character. Throughout, though, Tocqueville is measured and balanced in his opinions, and it could be argued that in general terms his writings offer a moderate critique of both pre- and post-1789 France.[17]

However, Tocqueville was not interested in the nature or course of the Revolution *per se*. As Furet – a great admirer – put it: 'Tocqueville concentrates on the *Ancien Régime* more than on the Revolution, on pre-1789 more than on post-1789 France.'[18] This was because, in his schema of things, the Revolution was but a fairly innocuous interlude, sandwiched as it was between the end of the monarchical era and the beginning of the Napoleonic period.[19] He asked many rhetorical questions about it – 'Now, was the Revolution, in reality, as extraordinary as it seemed to its contemporaries? Was it as unexampled, as deeply subversive as they supposed? What was the real meaning, what the true character of this strange and terrible revolution? What did it actually destroy? What did it create?'[20] – but he was not particularly concerned about the narrative of events. In fact, he 'shunned' this style of history.[21]

His concerns were many. He was wary of the fact that the Revolution had become almost synonymous with 'irreligion' and, for good measure, also viewed *itself* as a 'new religion'. Here he sees the permeating influence of the *philosophes* at work.[22] He was interested in the relationship between the Consulate and the Revolution.[23] And the antennae that Tocqueville developed were particularly sensitive to any signs of 'despotism', to any kind of 'liberty deficit'. His characterisation of the post-1789 regime is vivid:

> a far stronger and more absolute government than the one the Revolution overthrew then seized and monopolised all political power, suppressed all the liberties which had been so dearly bought, and set up in their stead empty shams; deprived electors of all means of obtaining information, of the right of assemblage, and of the faculty of exercising a choice, yet talked of popular sovereignty; said

the taxes were freely voted, when mute or enslaved assemblies assented to their imposition; and, while stripping the nation of every vestige of self-government, of constitutional guarantees, and of liberty of thought, speech and the press – that is to say, of the most precious and the noblest conquest of 1789 – still dared to claim descent from that great era.[24]

His underlying contention is that the revolutionaries had placed a premium on equality, but to the detriment of liberty. As a liberal – albeit an aristocratic one – this was distasteful.

But most of Tocqueville's time was spent enquiring into the relationship between pre- and post-1789 regimes, and also weighing up the comparisons and contrasts that could be made between the two. In general terms, Tocqueville's judgement was that the regime of the revolutionaries was *not* superior to that of the Bourbon monarchs, nor did it in any way mark a 'break'. Rather, in his view, the Revolution was a 'continuation' of the *Ancien Régime*. He makes this plain from the outset of his book. Paragraphs 2 and 3 of his Preface read as follows:

> The French made, in 1789, the greatest effort that has ever been made by any people to sever their history into two parts so to speak, and to tear open a gulf between their past and their future. In this design, they took the greatest care to leave every trace of their past condition behind them; they imposed all kinds of restraints upon themselves in order to be different from their ancestry; they omitted nothing which could disguise them. I have always fancied that they were less successful in this enterprise than has been generally believed abroad, or even supposed at home. I have always suspected that they unconsciously retained most of the sentiments, habits, and ideas which the old regime had taught them, and by whose aid they achieved the revolution; and that, without intending it, they used its ruins as materials for the construction of their new society.[25]

One of the key words in this passage is 'unconsciously' (perhaps it should be 'subconsciously'). Obviously the revolutionaries had a plan and a vision, but there is no way that they purposefully set out to emulate the monarchical regime. What Tocqueville is saying is that, when they were presented with the realities of power, the revolutionaries resorted to the kind of expedients that previous administrations had employed. Perhaps this is a warning against over-reliance on dogma and ideology – for in government the revolutionaries had to go with the flow and were not going to be able to change the world overnight. Tocqueville goes on to claim that, for this reason and others, the uniqueness of 1789 has been overstated – 'Radical as it was, the Revolution introduced fewer innovations than has generally been supposed'[26] – and that its achievements have been overplayed. Here again he sees continuities between the work of *Ancien Régime* monarchs and post-1789 radicals: 'The Revolution effected suddenly, by a convulsive and sudden effort, without transition, precautions, or pity, what would have been gradually effected by time had it never occurred.'[27]

In the course of his writings, Tocqueville identifies several areas in which there were pre- and post-1789 similarities:

- 'monarchical government' – which existed for several years *after* the Fall of the Bastille,
- the sub-division of property,
- legal rights for government officials,
- the offices and agencies of central and local government.

At times he is fairly blunt in the way that he identifies these 'continuities'. He quotes Mirabeau in 1790 as saying, 'the greater part of the acts of the national assembly are decidedly favourable to a monarchical government'; he claims it is 'a vulgar error to suppose that the subdivision of property in France dates from the Revolution'; he says that government officials are 'in error' if they think that 1789 brought them significant rights; and he argues that the 'principles of government' adopted by the revolutionaries were regularly those of the old monarchy.[28]

An interest in state administration and the mechanics of how France and other countries were governed is an obvious, ongoing theme in his writings. Tocqueville is fascinated, and also alarmed, by the 'centralising' tendencies of French governments pre- and post-Revolution – the 'mania' that involved 'managing everything at Paris'.[29] When he came to consider the various organs of government under the Bourbons, the Revolution and the post-1799 Napoleonic regime, he declared:

A single body, placed in the centre of the kingdom, administering government throughout the country; a single minister managing nearly all the business of the interior; a single agent directing the details in each province; no secondary administrative bodies, or authorities competent to act without permission; special tribunals to hear cases in which government is concerned, and shield its agents. What is this but the same centralization with which we are acquainted? As compared with ours, its forms are less sharply marked, its mode of action less regular, its existence less tranquil; but the system is the same. Nothing has been added, nothing taken away from the old plan; when the surrounding edifices were pulled down, it stood precisely as we see it.[30]

He goes on:

I once heard an orator, in the days when we had assemblies, call administrative centralization 'that noble conquest of the revolution which Europe envies us'. I am willing to admit that centralization was a noble conquest, and that Europe envies us its possession; but I deny that it was a conquest of the Revolution. It was, on the contrary, a feature of the old regime, and, I may add, the only one which out-lived the revolution, because it was the only one that was suited to the new condition of society created by the Revolution.[31]

There is a corollary too. If France, under the monarchy and under the Revolution, was so utterly Paris-centric, what of the provinces? In this part of his work, Tocqueville demonstrates a powerful attachment to the institution of the *intendant* ('The correspondence between the *intendants* and their sub-delegates shows that the government had a hand in the management of all the cities in the kingdom, great and small. It was consulted on all subjects, and gave decided opinions on all; it even regulated festivals.').[32] He also believes that *independence*, rather than 'capital-city *dependence*', should be the order of the day for the biggest French town right down to the smallest French village.[33]

Tocqueville goes on to demonstrate the continuities at play in other key areas. As a man who had taken up a career in the law, before his interest in political matters intervened, Tocqueville was especially interested in France's legal system and judiciary. 'Modern legalists assure us that we have made great progress in administrative law since the Revolution', he stated.

They tell us that 'before that event the powers of the judiciary and those of the administration were intermingled and confused, but that since then they have been severed, and a line drawn between them'. A right appreciation of the progress here mentioned can only be formed when it is well borne in mind that if the judiciary under the old regime occasionally overstepped its natural sphere, it never filled the whole of that sphere. Both of these facts must be remembered, or a false and incomplete view will be taken of the subject.[34]

Moreover, Tocqueville ridicules the frenzy of constitution-making that dominated the period 1789–1848. He argues that the old monarchy could guarantee key rights in just the same way as the myriad constitutions of the late-eighteenth and early-nineteenth centuries were intent on doing:

In one of the nine or ten constitutions which have been established in France within the last sixty years, and designed to last forever, an article was inserted declaring that no government official could be prosecuted before the common courts until permission had been obtained from the executive. The idea seemed so happy that, when the constitution was destroyed, the article in question was rescued from destruction, and has ever since been carefully sheltered from revolution. Officials commonly allude to the privilege secured to them by this article as one of the great triumphs of 1789, but here again they are in error. The old monarchy was quite as solicitous as more modern governments to protect its servants from responsibility to the courts, like mere citizens. Between the two eras the only substantial difference is this: before the revolution government could not come to the rescue of its agents without having recourse to arbitrary and illegal measures; since then it has been legally authorized to let them violate the law.[35]

Here, Tocqueville not only emphasises the similarity of pre- and post-1789 regimes; as if to emphasise his aristocratic background and *Ancien Régime* sympathies, he also pokes fun at the 'new France', lost as it is in a maze of written constitutions. It is perhaps on occasions such as this that Tocqueville's mask slips and his slightly partisan attitude comes through. Arguably, the idea of continuities is as fundamental to Tocqueville's work as the notion of class struggle is to Marx. This is no idle analogy. Hampson, surveying revolutionary historiography from the perspective of the late twentieth century, sees similarities in the way that both men thought about history, while Furet points to the dialectic at the heart of Tocqueville's work on more than one occasion, as if he is trying to highlight the latter's partial affinity with Marx's analysis of revolution.[36] (In their writings on the 1848 Revolution, too, there are interesting similarities as well as dissimilarities).

Tocqueville's final, and hardest-hitting, conclusion is that the Revolution was anything but 'a casual accident'[37] – instead, it was a sequel, or follow-on (to the previous regime), in terms of the strengthening of the administrative state, political ideas, and even foreign policy.[38] In short, 1789 had witnessed the substitution of one despotic regime for another. Hampson offers us this evaluation:

> No one knew better than Tocqueville of the *continuities* that can and do underlie revolutionary transformation. For him, the French Revolution created neither a new people nor a new France. It was the culmination, rather, of long-term trends in the society of the *ancien régime* – some of them radical (trends toward democracy), some of them bureaucratic-administrative (trends toward the centralization of power that emerged from the victory of absolutist monarchs over the true feudal aristocracy). Implicit in Tocqueville's analysis of the passion displayed in and engendered by the Revolution, however, and implicit in the position the French Revolution occupied and occupies in the consciousness of the world around it, is the recognition that it constitutes not only the culmination of past histories, but the dawn of a new ideological age.[39]

Hampson is surely right to point to this aspect of his work as both significant and poignant.

It is a fact that Tocqueville's book has run into countless reprints and translations – Anchor Books, Doubleday, Dent, University of Chicago Press – right up until today. But that said, it is almost impossible to quantify the impact and influence of Tocqueville's writings. His book was a landmark in revolutionary historiography. He mixed sociology with traditional history, and an aristocratic mentality with genuine sympathy for liberal values. He offered a unique thesis that was both rigorously prepared and staunchly argued.

Unquestionably, he became a key reference point for future historians. Hampson implies that for some writers, 'trailing Tocqueville as a reluctant captive behind one's own triumphant chariot' has been a definite tactic. And he goes on: 'It is almost impossible for anyone to put forward a view of the nature and significance of the French Revolution that has not been anticipated, in one form or another, by Tocqueville.'[40] Hampson, like Tocqueville, situates himself outside the 'Great Tradition', so perhaps this is a very personal observation. Furthermore, the fact that both Lefebvre and Furet – two historians with virtually nothing in common – have paid their professional respects to Tocqueville is a sure sign of his influence.[41] Furet, in particular, is mesmerised by Tocqueville, and devotes a quarter of his own book, *Interpreting the French Revolution*, to analysing his significance. He writes: 'Tocqueville's attachment to history did not spring from a love of the past but from his sensitivity to the present ... He began his quest not in time, but in space, using geography as a kind of comparative history.[42]

The image of Tocqueville inhabiting two zones ('space' and 'time') not normally frequented by other writers is a nice one, and enables us to appreciate the uniqueness and the profundity of his writings. More than anything perhaps, Tocqueville had a fear of revolution. We can see this in his attitude to 1848, and also 1789. 'Revolution has several faults in Tocqueville's point of view', writes Stephane Dion. 'It exacerbates the egalitarian passion and causes it to degenerate into envious passion, to the point that men come to prefer equality in servitude to inequality in liberty. Revolution develops the taste for general ideas in politics and wants to make a clean sweep of the past, whereas democracy has need of pragmatism and experience.'[43] This is where his ideas on democracy, revolution and continuities merge.

Essentially, Tocqueville was a moderate: an aristocrat who was also a liberal and a man who, more than anything, valued order and stability. His uniqueness as a historian was threefold: he analysed rather than described, he was interested in the *Ancien Régime* more than the Revolution, and he delineated continuities in French history in an era when the country was being destabilised by revolution after revolution. This was an interesting blend of ideas and attitudes. Very few historians, if any, could boast admirers in Taine, Marx, Cobban *and* Furet. But that would have been Tocqueville's claim.[44]

Perhaps the last word should go to Cobban, who has a place alongside Tocqueville in the pantheon of great revolutionary historians:

Since de Tocqueville wrote, nearly a century ago, historical research has added a mountain of detail to the little heap of facts he had garnered, yet his remains one of the best books on the Revolution that has ever been written. Some of the books on our list illustrate the dangers of writing history to a theory. Many literary histories of the Revolution have now not even a literary value. De Tocqueville's work shows that intellectual content and historical integrity, even without the highest literary qualities, can give a history a place in the small and select rank of historical classics.[45]

Few students of the Revolution would disagree with this statement. For later historians of the Revolution, he was a writer and a thinker who was almost impossible to ignore.

Notes

1 A. de Tocqueville, *The Ancien Régime* (Dent, 1988), p. 7.
2 A. Cobban, *Aspects of the French Revolution* (London, 1968), p. 40.
3 R.R. Palmer, *The World of the French Revolution* (London, 1971), p. 262.
4 A. de Tocqueville, *Recollections* (Oxford, 1987), p. 98.
5 Tocqueville, *Ancien Régime*, pp. xxiii, xxiv.
6 Ibid., p. xxii.
7 Ibid., p. xxiii.
8 Ibid., p. 13.
9 Ibid., pp. v, xiii.
10 Ibid., p. 15.
11 F. Furet, *Interpreting the French Revolution* (London, 1981), p. 133.
12 E. Kamenka, 'Revolutionary Ideology and "The Great French Revolution of 1789–?"', in G. Best (ed.), *The Permanent Revolution* (London, 1989), pp. 75–6.
13 Ibid., p. xxv.
14 Ibid., p.vi.
15 Ibid., pp. 17–25.
16 A. Forrest, *The French Revolution* (Oxford, 1993), p. 15.
17 Cobban, *Aspects*, p. 39; see also G. Kates, *The French Revolution* (London, 1988), p. 69.
18 Furet, *Interpreting*, p. 133.
19 This is a general theme in the book.
20 Ibid., p. 4.
21 Furet, *Interpreting*, p. 140.
22 Ibid., pp. 4–5.
23 This is one of the major recurring themes of the book.
24 Ibid., p. xxiv.
25 Ibid., p. xxi.
26 Ibid., p. 16.
27 Ibid., p. 16.

28 Ibid., pp. 6–7, 20, 44, 47–8.
29 Ibid., pp. 48–9.
30 Ibid., pp. 45–6.
31 Ibid., p. 25.
32 Ibid., p. 37.
33 Ibid., pp. 37–8.
34 Ibid., pp. 43–4.
35 Ibid., p. 44.
36 See Furet, *Interpreting*, pp. 142–3, for example. Tocqueville, *Ancien Régime*, pp. xvi/xvii.
37 Tocqueville, *Ancien Régime*, p. 16.
38 See Cobban, *Aspects*, pp. 40–3 and A. Soboul, 'The French Revolution in the History of the Contemporary World' in G. Kates (ed.), *The French Revolution* (London, 1998), p. 32.
39 Kamenka, 'Revolutionary Ideology', pp. 75–6.
40 Tocqueville, *Ancien Régime*, p. xvi.
41 Ibid., pp. xv, xvi.
42 Furet, *Interpreting*, p. 132.
43 Stephane Dion, www.utpjournals.com/product/chr/712/democracies6.html.
44 See later chapters for more on these historians' links to Tocqueville.
45 Cobban, *Aspects.*, p. 43.

5

Third Republic historians

I do not think I have overlooked a single important source, nor have I made a single assertion that is not directly drawn from these sources.[1]

Against the backdrop of a new, progressive regime – the Third Republic – historians came to re-evaluate the Revolution, often in overtly political and ideological terms. It is also important to note that the centenary of the Revolution was celebrated during the post-1870 period, a significant landmark that gave rise to an increase in historiographical writings. The two most important names of this era were Hippolyte Taine and Alphonse Aulard.

Taine offered a sociological interpretation of events that, in time, marked him out as the archetypal conservative onlooker. One modern commentator stated: 'Despite the somewhat mechanical rigor of his mind, Taine had a gift for the telling detail and for imaginative description, and, although some historians have complained that he piles anecdote upon anecdote, he understood very well that, in the case of the Revolution, the devil was truly in the details.'[2] By contrast, Aulard was the first professional historian of the French Revolution, and he devoted his life to this study. A professor at the University of Paris – a position he gained on the centenary of the event in 1889 – he founded the Société de l'Histoire de la Révolution and the bi-monthly review *Révolution Française*. Instead of monarchy, Aulard favoured a brand of democratic republicanism that was very much in vogue with the establishment of the Third Republic.

Essentially, Aulard saw the conservative interpretation of Taine as defective, and so, as some kind of corrective, he devel-

oped what was, to all intents and purposes, a republican, bourgeois, and anti-clerical view of the Revolution, which focused
almost exclusively on politics and political history. This is just
one example – perhaps one of the most famous – of the way in
which historians have 'confronted' each other over the meaning
of the Revolution. The disagreement between Taine and Aulard is
central to this chapter, but we also touch on other themes: the
(republican) political context, the centenary of the Revolution, as
well as the gradual professionalising and radicalising of revolutionary historiography.

Hippolyte Adolphe Taine's fame rests on the fact that he was,
in Hampson's words, the second 'heterodox historian' in the
history of French revolutionary historiography.[3] Certainly, it is
true that the 'Great Tradition', or 'classical' tradition, that
enveloped historians such as Michelet and Aulard, did not interest him. In a way, it is intriguing to encounter someone who
swam against the tide so much, with such obvious disregard, and
with so little care for the consequences. Taine's main concern was
to comment on the Revolution as he saw it, warts and all. If he
went against the grain, so be it. As such he produced one of the
great 'anti' histories of the Revolution. The event was not the
climax of French history, but rather its nadir. Moreover, he
himself was writing during a period of great political instability.
France had been humiliated by Prussia in the war of 1870–1 and
the Third Republic – established officially in 1875 – was viewed
as merely the 'least unpopular' solution to the country's political
troubles.

Thus, as Taine set to work on what came to be regarded as
his greatest work, *Les Origines de la France contemporaine*, the
country was in crisis. The debacle of 1871 was still fresh in
people's memories and, what is more, the new Republic was
tottering, with the monarchist right on the offensive and the
emergence of the new 'nationalist right' of Boulanger and Barrès
just around the corner. Taine, the 'heterodox' historian, therefore, had a conducive environment in which to work. From the
left, Comninel puts it like this: 'During the early days of the
Third Republic, right-wing opposition to the Revolution's liberal-
radical legacy found its pre-eminent historiographical expression
in the work of Hippolyte Taine ... Until the Republic had weath-

ered the crises of its first decades, this interpretation hung over it like a pall.'[4] Taine struck while France was vulnerable. But the Republic was resilient. In its formative years it withstood a range of grave political crises – the Commune, Boulangism, the Dreyfus Affair – and it would parry the words of Taine, too.

Most onlookers are agreed that even though Taine had pretensions to writing history, he was not a historian *per se*. Perhaps he dealt too much in sociological and psychological insights to be a historian in the strictest sense of the term. Further, it could be argued that instead of exploring the sources and then arriving at some plausible conclusions, Taine worked in exactly the opposite way: he presented an opinion, or prejudice, or conspiracy theory, and then tried to locate the facts and evidence to prove it. It is in this sense that critics have attacked him for 'reading history backwards' and for assessing primary sources uncritically.[5]

Taine also liked his 'systems', 'laws' and 'formulas'. He sought to explain history in these mechanistic terms and hoped that the 'rationalism' and 'mathematical logic' of his arguments would win favour and impress people. Unfortunately, this rarely happened and he was invariably lampooned as a simplistic thinker. As if this is not enough, it is argued that Taine relied too heavily on colourful language and metaphor, to the detriment of evaluation and analysis. At one point, for example, he describes the Jacobins as being, 'born out of social decomposition like mushrooms out of compost'.[6] The analogy is vivid, but there is not very much reasoned discussion or interpretation. As a result, Hampson says his tone was 'monotonously strident and his judgement unbalanced', which is probably close to the mark.[7]

In terms of what he said, rather than how he said it, or how he 'did' history, there seem to be a number of undercurrents to Taine's writings on the Revolution. First, it is interesting to note the labels that have been pinned on him over the last century and a half. On account of his early work he has been depicted as a 'liberal', 'individualist' and 'moderate constitutionalist'.[8] Here it is pertinent to point out that in 2002 his work on the Revolution was reprinted by the Indianapolis-based Liberty Fund.[9] As if making a statement about what they see in Taine's writing, the Fund describes itself as 'a foundation established to encourage study of the ideal of a society of free and responsible individuals',[10] But as a result of his later, more famous and colourful writings, he has been pigeon-holed as a 'conservative' and an archetypal 'man of the right'. As Hampson, in his survey of revolutionary historiography, puts it, 'Taine abandoned his initial liberalism as a result of the Paris Commune [of 1871], which left him with a permanent hatred and fear of the mob.'[11] But he also argues that Taine was in no way a counter-revolutionary – he despaired of the nobility and clergy just like historians on the left.[12] That said, if we were to draw up a 'family tree' to represent the various generations of historians of the Revolution, we would have to make a clear link between Taine and Burke (in the late eighteenth century) and de Tocqueville (in the mid-nineteenth).[13] There are definite connections between the works of all three writers.[14]

Second, it is fascinating to trace the factors that provoked Taine into writing about the Revolution. Obviously, the fundamental theoretical issue was 1789 and the crossroads at which France had arrived. But beyond this there were other reasons. Taine had been horrified by the experience of war with Prussia (1870) and the Paris Commune (1870–1). 'He was shaken to the core ... by France's defeat in the Franco-Prussian War and by the insanity of the Paris commune', writes Thomas Fleming. 'He determined on writing what he hoped would be an objective account of France's progress from the *ancien régime* to the France of his own day. This was the genesis of the three-part plan of his *Origines de la France Contemporaine*.'[15]

Third, we need to be aware of Taine's attitude towards the origins of the Revolution. Causation is not a simple matter, and nor is Taine's perspective on causation. On one level, he does try to analyse, and attempts to reach some rounded conclusions. In the end, though, he tends to ignore the idea of there being *several* revolutions within the main revolution, and also dismisses the idea that the revolutionaries were motivated primarily by economic grievances. Eventually, he settles for an interpretation that blends several key theories: that the *philosophes* of the eighteenth century were effective in disseminating a package of new abstract ideas, that the bourgeoisie were receptive to these ideas, and that 'popular passions' also played their part. As such, he slightly downplays the political narrative.

On the Revolution itself, Taine is scathing. In his depiction of its early years he plays on themes of chaos and illegality. 'So far, the weakness of the legal government is extreme. For four years, whatever its kind, everywhere and constantly, it has been disobeyed; for four years, whatever its kind, it has never dared enforce obedience', he says, as if writing in 1793.

> Recruited among the cultivated and refined class, the rulers of the country have brought with them into power the prejudices and sensibilities of the epoch; under the empire of the prevailing dogma they have deferred to the will of the multitude and, with too much faith in the rights of man, they have had too little in the rights of the magistrate; moreover, through humanity, they have abhorred blood-shed and, unwilling to repress, they have allowed themselves to be repressed. Thus, from the 1st of May 1789 to 2 June 1793, they have carried on the administration, or legislated, athwart innumerable insurrections, almost all of them going unpunished; while their constitutions, so many unhealthy products of theory and fear, have done no more than transform spontaneous anarchy into legal anarchy.[16]

There are key markers in this passage. The talk of 'insurrections' and 'the multitude' helps us to understand the main thrust of Taine's message. He is wary of the people, and probably feels that they do not deserve recognition, hence his attack on the early revolutionary leaders for putting too much faith in the 'rights of man'. Taine also talks about the 'legal government', as if contrasting it with some emerging *'illegal'* force. It is clear what he is hinting at. He goes on to complain about the revolutionaries' lack of respect and, de facto, their *illegitimate* behaviour:

> Willfully and through distrust of authority they have undermined the principle of command, reduced the King to the post of a decorative puppet, and almost annihilated the central power: from the top to the bottom of the hierarchy the superior has lost his hold on the inferior, the minister on the departments, the departments on the districts, and the districts on the communes; throughout all branches of the service, the chief, elected on the spot and by his subordinates, has come to depend on them. Thenceforth, each post in which authority is vested is found isolated, dismantled and preyed upon, while, to crown all, the Declaration of Rights, proclaiming 'the jurisdiction of constituents over their clerks', has invited the assailants to make the assault. On the strength of this a faction arises which ends

in becoming an organized band: under its clamorings, its menaces and its pikes, at Paris and in the provinces, at the polls and in the parliament, the majorities are all silenced, while the minorities vote, decree and govern; the Legislative Assembly is purged, the King is dethroned, and the Convention is mutilated.[17]

Here Taine reveals his hand. He has a natural attachment to 'hierarchy' and 'authority', and thus cannot tolerate the fact that the King has been 'dethroned' and reduced to the status of 'decorative puppet'.

He identifies a new faction emerging. He implies that it is a 'minority' grouping interested primarily in violence ('its menaces and pikes'). He could be referring to the 'people' as a group – they famously attached the head of the governor of the Bastille to a pike on 14 July – or he could be hinting at the emergence of the Jacobins as an organised or semi-organised faction. Either way, he soon moves on to an in-depth examination of the Jacobins as a political formation. He has very little positive to say about them:

> Of all the garrisons of the central citadel, whether royalists, constitutionalists, or Girondists, not one has been able to defend itself, to re-fashion the executive instrument, to draw the sword and use it in the streets: on the first attack, often at the first summons, all have surrendered, and now the citadel, with every other public fortress, is in the hands of the Jacobins. This time, its occupants are of a different stamp. Aside from the great mass of well-disposed people fond of a quiet life, the Revolution has sifted out and separated from the rest all who are fanatical, brutal or perverse enough to have lost respect for others; these form the new garrison – sectarians blinded by their creed, the roughs (*assommeurs*) who are hardened by their calling, and those who make all they can out of their offices. None of this class are scrupulous concerning human life or property; for, as we have seen, they have shaped the theory to suit themselves, and reduced popular sovereignty to their sovereignty.[18]

Taine does not hide his emotions. Again he talks about their disrespectful behaviour, but now he also chides them for their fanaticism and sectarianism, and their blinkered attitude to issues. He implies that they are dirty and also corrupt and self-seeking. The last line is reminiscent of the charge laid at the door of the Russian Bolsheviks in 1917: they had talked impressively about the 'dictatorship of the proletariat', but when push came to shove, they resorted to the 'dictatorship of the Bolshevik party'.

There follows an all-embracing personal attack on the 'typical' Jacobin agitator. 'The commonwealth, according to the Jacobin, is his; with him, the commonwealth comprises all private possessions, bodies, estates, souls and consciences; everything belongs to him; the fact of being a Jacobin makes him legitimately tsar and pope. Little does he care about the wills of actually living Frenchmen; his mandate does not emanate from a vote; it descends to him from aloft, conferred on him by Truth, by Reason, by Virtue. As he alone is enlightened, and the only patriot, he alone is worthy to take command, while resistance, according to his imperious pride, is criminal.' He continues:

> If the majority protests, it is because the majority is imbecile or corrupt; in either case, it merits a check, and a check it shall have. Accordingly, the Jacobin does nothing else from the outset; insurrections, usurpations, pillagings, murders, assaults on individuals, on magistrates, on assemblies, violations of law, attacks on the State, on communities – there is no outrage not committed by him. He has always acted as sovereign instinctively; he was so as a private individual and clubbist; he is not to cease being so, now that he possesses legal authority, and all the more because if he hesitates he knows he is lost; to save himself from the scaffold he has no refuge but in a dictatorship. Such a man, unlike his predecessors, will not allow himself to be turned out; on the contrary, he will exact obedience at any cost. He will not hesitate to restore the central power; he will put back the local wheels that have been detached; he will repair the old forcing-gear; he will set it agoing so as to work more rudely and arbitrarily than ever, with greater contempt for private rights and public liberties than either a Louis XIV or a Napoleon.[19]

There are interesting dimensions to this passage – the sarcastic description of the Jacobin as 'enlightened', the vehement critique of Jacobin-style centralisation – but probably the most striking thing is its general tone. This kind of diatribe is similar in style to the most vicious of anti-Semitic rants. It appears that Taine is singling out the Jacobin as the source of all evil, as the ultimate scapegoat, in much the same way as later fascists and racists would pick on the Jew. But who was ultimately responsible for the madness of the Revolution – the 'minority' (the Jacobins in government) or the 'majority' (the mass of ordinary people)? At various junctures, Taine appears to offer different answers and sometimes even confuses the two.

Suffice it to say that the Revolution, for Taine, was a catastrophe. It equated with the Terror, violence and disaster. This was his 'simple', 'logical' formula. He portrayed it as a period of unadulterated evil and vice. As one commentator puts it: 'To Taine's great credit, he was not taken in by the myth of two revolutions: the British-style reformist revolution of 1789, followed by the Jacobin Terror caused by a few bad men who betrayed the spirit of 1789.'[20] Crucial, finally, is the nature and tone of Taine's attack on the overarching ideology of the Revolution. His main bugbear is its exaggerated intellectualism, in particular its glorification of abstract ideas such as 'liberty', 'equality' and 'fraternity'. On top of this, Taine was very much a provincialist. As such, he objects vociferously to the Paris-centric nature of the Revolution and the rapid process of centralisation that was put in motion by Robespierre and the Committee of Public Safety. Thus, as much as Taine interpreted the Revolution as a conflict between good and evil, and between right and left, he also saw it as a battle between 'the provinces' and Paris.

In general, Taine looked on the 'Great Tradition' in the late nineteenth century with just the same total disdain with which some eccentric right-wingers look on the ideology of political correctness in the twenty-first century.

The legacy of Taine was not insignificant. Not every historian of the Revolution gives birth to a philosophical 'school' but the distinctiveness and peculiarity of his ideas ensured, at best, longevity for some of his principal assertions, and, at the very worst, he remained an important reference point for future scholars. In particular, Roustan, Funck-Brentano and Cochin all took on board Taine's argument, or conspiracy theory, which laid the blame for the Revolution at the door of the eighteenth-century *philosophes*. Furthermore, in his glorification of the 'provinces', Taine certainly touched a nerve with Maurice Barrès, the novelist-turned-politician who on one level was a very traditional French conservative, and on another has been labelled 'France's first fascist'.[21] Fleming takes up the story:

> [Barrès] inserts a wonderful portrait of the ageing critic [Taine] into his novel *Les déracinés*. The courtly old man goes to visit a young

admirer from Lorraine and takes him on a walk to Les Invalides (where Napoleon is buried), where he shows him a great plane tree, which he describes in beautiful detail, intimating (I am oversimplifying) that the organic interrelationship of parts is a better model for the young man and his provincial friends in Paris than the rootless individualism taught by the liberals. See what pure health it is in. There is no predominance in its trunk, its branches, its leaves. It is a rustling federation. It is its own law, and it flourishes ... What a good lesson for rhetoric, and not only for the art of literate people but also what a guide for thinking. For Barrès, Hippolyte Taine offered confirmation of his own provincialism, his attachment to the roots of his family and history in Lorraine; he also represented an alternative to the sterile rationality of all internationalisms. The French Revolution was, among other things, a war of the center against the provinces, just as it was a war for an abstract international ideal of liberty, equality, and fraternity (identified by the Jacobins with France itself) that would destroy the real France.[22]

In terms of popularity, however, Taine was never going to make a concrete mark. Hampson – who like the author of *Origines de la France Contemporaine* also situates himself outside the 'Great Tradition' – explains his lack of real influence:

> He wrote ... at a time when the Third Republic, struggling to assert its legitimacy, was calling on all Frenchmen to unite in defence of its own particular version of the meaning of the Revolution, and he suffered the common fate of those who rock boats. He was denounced by Aulard and there was enough unreasonableness in his work to allow anyone to dismiss it all with an easy conscience.[23]

This is certainly true – it is relatively easy to sideline someone with unorthodox, sometimes eccentric, opinions.

François Victor Alphonse Aulard was the Sorbonne's first professor of the Revolution and his most famous work was *The French Revolution: A Political History*. Some commentators have implied that Aulard was a rather idiosyncratic editor.[24] But, there is no doubting his skills and pedigree as a historian. More than anything, he put the emphasis squarely on 'the sources'. The modern historian may take it for granted that these are, and always will be, the essential tools of the trade, but in Aulard's time this was not always the case. And as we will see with other historians whose writings are examined in this book, those who wrote about the Revolution did so not only from a variety of perspectives, but also making use of many different methods, some of which are now ridiculed.

Aulard's interpretation of the Revolution was an interesting blend. On the one hand, he has gained the reputation for moderation, detachment and neutrality, for the professionalism and modernity of his approach, perhaps as a result of his high-profile, overarching, and slightly institutionalised role as the unofficial 'Dean' of revolutionary studies in France. As he himself says in the Preface to *The French Revolution: A Political History*: 'As for the state of mind in which I have written this book, I will say only that I have tried, as far as in me lay, to write a historical work, and not to advance a theory. I should wish my work to be considered as an example of the application of the historical method to the study of a period disfigured by passion and by legend.'[25] Thus, he places a premium on his 'unbiased' and 'untheoretical' approach, and this is why he has come to be viewed as leader-in-chief of the 'official school of [revolutionary] historians'.[26]

However, on the other hand, Aulard is seen by some as overtly biased and partisan in the way that, as a supporter of the Third Republic, he attempts to buttress that regime by proclaiming the oneness of 1789 and 1871.[27] At times this is quite explicit, especially where he plays on the radicalism, secularism and anti-clericalism of the Revolution and transposes this into the world of post-1871 France. His espousal of the notion of 'bourgeois revolution' is a nod in the direction of future Marxist historians, and in general terms it is clear that he approves of the 'socialist' undercurrents to certain phases of the 1790s. He displays little sympathy for the monarchy and comes across as a loyal republican. Probably the best indication of this is the titles he chooses for his chapters in Volume I of *The French Revolution: A Political History*. A selection include: 'Democratic and Republican Ideas before the Revolution', 'Democratic and Republican Ideas at the Outset of the Revolution', 'Formation of the Democratic Party and Birth of the Republican Party (1790, 1791)', 'The Flight to Varennes and the Republican Movement (June 21–July 17, 1791)', 'The Republicans and the Democrats after the Affair of the Champ de Mars'. There is a clear thread to Aulard's writing –

the notion that democratic and republican ideas were fundamental to the Revolution.

It would be fair to say that Aulard is not particularly interested in the issue of causation. He talks about the 'weakness' of royalty[28] and is aware that reformist ideas ('The idea that the King should be only a citizen subject to the law') were gaining ground in the middle and latter decades of the eighteenth century.[29] At the same time he refers to 'certain writers'[30] – like Montesquieu, Voltaire, Condorcet and Sieyès, to name but four – whose ideas affected the political and intellectual climate in 'pre-revolutionary' France. He also examines the impact of Anglo-American political ideas on the genesis of revolution. In general terms, Aulard's interpretation of the revolutionary decade is political rather than socio-economic in emphasis.

> The economic and social history of the Revolution is dispersed over so many sources that it is actually impossible, in one lifetime to deal with them all, or even with the most important. He who would write this history unaided could only here and there attain the whole truth, and would end by producing only a superficial sketch of the whole, drawn at second or third hand. But in the case of political history, if it be reduced to the facts I have chosen, it is possible for a man, in the course of twenty years, to read the laws of the Revolution, the principal journals, correspondences, deliberations, speeches, election papers, and the biographies of those who played a part in the political life of the time.[31]

In a way, this is a strange admission for a historian to make, especially when the historian in question is Chair of the History of the Revolution at the Sorbonne. It is possible to admire his candid attitude, but the manner in which he divides history into three distinct fields strikes the modern observer as slightly simplistic. It is also questionable whether there is such a gulf between the quantity of sources available in the areas of social and economic history on the one hand and political history on the other.

Aulard is much more convincing when he talks about the sources that he has actually used. He does not think much of memoirs as a tool, stating: 'Not only are there very few memoirs which may be taken as absolutely authentic: there are still fewer whose authors have not thought more of the figure they cut than of the truth. Written after the event, mostly under the

Restoration, they have one very serious failing in common: I mean the distortion of memory which disfigures almost every page.'[32] He goes on to say:

> The laws, in their authentic and official form, are to be found in the Baudoin Collection, in the Louvre, in the *Bulletin des Lois*, in the *procès-verbaux* of the legislative assemblies, and also, singly, in special impressions ... Decrees of the Government, of the Committee of Public Safety, of the executive Directory, and of the Consuls, ministerial decisions, &c., have been taken from the official texts, from the register and the minutes of the Committee of Public Safety ... from the *Bulletin* of the Convention, from the papers of the Executive Directory, from the *Rédacteur*, the organ of the Directory, and from the *Moniteur*, the organ of the Consular Government.[33]

This is a firm and comprehensive statement. Cobban, who in the 1970s diverted away from the classical tradition (of which Aulard was a part), puts his uniqueness into perspective: 'The secret of what he did for the history of the Revolution is to be found in the first three of the ten commandments which he was accustomed to give to his students at the beginning of each academic year: 1. Always go to the sources; 2. Say nothing which you do not know from an original source; 3. Write nothing without giving your references. With these principles he transformed revolutionary historiography.'[34] Aulard, surely, would have approved of Cobban's summary.

Contrasted with the methodologies of the past, which based themselves on hearsay, anecdote and gossip, this *Aulardiste* mantra was obviously a significant step forward. But, it is also true that, in the early years of the twenty-first century, no degree-level student worth their salt would contemplate doing anything else but follow Aulard's dictum. That is the mark of Aulard: he revolutionised a profession and created the principles upon which it would stand thereafter. Here he sounds much more like a text-book historian, and as he has already conceded, interested exclusively in the 'hard politics' of the era.

One aspect of his exposition on sources is worthy of further comment. Aulard indicates that *Moniteur* was a key source when he was trying to piece together the politics of the Napoleonic years. But why was he interested in the Napoleonic period when most other historians confine their histories of the Revolution to the era 1789–95 or 1789–99? Aulard gives us an answer on page 2 of the first volume of *The French Revolution: A Political History*. For him:

> The history of Democracy and the Republic during the Revolution falls naturally under four headings:
> 1 From 1789 to 1792 the period of the origins of Democracy and the Republic – that is, of the formation of the Democratic and Republican parties under a constitutional monarchy by a property-owners' suffrage.
> 2 From 1792 to 1795 was the period of the Democratic Republic.
> 3 From 1795 to 1799 was the period of the Bourgeois Republic.
> 4 From 1799 to 1809 was the period of the Plebiscitary Republic.[35]

His loyalty to republicanism means that in deciding on the parameters of the Revolution (with his history in mind), he was always going to be 'led' in a certain direction. For Aulard, the Revolution meant the Republic and vice-versa. Thus, right up to 1809 he could see the Revolution at work, even though he cut short his own history in 1804. (His republicanism also means that he interprets the Terror as a product of 'circumstance' rather than 'dogma' or 'ideology', and that he sympathises with Danton rather than Robespierre).

The way that Aulard sees the Revolution as a post-1800, as well as a pre-1800, phenomenon is curious, for in 1799 Napoleon came to power via a *coup d'état*. And, even though Aulard is right to point out that the 'Plebiscitary Republic' existed in name for a decade after this date, it is strange that he does not see in Bonaparte's authoritarianism, not to mention his officious and overbearing demeanour, a definite move away from his cherished ideals of 'Democracy' and 'Republicanism' – words that, significantly, were always spelt with capital letters in his work. By contrast, Aulard is pretty unenthusiastic about the King. In assessing the nature and significance of the *cahiers*, he acknowledges the popularity of the monarch:

> It would seem that none of the petitioners dream of attributing their stated grievances to the Monarchy, nor even to the King. In all these documents, the French are seen imbued with an ardent royalism, a warm devotion to the person of Louis XVI. Above all, in documents of the more humble kind, petitions from parishes, and the like, there

is a note of confidence, love and gratitude. 'Our good king! The King our father!' – so the peasants and the workers address him. The nobles and the clergy, less ingenuously enthusiastic, appear equally loyal.[36]

However, he also plays on the 'despotism' of the King[37] and the opposition to him that developed, especially in the *parlements*.[38]

It is interesting, though not surprising, that Aulard detects radical and progressive ideas quite early on in the Revolution. As he says, 'If the democratic party showed republican tendencies in 1790 and 1791, it also showed socialistic and feministic tendencies.'[39] He goes on to quote from a journal, *Révolutions de Paris*, that was beginning to speak for the 'people' and to advise them on political tactics, and also to identify socialists in groups such as Society of the Friends of Unity and Equality in the Family, founded in 1790.[40] There is no call for proletarian revolt,[41] but, 'it is very certain that there were other socialists in the democratic party besides Marat; and a few socialistic manifestations occurred in the early part of 1791'.[42]

More than other historians perhaps, Aulard recognised the role of women in the Revolution:

> If there were, at this time, democratic socialists, there were also democratic feminists, who wished to admit women to the body politic ... Women pleaded their cause by means of acts as well as words: they took part in the Revolution, to the success of which they contributed: some in the *salons*, some in the streets, some at the taking of the Bastille. They took a hand in the municipalisation of the country in July, 1789. The decisive character of October 5th and 6th was due to women. The Commune, in 1790, decorated a number of the women of Paris with medals ... Women had, indeed, really played the part of citizens when Condorect took their cause in hand, with more insistence and more publicly than in 1788, and published, in July, 1790 ... a vigorous and eloquent article, entitled: 'On the Admission of Women to the Rights of the State', which was a veritable feminist manifesto.[43]

It is in this sense that the Aulard era marks the end of 'conservative' or 'right-wing' revolutionary history (as epitomised by Taine in particular). He highlights aspects of the Revolution that others had ignored, and also anticipates the arrival of overtly and avowedly left-wing historians in the shape of, for instance, Jaurès,

Mathiez and Lefebvre. Yet, for all his radicalism and leftist inclinations, Aulard's reputation rests on his straight-down-the-line
republicanism and his achievement in modernising his profession.
The arch-revisionist Cobban explained: 'Aulard wrote at a time
when the Third Republic had overcome its early difficulties and
was beginning to acquire confidence. His political ideal was
embodied in the bourgeois, anti-clerical republicanism of the
Radical Socialist Party ... Aulard saw the Revolution as sowing
the seed which had reached fruition in the Third Republic.'[44]
Aulard himself would certainly not have disputed this characterisation.

Fundamentally, however, the elevation of Aulard to the Chair
at the Sorbonne helped to raise the profile of revolutionary historiography. Thereafter, the Chair has, 'been a symbol of historical
orthodoxy and – especially in view of the hierarchical nature of
the French educational system – a powerful means of defending
it'.[45] Moreover, he understood that, a hundred years on, he had a
huge advantage over writers who had either been involved in, or
had been close to, the Revolution. Speaking as a man of the late
nineteenth century, he stated:

> Yet we do see matters more clearly than those contemporaries who
> struggled in the dark; all ignorant of the issue of things, of the
> sequence of the drama; who (not unlike ourselves to-day perhaps)
> gave weight to matters of no consequence and ignored the signifi-
> cant facts. Certainly the knowledge of results is no infallible
> touchstone in the selection of facts, for the results are not final; the
> Revolution lives to-day in another shape and under other condi-
> tions; but we do at least see partial results, periods accomplished,
> and a development of things, which allow us to distinguish the
> ephemeral from the lasting, to separate the facts which have had
> their consequences in our history from those of no particular signifi-
> cance.[46]

Aulard was the first 'professional' historian of the Revolution and
his comments here seem to reflect this fact. He seems to be aware
that, writing 100 years on from the event, he has certain advan-
tages over other writers, those who 'struggled in the dark'. This is
an interesting insight into his own self-awareness.

In his discourse, Aulard emerged as both combative and
confrontational. For instance, he had a very public disagreement

with his most famous student, Albert Mathiez.[47] Whereas the former put a premium on politics and political history, the latter highlighted socio-economic issues. But differences of opinion like this one were a product of their time, and reflected the growing vibrancy of historical debate. Commenting on the state of revolutionary historiography in the 1980s, Douglas Johnson wrote: 'The days were past when history at the Sorbonne was dominated by such eminent specialists of the Revolution as Aulard and Mathiez, debating about Danton and Robespierre.'[48] Johnson's point was that things had changed: the Revolution was no longer venerated above all other events and modern historians were interested in 'long perspectives' rather than detail.[49]

But it was his feud with Hippolyte Taine that brought him most notoriety. One online source describes the disagreement in quite neutral terms: 'More recently (as of 1911), Taine's historical work has been adversely criticized, especially by A. Aulard in lectures delivered at the Sorbonne in 1905–6 and 1906–7 ... devoted to destructive criticism of Taine's work on the French Revolution.'[50] But this does not do it justice. It was more emotive, more fundamental than this. Here a republican confronted a conservative; a professional historian was forced to pit his wits against a man who, at times, was more sociologist and psychologist than orthodox practitioner of history; a man who stressed the role of ideas in the origins of the Revolution had to deal with a man who interpreted the event as some kind of 'plot'.

It was quite the opposite of a meeting of minds. But for all his bluff and bluster, Aulard took Taine seriously and 'concluded from his "close and impartial inspection" that in Taine's book "an exact reference, an accurate transcription of a text, or a correct assertion is the exception" ... "There are serious inaccuracies, insignificant inaccuracies, innocent inaccuracies, tendentious inaccuracies, but there are inaccuracies everywhere or almost everywhere."'[51]

Taine and Aulard were the heavyweight historians to emerge during the early decades of the Third Republic. But there were others too who contributed to the debate on the Revolution. Dr Jean François Eugène Robinet and Louis Madelin were primarily *Dantonistes*. The former was responsible for *Le Procès des*

Dantonistes and three other works on his 'hero' between 1879 and 1889; the latter, *Danton*, a celebrated biography published in 1879.

In their pro-Danton musings, Robinet and Madelin follow in the tradition of Aulard. By contrast, Frantz Funck-Brentano and Pierre Gaxotte link back to Taine. Funck-Brentano offers us a very favourable picture of pre-1789, so much so that Cobban, writing in 1971, is forced to ask: 'Why then was there a Revolution?'[52] And like Taine, Funck-Brentano has been attacked for his 'unsound' historical methods, his 'one-sided' conclusions, and his 'superficial' general approach.[53] Meanwhile, Gaxotte has been described as one of the Revolution's 'most reactionary critics'.[54] Writing during the inter-war years, he feels it his duty to buttress the 'right-wing nationalist parties' in France by lauding the achievements of the *Ancien Régime* and minimizing its defects.[55] Neither Gaxotte nor Funck-Brentano are particularly celebrated historians, but they are interesting figures on account of their willingness to follow a counter-revolutionary line well into the post-1871 era, when the idea of France returning to a monarchical system was well and truly dead. Suffice it to say, the hegemonic status of the 'Great Tradition' was under little threat.

Finally, let us consider Augustin Cochin, another interesting historian of the Third Republic period. In many ways he is a peripheral figure in the story of French revolutionary historiography, but it is interesting to note that long after his death his reputation was restored by François Furet, possibly the most celebrated living historian of the Revolution. It is easy to understand why Furet – who conceptualised, rather than narrated, the Revolution in his work – was drawn to Cochin. The latter, in the words of Gail Bossenga,

> rejected the idea of plot and, indeed, all historical explanations that looked to human intention as the motor of historical change. Rather than examining human motivation, Cochin sought to uncover general laws conditioning human activity ... Half a century later, François Furet resurrected Cochin's ideas in his search for theoretical alternatives to a Marxist model of the French Revolution.[56]

Furet devoted a full chapter to Cochin's ideas in *Interpreting the French Revolution*, and pointedly labelled him the 'most neglected historian' of the Revolution.[57]

What this chapter has proved is that the seven decades of the Third Republic were particularly fertile years for revolutionary history. They produced the first 'professional' historian of the Revolution (Aulard) and also a giant of the counter-revolutionary tradition (Taine). Both, in their different ways, were inspired by the establishment of the Republic and its troubled early years. Essentially, Aulard tried to bolster it, while Taine attempted to destabilise it. In academic terms, the irresistible force had met the immovable object. Moreover, the fact that these two historians were willing to confront each other openly gave the debate on the Revolution added interest and a public face.

In the same period, the first Chair of revolutionary history was established at the Sorbonne, and we also witness the first stirrings of a new, socialist and Marxist historiography.

Notes

1 A. Aulard, *The French Revolution: A Political History* (London, 1910), pp. 15–16.
2 www.chroniclesmagazine.org/Chronicles/July2003/0703Fleming.html.
3 N. Hampson, 'The French Revolution and its Historians' in G. Best (ed.), *The Permanent Revolution* (London, 1989), p. 225. Tocqueville was the other.
4 G. Comninel, *Rethinking the French Revolution* (London, 1990), pp. 12–13.
5 See A. Cobban, *Aspects of the French Revolution* (London, 1971).
6 H. Taine, *The French Revolution*, 3 Vols (1878), at http://oll.libertyfund.org /ToC/0178.php, p. 426.
7 Hampson, 'Revolution and Historians', p. 226.
8 Ibid., p. 226.
9 Interestingly, the Liberty Fund has also re-published Acton's *Lectures on the French Revolution* – another great liberal treatise on the period.
10 Introduction to Taine's book at http://oll.libertyfund.org/ToC/0178.php.
11 Hampson, 'Revolution and Historians', p. 225.
12 Ibid., p. 225.
13 Tocqueville is Hampson's 'other' heterodox historian.
14 Hampson, 'Revolution and Historians', p. 225.
15 www.chroniclesmagazine.org/Chronicles/July2003/0703Fleming.html.
16 http://oll.libertyfund.org/ToC/0178.php
17 Taine, *Revolution.*, pp. 2–4.
18 Ibid.
19 Ibid.
20 www.chroniclesmagazine.org/Chronicles/July2003/0703Fleming.html.
21 R. Soucy, *Fascism in France: The Case of Maurice Barrès* (Berkeley, 1972).
22 www.chroniclesmagazine.org/Chronicles/July2003/0703Fleming.html.

23 Hampson, 'Revolution and Historians', p. 226.
24 Cobban, *Aspects.*, p. 253.
25 Aulard, *Political History*, p. 18.
26 Cobban, *Aspects*, p. 52.
27 Ibid., p. 49.
28 Aulard, *Political History*, p. 100.
29 Ibid., p. 99.
30 Ibid., p. 6.
31 Ibid., p. 1.
32 Ibid., pp. 16–17.
33 Ibid., pp. 15–16.
34 Cobban, *Aspects*, pp. 252–3.
35 Aulard, *Political History*, p. 10.
36 Ibid., p. 81.
37 Ibid., p. 90.
38 Ibid., pp. 100–1.
39 Ibid., p. 225.
40 Ibid., p. 229.
41 Ibid., p. 228.
42 Ibid., p. 226.
43 Ibid., pp. 231–2.
44 Cobban, *Aspects*, p. 49.
45 Hampson, 'Revolution and Historians', p. 221.
46 Aulard, *Political History*, pp. 11–12.
47 See Chapter 6.
48 D. Johnson, 'The Twentieth Century: Recollection and Rejection', in G. Best (ed.), *The Permanent Revolution* (London, 1989), p. 193.
49 Ibid., p. 193.
50 See www.answers.com/topic/hippolyte-taine.
51 See www.historycooperative.org/journals/ahr/108.1/ah0103000001.html.
52 Cobban, *Aspects*, p. 54.
53 Ibid., p. 54.
54 http://muse.jhu.edu/cgi-bin/access.cgi?uri=/journals/french _historical_studies.
55 Cobban, *Aspects*, pp. 54–6. Gaxotte's book, *The French Revolution*, was published in 1928. He also wrote a volume entitled *Louis XV and His Times*.
56 *H-France Review*, Vol. 3 (July 2003), No. 75.
57 F. Furet, *Interpreting the French Revolution* (Cambridge, 1981), pp. 164–204.

Part II

Twentieth century

6

Marxist 'orthodoxy'

The bourgeoisie stopped talking of despotism. Making an idol of Louis XVI, they turned their attack against the aristocracy. A social struggle, a 'class war' as M. Sagnac has said, broke out openly.[1]

In the first half of the twentieth century, the historiography of the Revolution was to undergo a seismic shift. In the wake of liberal, conservative and republican interpretations came a new 'family' of theses. These were explicitly socialist and Marxist theories, although, as if to forestall criticism, the individuals who put them forward also described them as 'republican'. In itself this was a momentous development. But what also happened was that the socialist/Marxist interpretation of the Revolution became the historical 'orthodoxy'. For *any* thesis to acquire such widespread acceptance was remarkable. But for a *new*, and what is more a *new, left-wing*, theory to gain such legitimacy was extraordinary. As it turned out, for most of the twentieth century – perhaps sixty or seventy years – the Marxist line on the Revolution was the accepted one. (Perhaps this situation should be contrasted with the scenario in England, where English Marxist writers – Hill, Thompson, Hobsbawm, for example – were both effective and influential, but never really acquired a position of hegemony or security.)

The key landmarks in French Marxist historiography were as follows:

1898 – Jean Jaurès, *Histoire Socialiste de la Révolution française*
1927 – Albert Mathiez, *The French Revolution*
1939 – George Lefebvre, *Quatre Vingt Neuf*
1965 – Albert Soboul, *A Short History of the French Revolution*

Noteworthy also were two other facts. The writers who put forward the Marxist line on the Revolution began to coalesce under the banner of the 'Annales School'. It was also interesting that many of the key left-wing historians were not just *historians*, but political activists too, involved either in the French socialist or communist parties. This chapter deals with a number of key issues: What was the left-wing view of the Revolution? How exactly did the Marxist interpretation become the 'orthodoxy'? How should we measure the contribution of the key historians and thinkers? And what were the strengths and weaknesses of the socialist/Marxist view of events?

The question that has to be addressed initially is a crucial one. How, in the first half of the twentieth century, did overtly left-wing interpretations of the Revolution start to emerge? The answer to this conundrum is not straightforward. Initially, we need to place the emergence of Marxist interpretations in context. Marx and Engels had published *The Communist Manifesto* in 1848, and then decades later, after witnessing the Franco-Prussian War and the Paris Commune (from afar), Marx was responsible for *The Civil War in France*, a pointed examination of political developments in France. Given Marx's interest in France as a seedbed of radical ideas, it was only natural that he and his followers would eventually turn their attention to the events of 1789. For Marx himself, the Revolution was an important reference point.[2] He refers to it often in his writings, and talks about it as the 'old', and 'great', as if in veneration.[3] He was curious about the whole revolutionary tradition in France, and also, for partisan reasons, concerned, if not obsessed, about the idea of 'revolution' as an idea.[4]

Here we should be aware that Marx was also interested in the English Revolution. He wrote extensively on the subject and saw it as an important historical episode worthy of serious investigation. He interprets it as laying the foundations for capitalism. He sees 'new' and 'old' nobilities present, and also a mass of embryonic proletarians. But, for Marx, the French Revolution was more recent and also closer to home. Moreover, it fitted slightly better into his 'model' of how revolutions occur and, arguably, left less of the body politic intact than its equivalent in England.

There are important undercurrents to Marx's writings on the

Revolution. He applauds its achievements in eradicating feudalism and establishing 'national unity' (he depicts it as a 'gigantic
broom' and as the harbinger of the 'modern world');[5] he explains
its increasing radicalism;[6] he lauds its impact on other countries,[7]
and he is constantly comparing and contrasting it with the 1848
Revolution in France. And when he is not advancing his 'scientific' interpretation of history, he does acknowledge that political
developments in England and the battle between the *parlements*
and the monarchy played their part in the origins of the
Revolution.[8] But, Marx's writings demonstrate that he was
primarily interested in the role of the bourgeoisie in 1789. 'Each
step in the development of the bourgeoisie was accompanied by a
corresponding political advance in that class', he wrote in *The
Communist Manifesto*.

> An oppressed class under the sway of the feudal nobility ... taxable
> 'third estate' of the monarchy (as in France); afterward, in the
> period of manufacturing proper, serving either the semi-feudal or
> the absolute monarchy as a counterpoise against the nobility, and, in
> fact, cornerstone of the great monarchies in general – the bour-
> geoisie has at last, since the establishment of Modern Industry and
> of the world market, conquered for itself, in the modern representa-
> tive state, exclusive political sway. The executive of the modern
> state is but a committee for managing the common affairs of the
> whole bourgeoisie. The bourgeoisie, historically, has played a most
> revolutionary part.[9]

And again in *The German Ideology*:

> When the French bourgeoisie overthrew the power of the aristoc-
> racy, it thereby made it possible for many proletarians to raise
> themselves above the proletariat, but only insofar as they become
> bourgeois. Every new class, therefore, achieves its hegemony only
> on a broader basis than that of the class ruling previously, whereas
> the opposition of the non-ruling class against the new ruling class
> later develops all the more sharply and profoundly. Both these
> things determine the fact that the struggle to be waged against this
> new ruling class, in its turn, aims at a more decided and radical
> negation of the previous conditions of society than could all previ-
> ous classes which sought to rule.[10]

There are key themes here: the role of the bourgeoisie as 'agent'
in the revolutionary process, the connection between economic

and political power, and the catalysing effect that the ascendancy of the bourgeoisie had on the urban masses. Marx argued that bourgeois hegemony was a crucial prerequisite for further change in a socialist direction, and in line with his 'scientific' theory. And as if to demonstrate the inevitability of this process, he also pointed to the defects of bourgeois rule: the lack of real equality and the vindictive nature of class politics.

Before we move on, it is important to note that Marx, writing in *The Civil War in France* in 1871, seemed to concur with Tocqueville, who had written *The Old Regime and the French Revolution* fifteen years earlier. Marx stated:

> The first French revolution with its task to found national unity (to create a nation) had to break down all local, territorial, townish and provincial independence. It was, therefore, forced to develop what absolute monarchy had commenced, the centralization and organisation of state power, and to expand the circumference and the attributes of the state power, the number of its tools, its independence.[11]

This was straight out of Tocqueville. The liberal aristocrat and the left-wing revolutionary would disagree on a number of issues, but they both realised that, in some respects at least, the Revolution was the natural heir to the Bourbon monarchy.

Naturally, 'Marxism' as a new ideology was to affect and influence the historical community. It was not simply a 'set of ideas' but something more far-reaching: a way of thinking, a philosophy of life and society, a pseudo-scientific way of understanding the world. By the middle of the nineteenth century Marx had his apostles; by the 1880s and 1890s he had historians speaking in his name (Jaurès being the first major left-wing writer to grapple with the Revolution).

But, we must remind ourselves that 'republican' interpretations with (what seemed like) socialist sympathies had already seen the light of day well before 1900. In Chapter 5 we noted the work of Aulard, and in Chapter 4 we examined the writings of Michelet, who put forward possibly the most famous republican theory of the Revolution, with his love letter to *le peuple*. It is also fair to say that a momentum developed, with one historian's thesis encouraging another, and so on. Here we must single out the work of Lefebvre. The depth of his research and the scale and scope of his writings was a milestone in the historiography of the Revolution, let alone left-wing historiography. This gave the Marxist view credibility and, moreover, encouraged others to follow in his footsteps. However, it could be argued that, when we weigh up the factors that promoted the emergence of left-wing interpretations of 1789, the most significant event, or issue, was yet to arrive. This was the Russian Revolution. It is difficult to quantify the exact impact of February and October 1917 so immense and profound was it. For decades those on the left had been hoping for, and also dreaming of, political change. Many activists had plotted and conspired. They had taken part in still-born revolutions and been unsuccessful, disappointed, and sometimes even betrayed. And then came the fall of the Tsar and the establishment, and then consolidation, of Bolshevik rule.

Russia, 1917, was both a precedent and a source of great encouragement for those on the left. Political activists around Europe aimed for a re-run in their own country, while writers and historians saw in the Bolshevik victory a profound moment of working-class triumph. Although the story of the USSR demonstrates the folly of this view, it is still difficult to underestimate the power, poignancy and symbolism of the February and October revolutions. If Russia could journey from 'feudalism' (the *Ancien Régime* of the Tsars) through 'bourgeois capitalism' (the interregnum of Kerensky's Provisional Government) to 'socialist utopia' (Lenin's new regime) then, surely, so could other nations. What is more, was it not also possible that some countries had already begun their dialectic-induced trek through history? French historians who located themselves on the left asked themselves more specific questions: What was the relationship between the era of the Bourbons and the era of the revolutionaries? In what sense did 1789 mark a rupture between feudal and capitalist epochs? Was there any sense in which France, in the aftermath of 1789, had witnessed socialism or socialist ideas in power?

But the main question, the big question, was this: To what extent was the Revolution of 1789 a 'bourgeois revolution'? In other words, to what extent did the experience of France in the period 1789–99 conform to Marx's delineation of the key 'scientific' stages in history? And, looking back on the Revolution, with over a century's worth of hindsight, could the experience of France be *made*, or *forced*, to coincide with Marx's model? It was these major, fundamental questions that Marxist and left-leaning historians were forced to grapple with in the early years of the twentieth century. The point to be made about these Marxist historians is this: although, to a large extent, their research may well have been driven by ideology, there is no doubt that their ideas gained wide currency and acceptance.

Obviously, the plethora of Marxist historians did not agree on everything. They each had individual concerns and emphases, and expressed their ideas in different ways. However, it is possible to identify some general features of the Marxist position.

The general thrust of Marxist theory was that the Revolution was both inevitable and desirable. Marxists argued that the Revolution had been 'bourgeois' in inspiration, that the capitalist ethos had superseded the feudal idea, and that the bourgeois character of the Revolution was pre-eminent. However, at the same time, Marxist writers also acknowledged that other distinctive revolutions had taken place: the revolt of the nobility in the period 1787–89 and, 'on the back of' the bourgeois revolution, the separate but linked revolutions of the people and the peasantry. Even though Marxist writers put the prime emphasis on the bourgeoisie and the revolution that they had created, they also highlighted the role of ordinary people – those who lived in the towns and cities of France. These were the 'heroic' classes, the poorer people who were motivated by the price of bread, by the level of taxation, by famine. This is why, in time, Marxist writers came to glorify the group of Parisian radicals known as the *sansculottes*, and why they also became interested in the 'crowd' as a force in revolutionary politics.

In general, those on the Marxist left saw the Revolution as class based, as a 'class struggle', to use one of Marx's most famous phrases. The corollary of this position was that two other potential 'issues' were dismissed. First, it would be fair to say that Marxists attached little significance to the autonomous role of ideas in history, and in the build-up to 1789 more specifically. They acknowledged the existence of the *philosophes* and the Enlightenment, but they placed the emphasis on class relationships, rather than the independent power of ideas, when it came to origins and causation. (Of course, they *did* acknowledge that ideas and ideologies could be generated within distinct sets of socio-economic settings, but this was very different from saying that ideas and ideologies had the power to *cause* events).

Second, Marxist writers spoke very little about the King and his role in the pre- and post-1789 periods. He was generally viewed as a 'bystander', a man who was merely looking on as historical forces took shape around him. It was as if, on both counts, Marxists were so engrossed by issues of class that they minimised the role of any other factor or potential factor. When they turned their attention to the Revolution itself – to the period 1789–99 – Marxist writers made a number of fundamental points. They argued that 1789 as a revolutionary year was one of myriad achievements. Even when the peacefulness of 1789 was replaced by the anarchy of 1793–94, they felt that they could rationalise this. They argued, for example, that violence was a necessary accompaniment to revolutionary change and did not detract from the democratic nature of the Revolution. Thus, in general terms, Marxist writers found it possible, and actually quite acceptable, to justify and rationalise the Terror. Not only this, but in Robespierre – much more than in Danton – left-wing historians saw an icon.

In summary, it is clear that Marxist writers interpreted the Revolution as an opportunity for social change. That is why they have placed so much emphasis on the class struggle between bourgeoisie and aristocracy, and why they have glorified the role of the *sans-culottes*, who sought a revolution in economic relations rather than political systems. But, as we will now explore, the Marxist view of the Revolution was not as uniform or monolithic as some on the left, and the right, would have us believe. Of course there were central tenets, and principles, and ideas, but there were also quite specific concerns and emphases associated with particular individuals. And as with all traditions or schools of thought, the Marxist interpretation of the Revolution evolved over time and adapted itself to changing circumstances.

Jean-Joseph-Marie-Auguste Jaurès was a leader of the French Socialist movement during its formative years and, on a more general level, one of the most important figures in the history of the French left. His main achievement was the unification of the Socialist movement in the early years of the twentieth century, but he also came to personify the campaign to prevent the outbreak of war in 1914.

In terms of his writings on the French Revolution, Jaurès put forward an overtly socialist and sociological interpretation, focusing primarily on social and economic issues, and his ideas were warmly welcomed by Aulard. Jaurès' biographer, Harvey Goldberg, is impressed with his subject's method: 'Without doubt Jaurès understood and met the rigorous demands of the historical craft. In the years between 1899 and 1903, he was often seen at the Archives Nationales, the Bibliothèque Nationale, the Carnavalet – where he pored over many hundreds of printed and manuscript sources.'[12]

Jaurès argued that class struggle was a motivating force in historical evolution, and in 1780s France in particular. Alfred Cobban, whose revisionist theses of the 1960s eventually challenged the Marxist line, puts it like this: 'The general idea in which Jaurès sums up the causation of the Revolution is the rise of the bourgeoisie, which "through its economic growth inevitably took the road of its revolutionary destinies". Starting with Marxist assumptions, he takes the French bourgeoisie to be a class of wealthy capitalists and financiers, with a satellite class of *rentiers* – investors in state funds.'[13] This is a fairly accurate summation. As a politician and polemicist, Jaurès' main objective was the dissemination of socialist ideas and the gradual – nationwide and worldwide – adoption of democratic socialism. But this did not stop him putting huge energies into his historical research. 'His search into the revolutionary past enormously enriched his knowledge of social structure and historical change,' claims Goldberg. 'He learned, and consequently taught, more that was essential about the eighteenth century than any of his political contemporaries; in the process, he deepened his understanding of his own society and its evolution.'[14]

Albert Mathiez was arguably the most left-wing historian of the Revolution. Unlike other historians of the left, he was not a member of the Socialist or Communist party, but his major work, *La Révolution française* (3 volumes, 1922–27; translated 1928, reprinted 1962), stands as one of the landmarks of revolutionary historiography. As a budding historian, Mathiez was subject to two important influences. As a student at the Sorbonne he necessarily came under the influence of Alphonse Aulard, the Chair of French Revolutionary History. And it would be fair to say that the relationship that developed between Mathiez and Aulard has aroused much interest and comment.

The best way to sum up their relationship is to say that Mathiez adopted Aulard's methods and techniques but travelled in a very different direction as a historian. Kates says that 'Aulard was challenged by his most gifted student'; Cobban, the arch-revisionist, uses the word 'vendetta' over and over again to describe the essence of the relationship (which may be a little strong).[15] One area of tension was revolutionary 'personalities'. While Aulard put all his eggs in the *Dantoniste* basket, Mathiez looked towards Robespierre. The result, in the words of Comninel, was that, 'Mathiez pulled official republican historiography farther to the left'.[16] The other major influence on Mathiez was Jean Jaurès and his 'awesome legacy'.[17] Yet, if we are trying to detect the major conditioning influences on Mathiez – the man and the historian – we need to cast our eyes eastwards. Throughout the history of French revolutionary historiography, we have seen how external events can shape historians' thinking. Michelet reflected the 'pre-1848' mood in his heroic portrayal of 1789, while Taine was affected badly by the horrors of the Franco-Prussian War and what he eventually produced was a devastating critique of the revolutionary, republican tradition. But the symbiotic relationship that emerged between Mathiez on the one hand and political developments in Russia on the other was on an altogether different scale.

Mathiez was influenced enormously by the Bolsheviks' acquisition of power. Later historians have had a field day probing the context and the political climate in which Mathiez's ideas were shaped. No doubt with a wry grin on his face, Douglas Johnson has offered this assessment:

> When the French observed the Russian Revolution of 1917, the historian Mathiez wrote newspaper articles in which he tried to identify individuals and parties in Russia with their equivalents in the French Revolution (it was Mathiez, *Robespierriste* and critic of

the moderates in the French Revolution, who would apologize to a student who asked for a rendez-vous because he lived in the Vergniaud, named after a Girondin, but who would then cheer up, explaining that the student could take the 93 bus, a reference to the crucial year of the Revolution)![18]

Furet, who should know a thing or two about how external influences can affect a historian's judgement,[19] also acknowledges the relationship: 'Everything changed in 1917. The socialist revolution acquired a face; the French Revolution ceased to be a matrix of probabilities on which another liberating revolution could and should be modelled. It was no longer the field of possibilities, discovered and described by Jaurès; it had become the mother of a real event, dated, fixed, which had taken place and which was the Russian Revolution of October 1917.'

Norman Hampson, whose own work would also be affected by outside factors, identifies subsidiary contextual issues: 'Contemporary events merely sharpened his [Mathiez'] historical animosities ... The Russian Revolution, which Mathiez welcomed, served to justify the Terror. As always, the history of the Revolution was inseparable from contemporary politics.'[20] Hampson – who as a post-war revisionist helped to chip away at the Marxist orthodoxy – paints a picture of Mathiez as being almost perennially confused between history and present-day reality. There is more than a grain of truth in this. The sceptical view, of course, is that Mathiez and his comrades were scratching around for self-justification. They would latch on to *any* event or episode that had the potential to give their rigid, 'scientific' theories about the Revolution some kind of plausibility. They *would* see the French Revolution being played out in Russia in 1917, *wouldn't* they? Of course they would!

In terms of the story of the French Revolution, Mathiez was clear. It began as a struggle between the bourgeoisie and the aristocracy, but evolved into a conflict that pitted the middle class against the working class – thus raising the spectre of 'class struggle' (obviously, a crucial Marxist concept). As such, Mathiez has become vulnerable to criticism. The main charge against him is that he is too dogmatic, particularly in his economic analysis. Likewise, he has been attacked for his position on Robespierre and the Terror. He was fascinated by the man who came to personify Jacobinism and the Committee of Public Safety. He published many studies of Robespierre – though no complete biography – and it was as if he had almost privatised his memory for himself. Essentially, Mathiez viewed Robespierre in a positive light, as almost 'infallible'.[21] He was the embodiment of popular democracy and his overthrow in 1794 was a cause for regret. No wonder Mathiez ended his narrative history of the Revolution in 1794 with the demise of his hero. The corollary of this pro-Robespierre adulation was a willingness, or perhaps even a need, to justify the Terror. Mathiez saw the Terror as justifiable, as a necessary response to circumstances. His defence of it was 'passionate ... [he] argued that the cost of living for ordinary Parisians improved more during the Terror than at any other time. In Mathiez's view, Robespierre was not a dictator hungry for arbitrary power, but a democratic politician responding to popular pressures from Parisian workers.'[22]

As we have said on many occasions during the course of this study, a writer's attitude to the Terror is a sound general barometer of their attitude to the Revolution as a whole and helps us to discern exactly where we should place them in the historiographical spectrum. This is particularly the case with Mathiez. Another measure of significance is impact and influence, and there is no doubt that Mathiez was a guiding light for Georges Lefebvre, and also for Louis Gottschalk. Moreover, he left a concrete legacy in the form of the Société des Etudes Robespierristes, the group he founded. Among its many initiatives was the establishment of the journal, *Annales historiques de la Révolution française*. This became the forum *par excellence* for scholarly debate about the Revolution – hence the impressive list of general editors: Mathiez, Lefebvre, Soboul and Michel Vovelle.[23]

Georges Lefebvre was Chair in the History of the Revolution at the Sorbonne and, in many ways, the natural successor to Jaurès and Mathiez. It was his doctoral thesis that gave Lefebvre the platform on which to develop his ideas about French history. The study was entitled, 'The Peasants of the Nord Department during the French Revolution', and was duly published in book form. Comprising a major statistical examination of the peasant class in one French *département*, this work established Lefebvre's reputation as a high-class scholar who brought depth and rigour to the study of the Revolution. *Quatre-Vingt-Neuf* is his most famous work, written for the 150th anniversary of the Revolution in 1939, but it was so provocative, in the eyes of the Vichy government that assumed power in 1940, that it was immediately banned. This episode demonstrates, once again, the political significance and potency of historical writings on the Revolution.[24]

Lefebvre's is probably the most famous left-wing interpretation of the Revolution, and if one historian's writings can be taken to represent what has become known as 'Marxist orthodoxy', then it is probably his. He was fascinated by the 'stages in history' and the 'historical process' – key notions, of course, for Marxist writers. In his work he also placed great emphasis on anti-clericalism, the political mentality of urban and rural workers, and on 'history from below'. His interpretation is, simultaneously, social, economic and republican. The most controversial claim put forward by Lefebvre was that the Revolution equated to four revolutions that together comprised an 'integral whole':

> The first act of the revolution, in 1788, consisted in a triumph of the aristocracy, which, taking advantage of the government crisis, hoped to reassert itself and win back the political authority of which the Capetian dynasty had despoiled it. But, after having paralyzed the royal power which upheld its own social preeminence, the aristocracy opened the way to the bourgeois revolution, then to the popular revolution in the cities and finally to the revolution of the peasants – and found itself buried under the ruins of the Old Regime.[25]

Thus, he talked about 'aristocratic', 'bourgeois', 'urban' and 'rural' uprisings. But throughout his writings, Lefebvre maintained that the central 'cog' in the 'wheel' of 1789 was the bourgeoisie. They were the central reference point. And they did not just emerge 'out of nothing'. The Tennis Court Oath of June 1789 was merely the crowning symbol of their growth. They had a 'full consciousness of historic mission' and 'a common detestation of the aristocracy'.[26] Moreover:

> the growth of commerce and industry had created, step by step, a new form of wealth, mobile or commercial wealth, and a new class, called in France the bourgeoisie, which since the fourteenth century

had taken its place as the Third Estate in the General Estates of the kingdom...For centuries the bourgeois, envious of the aristocracy, had aimed only at thrusting himself into its ranks. More than once he had succeeded, for a great many nobles descended from ennobled bourgeois. This ambition was not extinct ... The exclusiveness of the nobility in the eighteenth century made the ascent even more arduous than before, especially when the nobles tried to reserve the most distinguished public employments for themselves. At the same time, with increasing wealth, the numbers and the ambitions of the bourgeois continued to mount ... With the doors shut, the idea arose of breaking them down.[27]

What defines Lefebvre, though, is his examination of the lower classes: the peasants and the urban population. This is where the depth of his research is most evident. He produced several studies on the rural dimensions of the Revolution. His view was that the peasants, after having their demands and grievances neglected for so long, 'suddenly ... revolted, taking their cause into their own hands and delivering a death blow to what was left of the feudal and manorial system. The peasant uprising is one of the most distinctive features of the revolution in France.'[28] In the cities, Lefebvre identifies the component members of 'the wage-earning class': 'woodworkers', 'master craftsmen', 'tanners', 'journeymen' and 'shopkeepers'.[29] He argues that, more than anything, these groups were provoked into revolt by economic conditions, specifically 'food shortage' and a reduction in 'the purchasing power of the masses'.[30] Further, Lefebvre shows that he is interested in the Revolution as a whole, not just 1789 or 1793. His book, *The Thermidorians*, is the most revealing proof of this.

Lefebvre's legacy is summed up best by Geoffrey Symcox, the man who translated *A Short History of the French Revolution*, a keynote work by Albert Soboul, one of Lefebvre's pupils: 'Lefebvre's work embraced the whole field of French revolutionary studies, and his contribution was above all to enrich our understanding of the social forces lying behind the apparent confusion and flux of political events ... Lefebvre really inaugurates what we may term the scientific study of the Revolution "from below", and in his work, for the first time, the masses move to center stage.'[31] Symcox goes on to argue that Lefebvre gave flesh to ideas and ways of 'doing' history that had been touched on, but *only* touched on, by others: 'Whereas before even sympathetic historians like Michelet had treated the popular movement as at best a shadowy abstraction, Lefebvre anatomized it and revealed the multiplicity of often conflicting forces that it comprised.'[32]

R.R. Palmer translated Lefebvre's 1947 work into English, and then published his own history, *The Age of the Democratic Revolution: A Political History of Europe and America* (2 Vols, 1964). Palmer was not a Marxist, but he did admire Lefebvre's work, and endorsed the notion of 'bourgeois revolution'. His significance as a historian comes in the fact that he broadened out the notion of revolution in geographical terms. But, as Hampson puts it, '[According to Palmer] The Americans began a series of revolutions, of which that in France was the most important. This was unlikely to commend itself to the custodians of the Great Tradition, since it denied the uniqueness of the French Revolution.'[33] This theme – the tension between French and non-French historians – will raise its head again in Chapter 7.

Albert Soboul wrote *A Short History of the French Revolution* (1965) and *The French Revolution 1787–1799* (2 Vols, 1975), and is generally viewed as Lefebvre's successor. Like Lefebvre he was attracted to the notion of 'history from below' and wrote extensively on the role of the Parisian *sans-culottes* in the Revolution. The commentator who reviewed Soboul's book, *The Sans-Culottes: The Popular Movement and Revolutionary Government, 1793–1794* (1981), for *The New York Times Book Review* declared: 'I know of no book as good as this that brings the revolutionary masses so vividly to light.'[34]

Essentially, Soboul stuck close to the main tenets of Marxist historiography, emphasising the socio-economic over the political and the principle of 'history from below'. He also stuck firmly and rigidly to the notion of bourgeois revolution. The opening paragraph of *A Short History of the French Revolution* illustrates this superbly:

> The Revolution marks the advent of bourgeois, capitalist society in French history. Its essential achievement was the creation of national unity through the destruction of the seigneurial system and the privileged orders of feudal society; as de Tocqueville observed in

The Old Regime and the Revolution ... the Revolution's 'real purpose was to do away everywhere with what remained of the institutions of the Middle Ages'. Its final outcome, the establishment of liberal democracy, provides a further clue to its historical meaning. From this double point of view, and considered within the perspective of world history, it may be regarded as the definitive model of all bourgeois revolutions.[35]

The references to 'bourgeois, capitalist society', 'national unity' and 'liberal democracy' are standard stuff. The nod towards Tocqueville is also interesting.

On the whole it would be fair to say that Soboul went slightly further than Lefebvre in his analysis. This explains why his name is often prefixed by the descriptors 'Marxist-Leninist' or 'Stalinist'. He offers enormous depth on the question of the peasantry's role. It was easy for other (earlier and later) historians to dismiss the peasants as 'unpoliticised' and, if they did harbour some political instincts, as 'backward', 'conservative' and 'reactionary'. Soboul's angle was radically different: 'The peasants played [a. . .] significant part in the French Revolution; this was one of its most distinctive characteristics. In 1789 the vast majority of the peasantry had long been free, for serfdom only survived in a few regions, chiefly the Nivernais and the Franche-Comté. It remains true nonetheless that the feudal mode of production still dominated the countryside, as is evidenced by the rents and dues paid to the seigneurs, and the tithes paid to the Church.' He continues:

> Tithes had frequently been diverted from their original purpose and furthermore aroused the odium that always attached to taxes in kind; in periods of rising prices their profitability increased, while in times of shortage they were levied at the expense of the peasant's own subsistence. The surviving seigneurial dues were even more unpopular and were just as heavy. Some historians have tended to minimize the weight of seigneurial exactions at the end of the Old Regime, but de Tocqueville anticipated their arguments long ago in the chapter of *The Old Regime and the Revolution* entitled 'Why Feudal Dues Were More Hated in France than Anywhere Else'.[36]

Again, there is an emphasis on class relations and an allusion to Tocqueville. Soboul's interest in the peasantry was not unique – it was shared by Lefebvre and Vovelle, to name but two other historians – but it was certainly distinctive.

Equally important, and perhaps even path-breaking, were Soboul's enquiries into the role of the urban masses, the *sans-culottes*, who emerged as an influential force during 1793 and 1794. He attaches profound significance to the *sans-culottes* as a complicating factor in the Revolution. He argues that in 1793 revolutionary leaders had to pursue a programme that was 'acceptable' to the *sans-culottes* and cognizant with their demands. At the same time, however, he also claims that the actions of the *sans-culottes* helped to 'stabilise' and 'consolidate' the government.[37] They were, thus, an omnipresent force, one that revolutionary leaders could not ignore. This is illuminated best by Soboul's use of case studies and examples. First:

> The *sans-culottes* attacked the institutions that supported commercial capital. They demanded the closing of the stock exchange and the suppression of joint-stock companies. On May 1, 1793, the Parisian section of Faubourg-du-Nord demanded the closing of the stock exchange; the next day the Contrat-Social section supported this petition. It was necessary to wait for the elimination of the Girondists: the Convention ordered the closing of the Paris Stock Exchange on June 27, 1793. As for joint-stock companies, they had proliferated by the end of the *Ancien Régime*. In July 1793, a citizen of the Sans-Culottes section was astonished to see appear 'here a mutual aid association, over there a commercial bank, in another place a savings bank, farther on a subscription insurance office for the elderly, here a life insurance office, at this address the patriotic Lottery of the street of the Bac. (These are nothing but businesses to grab money.) These rich men, owners and entrepreneurs of banks, are the ones to fear most.' On August 24, 1793, the Montagnard Convention banned financial companies; on April 15, 1794, it prohibited all companies without distinction.[38]

Second:

> Even more significant was the position of the Parisian sans-culottes on the subject of the manufacture of war materiel. Since nationalization had been adopted only for the manufacture of weapons, the revolutionary government was forced to turn to private enterprise for equipment and supplies. Following the tradition of the *Ancien Régime*, the government ordered from a handful of businessmen-wholesale merchants, important manufacturer-contractors instead of dispersing orders among many small workshops of independent producers: commercial capital would still dominate industrial

production, not the reverse. This situation was a source of conflict between the revolutionary government and the Parisian sans-culottes throughout the year II and contributed to the worsening of their relationship.[39]

So, at one and the same time, the *sans-culottes* were allies and enemies of the government in power. Earlier historians may have chosen to neglect their role, but Soboul saw it as his job to present the facts and to restore the *sans-culottes* to their rightful place in the story of the Revolution.

Underscoring this position was anger and frustration. Soboul was conscious of the way in which 'ordinary people' and their motivations/political instincts had been treated by historians and writers in the past:

> The masses in the towns and the countryside were not stirred up to revolt in 1789 by bourgeois intrigues and agitation. This was the conspiracy theory put forward by the abbé Barruel in his *Memoirs to Illustrate the History of Jacobinism,* published in Hamburg in 1798, and taken up again after a fashion by the historian Augustin Cochin in *The Philosophical Societies and the Revolution in Brittany* (1925). Nor did the popular masses rebel because of innate bloodthirstiness, as Taine argued in his *Origins of Contemporary France,* published in 1875, a splenetic and vituperative work. What aroused the masses was hunger; Michelet had already emphasized this self-evident fact ('Come, I pray you, and see the people lying down to sleep on the cold earth, patient as Job ... Famine is a normal condition of existence; hunger comes by royal decree'), and the work of C. E. Labrousse has now grounded it on a solid basis of scientific evidence.[40]

This, in essence, was the defining feature of the Marxist perspective, and Soboul's in particular: that economic deprivation had provoked the lower classes into organised revolt.

We should also make two other points about the historiographical tradition and Soboul's place in it. First, it is interesting that Soboul, above, makes reference to a number of historians who ignored the people's 'suffering' (Barruel, Cochin, Taine). Only Michelet is spared Soboul's wrath. Obviously it would be absurd to categorise Michelet as a 'Marxist' or even a 'pre-Marxist' – he shared none of the assumptions or premises of Jaurès, Lefebvre, Mathiez, Soboul and company. But, in his concern for the common man, and for the 'people' as a social force, Michelet foreshadows, in some very specific respects, the main thrust of Marxist historiography. Parker helps us here. He says that, 'Jaurès and Mathiez [among others]...added a socialist dimension to Michelet's enthusiasm for the people and the Revolution.'[41] Second, it is worthy of comment that, in two of the three passages cited above, Soboul pays tribute to Tocqueville's work on the Revolution. This is indicative of the fact that the majority of historians are able to see something important and relevant in the writings of the aristocrat. It is also testament to Tocqueville's uniqueness. He is impossible to classify or pigeon-hole and, as a result, historians – regardless of political viewpoint or historiographical angle – have felt themselves attracted to him.

Symcox puts Soboul's writings into perspective: 'For [him], class analysis is the only satisfactory way to interpret the enormous complexity of the French Revolution and to comprehend the movement as a whole, rather than as a series of disconnected events without real meaning.' He goes on: 'Soboul argues that the Revolution was more than just a straightforward conflict between the old dominant force of the aristocracy and the emergent power of the bourgeoisie, borne upward by the expansion of trade and industry: things were more complicated than that. At certain crucial moments the masses intervened, under the pressure of famine and dire economic necessity, or impelled by their own vision of social and economic justice.[42] As such, Soboul's legacy is the notion of 'bourgeois-peasant revolution' – a major contribution to the historiography of the period.

We should not restrict ourselves to the 'Big Four' left-wing historians, Jaurès, Mathiez, Lefebvre, Soboul. Jacques Godechot is a curious case. The socio-economic analysis he puts forward has much in common with the Marxist view. He understands that the Revolution was a bourgeois project. He states: 'The essential goal of the National Constituent Assembly was to construct a new regime which would guarantee to the bourgeoisie the peaceful exercise of power and eliminate the possibility of either a return to absolute monarchy, or rule of the aristocracy, or rule of the mass of the people.'[43] At the same time he acknowledges that there was no 'industrial revolution' or 'proletariat' in late-eigh-teenth-century France; but he does claim that 500,000 of the 600,000 people who lived in Paris were 'future *sans culottes*'.[44]

Prior to Godechot only non-French historians – R.R. Palmer in particular – had 'dared' to situate the French Revolution in a European or transatlantic context. But Godechot broke the taboo. He may have been French, and also a Marxist, but his first instinct was to place the Revolution of 1789 in a wider, broader schema. His starting point is Geneva 1768 but he also takes in disturbances in Ireland and other parts of western and northern Europe. He talks about 'revolutionary disorders' and an umbrella Europe-wide revolution that was discernible in the period 1787–1815. His conclusion, therefore, is that the Revolution of 1789 in France was anything but a 'bolt from the blue'.[45]

In 1976 Daniel Guérin produced *La Révolution française et nous*.[46] In previous works he had explored topics such as fascism and the Front Populaire government of 1936. Guérin was a self-proclaimed Trotskyite, and in *La Révolution française et nous* he nails his colours firmly to the mast, quoting Engels at the outset and throwing in references to 1917 as and when appropriate (or actually even when inappropriate). He goes on to argue that the Revolution was not just a bourgeois revolution. The thrust of his argument was that the bourgeoisie 'couldn't do it alone'. They had neither the ability nor the mentality to take the Revolution onto the 'streets', for example. That is why Guérin glorifies the 'people' as an 'autonomous mass movement' and a 'collective force'. And why one commentator has talked about his 'particu-larly affectionate (and for that reason misguided) account of mass movements in the Revolution, and their defeat or betrayal ...'[47] Ernest Labrousse specialised in economics, Marcel Reinhard made Carnot his focus and Eric Hobsbawm pursued the idea of revolution. There was also George Rudé and his work on the 'crowd' in the Revolution.

During the inter-war years, Rudé was a leading light in the Communist Party Historians' Group. In 1952 he was instrumen-tal in the founding of the journal *Past & Present* devoted to the study of 'history from below'. Essentially, what he did was steer 'Marxist' thinking in a new direction. He questioned many core Marxist assumptions – for example, the view which said that the

Revolution had been a catalyst for capitalist development in France. At the same time, he delved into new areas of research, most notably the role of the 'crowd', and of ordinary people, in the Revolution. Here, his key works are *The Crowd in the French Revolution* (1959), *The Crowd in History* (1964) and *The Face of the Crowd* (1988).

In *The Crowd in the French Revolution*, Rudé certainly puts down a marker. The first line of the Introduction reads: 'One aspect of the French Revolution that has been largely neglected by historians is the nature of the revolutionary crowd.' He then proceeds to examine the writings of Burke, Taine, Michelet and others, and concludes that the nature of revolutionary movements – particularly in the period 1787–89 – has been slightly neglected.[48] Thus, he presents himself as breaking new ground and of taking revolutionary historiography on to a new level where sociological and psychological methods are employed to complement traditional historical approaches.

In one sense Rudé was genuinely a free thinker and a different kind of Marxist. In another, he was tarred with the same brush. He was blacklisted and found it difficult to find employment in the academic world because of his left-leaning views.

The emergence of the Marxist interpretation of the French Revolution in the early twentieth century was unquestionably a major landmark in the historiography of the event. Jaurès, Mathiez, Lefebvre, Soboul all had their influences. The rise of socialism, the Russian Revolution, world war, the Cold War: these were external factors that could not but impact on the writings of left-leaning academics in France, just as the English Revolution had been utilised as a useful measure by earlier historians of various hues (Burke, Carlyle, Guizot, for example). That said, we should not be blinkered into thinking that the left-wing, Marxist view – in as much as there was a single view – was a giant departure from what had gone before. Obviously, it was the dawn of a new era in historiographical circles but, as we have noted previously, there was not a great deal of daylight between the Marxist view and the view of someone like Michelet, who glorified 'the people' but who did not add on layer upon layer of nuanced class analysis.[49]

Although it became, in time, the 'orthodox' interpretation of 1789, the Marxist view is certainly open to criticism. First, it appears that those on the left want to 'have their cake, and eat it'. They want to promote the notion of an all-encompassing 'bourgeois revolution' – a plausible standpoint in itself – but they also want to integrate into this position a belief that *other* revolutions occurred as well, namely those associated with the aristocracy, the urban population and the peasantry. The linked criticism is that for all their emphasis on class and class relations, Marxist historians are often remarkably simplistic and unsophisticated in their demarcation of classes and in their commentary on inter-class relations. Second, it is slightly unclear whether, in the Marxist interpretation, the bourgeoisie is envious of the aristocracy, or actually despises it as a class. This ambiguity is most apparent in the writings of Lefebvre. Third, the Marxist view is vulnerable on account of what it chooses to ignore rather than what it chooses to emphasise. Thus, the manner in which many left-wing writers neglect to find a role for ideas (for example, the Enlightenment) or key personalities (such as the King) is controversial to say the least.

Finally, and here we can sympathise to some extent, there seem to be a number of inconsistencies between Marxist historians. For example, whereas Lefebvre and Soboul place significant emphasis on the peasants as a revolutionary force in 1789, others do not. Of course, we should not expect total uniformity and homogeneity, even from Marxist writers, but these variations are worth noting. Similarly, it is interesting that some tension is evident between French and Anglo-American historians. For all these reasons, and others, it was not going to be long before the Marxist line on the Revolution came up against some serious scrutiny. This happened in the post-war years when Alfred Cobban and other revisionist historians set to work on undermining the reigning orthodoxy.

Notes

1 G. Lefebvre, *The Coming of the French Revolution* (New York, 1947), pp. 44–5.
2 The number of references to 'French Revolution' in the indexes of Marx's major works confirms this.

3 Marx also tends to use a lower-case rather than capital 'r' when he refers to the 'French revolution'. The implication here is that 1789 was just one of many French revolutions and emphasises that Marx is interested in the tradition rather than 1789 as a stand-alone event.

4 The ultimate aim of his writings, of course.

5 K. Marx, *The First International and After* (London, 1981), p. 206; see also, K. Marx, *Surveys from Exile* (London, 1992), pp. 241, 246, 248, 251.

6 K. Marx, *Surveys*, p. 169.

7 For example, Poland. K. Marx, *First International*, p. 389.

8 K. Marx, *Surveys*, p. 252.

9 www.marxists.org/archive/marx/works/1848/communist-manifesto/ch01 .htm.

10 Ibid.

11 K. Marx, *First International*, pp. 246–7.

12 H. Goldberg, *The Life of Jean Jaurès* (London, 1968), p. 284.

13 A. Cobban, *Aspects of the French Revolution* (London, 1968), p. 57.

14 Goldberg, *Jean Jaurès*, p. 288.

15 G. Kates, *The French Revolution* (London, 1998), p. 2; see also Cobban, *Aspects*.

16 G. Comninel, *Rethinking the French Revolution* (London, 1987), p. 14.

17 Kates, *Revolution*, p. 2.

18 D. Johnson, 'The Twentieth Century: Recollection and Rejection', in G. Best (ed.), *The Permanent Revolution* (London, 1989), p. 187.

19 See Chapter 8.

20 N. Hampson, 'The French Revolution and its Historians' in G. Best (ed.), *The Permanent Revolution* (London, 1989), p. 222.

21 Ibid., p. 223.

22 Kates, *Revolution*, pp. 2–3.

23 Ibid., p. 3.

24 The book was republished as *The Coming of the French Revolution* in 1947.

25 Lefebvre, *Coming of the Revolution.*, p. 5.

26 Ibid., pp. 42–3.

27 Ibid., pp. 4, 42–3.

28 Ibid., p. 113.

29 Ibid., pp. 86–7. This is just a selection.

30 Ibid., pp. 90–3.

31 G. Symcox, 'Translator's Preface' in A. Soboul, *A Short History of the French Revolution* (London, 1984), pp. viii, ix.

32 Ibid., pp. ix, x.

33 Hampson, 'Revolution', p. 227.

34 See http://pup.princeton.edu/titles/829.html.

35 Soboul, *Short History*, p. 1.

36 Ibid., p. 21.

37 Ibid., pp. 93, 97.

38 A. Soboul, *Understanding the French Revolution* (London, 1988), p. 60.

39 Soboul, *Understanding*, p. 60.

40 Soboul, *Short History*, p. 29.

41 N. Parker, *Portrayals of Revolution* (Hemel Hempstead, 1990), p. 204.

42 Symcox, 'Preface', pp. xi, xii.
43 J. Godechot, *France and the Atlantic Revolution* (London, 1965) p. 101.
44 J. Godechot, *The Taking of the Bastille* (London, 1970), p. 60.
45 Godechot, *Atlantic Revolution*, pp. 3–7.
46 *La Révolution française et nous* (Brussels, 1969).
47 Parker, *Portrayals*, p. 220.
48 G. Rudé, *The Crowd in the French Revolution* (Oxford, 1959), pp. 1–4.
49 Parker, *Portrayals*, p. 204.

7

'Soft revisionism'

> We shall not vainly search for a non-existent industrial revolution,
> in a country dominated by a landed aristocracy.[1]

'Soft revisionism' is the term coined to describe the efforts of a
range of post-war historians to discredit the Marxist 'orthodoxy'.
Led by Alfred Cobban, these writers still put the emphasis on
social and economic history; but they had serious concerns about
the narrowness and 'scientific' nature of the Marxist line. This
chapter explores the nature and significance of this school of
thinking.

Most commentators are agreed that the 'chief protagonist' or
'father of revisionism'[2] is Cobban, whose most important work
was *The Social Interpretation of the French Revolution* (1964).
Initially, this work was slightly neglected, but it gradually
acquired the reputation of a path-breaking work. On one level it
was a 'demolition' of the Marxist standpoint. On another it was a
'non-Marxist social interpretation'. It still placed the emphasis on
social and economic factors, but veered away from any kind of
'deterministic' approach.[3] In fact, Cobban objected strongly to
the notion that there were 'historical laws' – as hardline Marxists
just assumed. He went on to argue that the French Revolution
had no intrinsic unity (as Marxists had suggested) and that there
was no real class dimension to the event – in effect, that the 'aristocracy were not feudal and the bourgeoisie were not capitalist'
(both these assumptions had underpinned the Marxist view).

Other independent-minded, non-Marxist revisionists
buttressed the Cobban position. In the words of Kates, these
writers were 'not known for their political activism or political

labels'.[4] This is significant. It could be argued that whereas Marxist historians had a general line to uphold, this new breed of writers came to the subject without any obvious prejudices to propagate. Most notable in this context were G.V. Taylor, 'Non-capitalist wealth and the origins of the French Revolution', *American History Review* (1967), Norman Hampson, *A Social History of the French Revolution* (1963) and J.M. Thompson, *The French Revolution* (1966). Taylor's was a particularly important contribution as he, like Cobban, argued for an overlap between the bourgeoisie and the aristocracy as classes. It is relevant to point out that Cobban was English and Taylor was American for, very gradually, a shift in power was taking place – with French Marxist historians being usurped by Anglo-Saxon revisionists.

This chapter examines a series of issues: Why did the Marxist interpretation require 'revision'? How distinct are 'orthodox' and 'revisionist' interpretations? Why did Anglo-American historians have a different perspective on the Revolution from French historians? We begin by examining the essence of 'soft revisionism', and then move on to a consideration of individual historians. We finish by assessing the overall significance of this brand of revolutionary historiography.

'Soft revisionism' was based on a number of key tenets. First, Cobban and his co-accusers objected to the pseudo-scientific nature of Marxist theory. It seemed that Marxist interpretations were determined to put theory first and facts second; the revisionists placed a premium on the facts and nothing else. As Lewis put it: 'Cobban's attack was directed not so much against the importance of social and economic history as against the imposition of determinist, historical (that is marxist) laws of development.'[5] Cobban and his fellow revisionists also disliked the narrowness and rigidity of Marxist historians' thinking, especially the way in which classes were demarcated so strictly. Moreover, they felt that this kind of approach led to 'bad' history – in effect, putting the cart before the horse or, put more accurately, the 'dogma before the facts'. Thus, whereas Marxist thinkers viewed the aristocracy and bourgeoisie as distinct, mutually-exclusive classes, the post-war revisionists put forward the view that the two classes had 'merged' or almost 'merged' in late eighteenth-century France. Cobban argues this case very effectively:

> There can be no doubt that the new ruling class was above all one of landowners. These were the local notables. The basis of their wealth and influence was land, their prime aim to increase these by enlarging their estates. Perhaps Taine saw something fundamental in the revolution when he wrote, 'Whatever the great words – liberty, equality, fraternity – with which the revolution was ornamented, it was essentially a transference of property; that constituted its inmost stay, its prime motive and its historic meaning.' Curiously similar was the verdict of Lefebvre in his earlier, more empirical days. After the abolition of privileges, the nobles and *roturiers* joined, he wrote, in the same social class. The new bourgeoisie was one of *'propriétaires non-exploitants'*.[6]

He goes on:

> this was a revolution which bequeathed to France a ruling class of landowners ... It was, of course, to some extent a different class and type of landowner from that of the *ancien régime,* and one which possessed more political power than its predecessor. If such a class can be called a bourgeoisie, then this was the revolutionary bourgeoisie. If the latter is capable of being interpreted in such terms as these, at least it gives a great deal more sense to the subsequent history of France.[7]

One of the ironies of the situation in late-eighteenth-century France was that the bourgeoisie was so much in the ascendant, and so upwardly-mobile, that it was beginning to speculate in, and also gain ownership of, large swathes of land. Marxist historians would go along with the first clause in this sentence, but they would find it extremely difficult to accept the second, so keen were they on the notion of 'distinct' and 'separate' classes. And this, of course, was one of the many weaknesses of the Marxist argument – and one that the revisionists picked up on immediately.

Second, this wave of revisionists had serious reservations about the main claims of Lefebvre and his Marxist allies regarding the nature of the aristocracy and bourgeoisie – that is, *if they were actually* separate classes. In short, they argued that the aristocracy was not 'feudal', the bourgeoisie was neither 'united' nor 'capitalist', and it was the peasantry, rather than the middle-class bourgeoisie, who were responsible for the overthrow of the *Ancien Régime*. Likewise, the contention of the revisionists was that pre-1789 France was not totally feudal,[8] and that post-1789 France was hardly booming industrially or commercially. According to Lewis, 'Alfred Cobban rejected the notion that *revolution* was the essential midwife of the new bourgeois society in 1789, hence his emphasis upon the economic failure of the Revolution. In other words, revolutions can actually impede, rather than advance, the capitalist process.'[9]

Third, the revisionists could not hide the fact that, ultimately, they were actually questioning, and perhaps even downplaying, the significance of the Revolution and 1789 as a watershed (although Cobban, for one, denied this: 'It must not be supposed, though Georges Lefebvre did, that I am trying to deny the existence of the French Revolution; I merely want to discover what it was.')[10] And as such, the battle between Marxists and revisionists acquired the feel of a battle between French historians and non-French historians. And ironically perhaps, it was those on the left playing the 'nationalist' card.

During the post-war era, a clutch of historians began to air their doubts about the Revolution. John McManners' main argument was that money rather than privilege was the key to understanding the event and the era. This tended to undermine the Marxist thesis, which put enormous emphasis on feudalism and the feudal idea as the motor force of revolution.[11] Betty Behrens put forward a similar case in 'Nobles, Privileges and Taxes in France at the End of the *Ancien Régime*'. Her main argument was that the scale of noble 'privilege' under the *Ancien Régime* had been exaggerated.[12] Likewise, in *The French Pre-Revolution 1787–1788*, Jean Egret argued that the influence of the *parlements* had been embellished and exaggerated – something of a slap in the face for all those who had viewed the bodies as central to *Ancien Régime* society. Moreover, he identified a period immediately prior to the Revolution when the King's ministers showed themselves to be both weak and uninspired.[13]

But, at the vanguard of 'soft' revisionism was Cobban. He was Professor of History at the University of London and in his Inaugural Lecture, delivered in 1955, he attacked what he described as the 'myth' of the French Revolution.[14] But he did so in an understated way. His style was gentle and provocative, though what he was actually delivering was a grenade. He referred to the way in which 'explosions' occurred in certain historical fields, when 'accepted' theories and interpretations were dispensed with on account of new research being carried out and new ideas being aired. 'In the historiography of the English civil war the explosion has already occurred [he said], and it has blown up the supposed bourgeois revolution, leaving aristocracy and gentry, royal officials, lawyers, merchants, people, rising and falling classes, feudal and bourgeois society, landowners and peasants, scattered in fragments about monographs and textbooks'.

> Some eight or nine years ago I suggested that the same process of disintegration was likely to take place in the history of the French Revolution, and that the interpretation of the revolution in terms of the overthrow of feudalism by the bourgeoisie, always rather meaningless, was becoming increasingly incompatible with the results of modern research. This suggestion, although it was based in part on the results of Lefebvre's own researches, met with his criticism. The suggestion that the theory of the revolution as the overthrow of feudalism by the bourgeoisie was a myth, he took to be equivalent to a denial of the whole actuality of the revolution. At the same time, he agreed that, in a different and Sorelian sense, it was ... a myth.[15]

This was a provocative opening, but in a sense he was only doing what historians for generations had been taught to do: he was questioning everything – the sources and the latest historical interpretations.

Crucial here is the fact that the reigning orthodoxy was not just any old orthodoxy, but the *Marxist* one. Bolshevism had established itself in Russia in 1917 and after the Second World War Moscow had created satellite states throughout Eastern Europe and beyond. There was enormous symbolism in the construction of the Iron Curtain and the Berlin Wall. So, in a sense, it was no great surprise that the Marxist interpretation of the French Revolution gained almost total power and hegemony in the early and middle decades of the twentieth century. This is precisely what Marxism (as an ideology) was about: rigid dominance and control. Thus, Cobban's critique of Marxist historiography could in some way be likened to the first rumblings of discontent against the Soviet system. And just as the

Iron Curtain and Berlin Wall eventually came tumbling down, so the Marxist interpretation of the French Revolution was eventually superseded. Cobban's attack continued:

> Indeed, it is difficult to avoid the conclusion that the orthodox theory of the revolution has now assumed some of the characteristics of a religious belief ... This tendency of the Marxist theory of the revolution to culminate in a sort of semi-religious exaltation is far from being an accident. Marxism is a philosophy of history: its strength is that, like all philosophies of history, it embodies a view of the nature and ends of human existence. In other words, it is a sort of secular religion. However, the Marxist theory of the revolution would not have had the same general appeal if it had not also been something else. If one source of the strength of Marxism is the satisfaction it can give to the human desire for a purpose to justify and provide an end for the life of the human animal, another is its appearance of providing a scientific statement of the laws of social development. As well as a philosophy of history, it offers a theory of sociology. Particularly in the latter capacity it evidently appealed to Georges Lefebvre, who seems to have come to believe, in his later years, that Marxism could provide both a theoretical basis for his researches and a conclusion he could draw from them.[16]

Here Cobban pinpoints the aspects of the Marxist theory that he objects to: the 'religious' aura, the efforts at self-justification, the grand scientific and philosophical claims. It should also be pointed out that, even though Lefebvre comes under attack in this particular passage, it is Soboul – the 'Stalinist' and 'Marxist-Leninist' – who is the main target elsewhere.[17] The offensive against Marxist theorising grew stronger, and became even more explicit in Cobban's book:

> Amid the shifting sands of an uncertain and uncritical social terminology, the historian of eighteenth-century France has too often been content with broad generalisations possessing even at the time only a very rough relation to social realities, and now distorted by all the overtones of nineteenth-century sociological thought and present-day social conditions. The first necessity for writing the social history of the revolution is therefore to abandon the existing terminology. This is far from being a mere negative requirement. It is indeed a revolutionary step, for this terminology, with all its defects, embodies, as will be seen, a specific theory of the revolu-

tion, and to abandon the language is to abandon the theory. Adequately to deal with the social history of the revolution, an empirical examination of social facts is needed, such as a contemporary sociologist would make of his own society. An estimate of social position must not be based on a single criterion, legal, political or economic, as it often has been in the past, but on a plurality of tests – actual wealth and its nature, sources of income, social status and prestige, origin and direction of social movement of the individual and his family, legal order, political orientation, contemporary esteem, economic function, personal aspirations and grievances, and so on.[18]

In this passage no Marxist historians are mentioned by name, but the implication is clear: previous (for example, Marxist) writers had 'lost themselves' in a sea of over-complex 'jargon' and 'vagueness'. This was hard-hitting stuff. 'Not only the social classification but also the nature and direction of social movement in history needs to be considered afresh. The whole conception of rising and falling classes, which is closely involved with the idea of revolution, is in need of revision', argued Cobban.

> The movement of individuals from one class to another, if on a sufficiently large scale, has been equated with the rise or fall of a class. This is clearly unsound. However many sons of peasants, say, move into the town and become lawyers or merchants, this cannot be called the rise of the peasantry. A class has been compared to a hotel, which remains the same though a continually changing clientele passes through it! A class rises, properly speaking, when it acquires political power and increased economic well-being and yet remains the same class. Put in this way, the 'rise of the bourgeoisie' in the French Revolution ceases to be a platitude and becomes a problem. The essential thing is that we shall cease to take theories for facts. The distinguished French historian, M. Albert Soboul, almost in the same breath tells us that the triumph of the bourgeoisie is the essential fact of the revolution, and that we have no history of the bourgeoisie during the revolution. In other words, what he calls the essential fact is no more than an act of faith. We will have to choose whether we will believe M. Soboul when, as a theorist, he tells us that he knows for certain what the revolution was, or when, as an historian, he admits that only after many local and regional social studies have been made will works of synthesis on the different classes and social categories be possible. Of course, even while assuming that he knew in advance essentially what will be discov-

ered, it was a step forward to recognise that the research which should demonstrate it has not yet been done. I believe that we can go a little farther than this, and that quite a lot in fact has been done. If it has only very partially been used by historians, this is because much of it does not fit conveniently into the accepted theory. In this study, therefore, I do not propose to begin with any kind of theoretical discussion.[19]

Cobban does not pull his punches in his denunciation of 'simplistic' Marxist theorising. And the last line of the extract is highly significant: Cobban intends to stick to the 'facts' and not get bogged down in the kind of (self-fulfilling) theorising for which he attacks Marxist historians.

In the course of his book, Cobban addresses a number of important, specific issues. On feudalism he writes:

It must not be supposed, however, that historians invented the belief in eighteenth-century France that feudalism was the enemy. There can be no doubt that there was a widespread attack on something that was called feudalism, and that this attack was the expression of deeply-felt grievances. The problem is to identify these grievances and discover what, if anything, was feudal about them. It is reasonable to raise this question, because the revolutionaries had considerable doubts on the subject themselves. The Constituent Assembly, when it resolved to abolish feudal rights, found that it did not really know, and certainly was not agreed on, what were feudal and what were non-feudal among the various rights. The legislation of 4–11 August having in its first article 'entirely destroyed' the so-called feudal rights, in its subsequent ones partially restored them. The Feudal Committee tried to draw a line between *droits personnels* and *droits réels*, but this was a distinction derived from Roman Law and inappropriate to the extraordinary variety of seigniorial rights. Compromises favourable to the seigneurs were naturally those adopted by an Assembly and a Committee composed in large part of seigneurs, say the editors of the papers of the Committee! This was a practical as well as a legal problem. Its historic origins are easy to detect. Land changed hands rapidly in the later Middle Ages, passing from the possession of nobles into that of *roturiers*; but though the latter might acquire the land, they could not exercise the rights of a feudal lord over it.[20]

On the issue of the bourgeoisie, he comments:

The accepted view cannot be better given than in the words of M. Soboul. 'Thus', he writes, 'was the traditional economic order overthrown. Doubtless the bourgeoisie was before 1789 the master of production and exchange. But *laisser faire, laisser passer* freed its commercial and industrial activities from the fetters of privilege and monopoly. Capitalist production had been born and had begun to develop in the framework of a still feudal property system: the framework was now broken. The bourgeoisie of the Constituent Assembly accelerated the evolution by liberating the economy.' This seems an extremely plausible theory: difficulties only begin to arise when we look at the facts. In the first place, of course, we need not confine the judgement to the Constituent Assembly; nor apart from the interlude represented by the rule of the Committee of Public Safety do I think that M. Soboul intends to do so. Whether the organisation of industry in France was capitalist before the revolution has been a subject of some debate. Jaurès, Levasseur, Germain Martin, des Cilleuls, Picard, Ardachev, said that it was; Kovalesky, Tarle, Petrov, Loutchitsky argued that France remained a *pays agricole!* This is mainly a matter of terminology.[21]

Cobban is unfailingly polite, but his underlying objective is clear: to undermine the credibility of the Marxist line. He talks about 'the accepted view' and the 'facts' not tying in with the 'theory'. This is significant, coded language. Colin Lucas, who made his own input to the debate on the revisionist side, says: 'Cobban's essential contribution to the historiography of the French Revolution was to question the notion of the bourgeoisie as a capitalist or even proto-capitalist class. He thereby questioned the whole nature of the Revolution.'[22] This is a telling comment and, coming from a fellow revisionist, demonstrates the influence and impact of *The Social Interpretation of the French Revolution*. Cobban goes on:

> The essential point is to decide if the revolution does in fact represent an important stage in the economic history of France, and whether the direction in which its influence operated was in fact that which is suggested. The questions that need to be asked can be put in specific terms. Did the revolution promote a policy of freedom of trade and industry? Did it liberate, or in any way change, the role of finance? What was its influence on the commerce and the industry of France? These should not be regarded as superfluous questions, and in seeking for answers the fact that the revolutionary

bourgeoisie was primarily the declining class of *officiers* and the lawyers and other professional men, and not the businessmen of commerce and industry, should warn us against any preconceived conclusions.[23]

Again, talk of 'preconceived conclusions' comes across as a thinly-veiled attack on Jaurès, Lefebvre, Mathiez and Soboul. And the questions Cobban asks are pertinent. He seems to be sceptical on all counts.

Cobban was essentially a pioneer, a historian whose nationality and background meant that he had few qualms in questioning the established orthodoxy. Again, there are echoes of English Revolution historiography here. In the debate over the seventeenth century, English Marxist historians were always on the defensive and never really achieved a position of secure dominance, Hill's voluminous output notwithstanding.

Writing in 1968, in *Aspects of the French Revolution*, Cobban seemed genuinely pleased that the ideas he aired in *The Social Interpretation of the French Revolution* had been taken on board by other historians. Hinting that he had become slightly frustrated by the tit-for-tat nature of historiographical debate, he said: 'I am only encouraged to persist when I find that an historian who has made major and original contributions to the precise subject under debate, Professor George V. Taylor, can refer to "the theory that the Revolution was the triumph of capitalism over feudalism" as "what Cobban rightly calls 'the established theory of the French Revolution'".'[24]

George V. Taylor has been described as one of the 'Grand Old Men of Revisionism'.[25] Taylor was Professor of History at the University of North Carolina and devoted much energy to researching the nature of the middle and upper classes under the *Ancien Régime*. He was particularly interested in their economic activity and their attitude to each other. What emerged was a painstaking exercise in evidence-gathering. Kates refers to his, 'important articles in mainstream journals [which] added much empirical ammunition to the revisionist stockpile'.[26] The metaphor employed here was an apt one, for a fierce battle did seem to be developing between 'old-style' Marxists and 'new-style' revisionists. And Cobban's initial critique did seem all the more credible after Taylor's involvement.

Taylor did not make a secret of his preference for a 'social' interpretation of the Revolution. In one of his most celebrated phrases, he portrayed the Revolution as a 'political revolution with social consequences rather than a social revolution with political consequences'.[27] The minutiae of investment patterns were also of interest to Taylor. His conclusion was that there was little difference in the way that nobles and non-nobles invested their money. As a result, he put forward the view that upper and middle classes were actually part of one big 'class'. Taylor also questioned another 'orthodox' assumption. He said that it was wrong to assume that the middle classes automatically supported the various revolutionary governments during 1789–99. As regards terminology, Taylor let it be known that he did not favour the term 'bourgeoisie'. He is quoted as saying that the word is 'freighted with too many ambiguities to serve in research as a general analytical tool or operational category'.[28] (Cobban, Taylor's guiding light, was even more cutting: 'Since French historians themselves invariably use it, I may have to do so in referring to their views, but this must not be taken as implying any acceptance of a large, uniform, bourgeois class.')[29]

But we should not paint a picture of revisionists and Marxists being at loggerheads over everything. Taylor, for example, shared the left-wing line on the Enlightenment. He assigned little if any importance to its ideas – a position most Marxists would have endorsed. Nevertheless, Taylor's thesis was a milestone. Even before Cobban, historians were getting itchy feet about 1789. Take, for instance, Crane Brinton and his book, *Anatomy of Revolution*. Kates says Brinton adopted a 'sceptical position'.[30] Brinton himself was particularly candid: 'There is the compulsion – no weaker term will do – on the historian and particularly on the young scholar seeking to establish himself, to be original ... The creative historian, like the creative artist, has in our time to produce something new as "interpretation". He has, in short, to be a revisionist.'[31]

In 1963 Norman Hampson's book, *A Social History of the French Revolution*, was published. More than many historians, perhaps, Hampson – Professor of History at the University of York – was conscious of the fluctuations in interpretative work on the Revolution. In 1988 he offered his own commentary on the nature and trajectory of nineteenth- and twentieth-century historiography:

If we are all, up to a point, the products of our past, it is no less true that what men understand that past to have been owes a good deal to their present ... The particular conflicts of their times directed the attention of historians to specific aspects of the Revolution and inclined them to interpret what they found in ways that corresponded to the preoccupations of their own day. Any historian is someone with a foot in two different worlds ... What he writes is, or ought to be, of relevance to a public that relies on him for its knowledge of its past, and the more unstable the present, the more acutely it will be aware of that past ... All of these factors combined to give the history of the French Revolution a special resonance and to ensure its exceptional importance within French society ... Historians are also carried along by the general cultural movements of their own times, such as Romanticism, Positivism or Marxism. They are as much affected as anyone else by the evolution of ways of thinking about the behaviour of men in society.[32]

Writing in the modern era, Hampson had a good century and a half of revolutionary historiography – of constant ebbing and flowing – to dwell on and analyse. In fact, it could be argued that writing history against the backdrop of the Cold War, with Marxist and non-Marxist versions of France's history in competition, Hampson *was* affected by the 'climactic' factors he mentions above. As a British historian, he would also have been aware of the growing tension between French and non-French historians of the Revolution.

Hampson was not particularly close to Cobban – he once described Cobban's revisionist work as merely a 'non-Marxist economic interpretation of the revolution'[33] – but he did make a significant contribution to the revisionist canon, the canon with which Cobban was intimately associated with. Like other non-French and French historians, he pointed to the problems in using the term 'bourgeoisie' and also the crassness of trying to divide French society into a set of mutually-exclusive 'classes' (the Marxists seemed to be guilty on both counts). The bourgeoisie, Hampson says, was a concoction of businessmen, professional people and others. His turn of phrase is illuminating: '*Below* the financiers who were close to the Government and wealthy enough to be more or less immune from aristocratic hauteur, came the substantial businessmen, who were especially powerful in the seaports.' And also: '*All branches* of the upper middle class had therefore been inclined, to a greater or lesser extent, both to criticize the aristocracy and to aspire to noble status.'[34] The italics are mine. To Hampson, the bourgeoisie was neither homogenous nor coherent.

Unlike the Marxists, Hampson also made room for ideas in his theory of the Revolution. 'The "enlightenment" [he wrote] had been characterized by a noisy assault on the Church, the consequences of which it is difficult to assess'.

> The salon society of Paris was often inclined to agree with men like Condorcet that the historical role of Christianity had been one of persecution and obscurantism. Voltaire's attack on contemporary examples of intolerance like the iniquitous condemnations of Calas and the chevalier de la Barre also contributed to discredit the Church as a whole. Atheism was still rare and dangerous to profess, but the prevailing belief in intellectual circles was a vague deism that ranged from Voltaire's divine watchmaker to the emotional vision of Rousseau's *vicaire savoyard*. Reason and sensibility both accommodated themselves to violent onslaughts on the organization and theology of the Roman Catholic Church – the Calvinists, whose republican city-state of Geneva was more to the tastes of the age, had a better Press. To a limited extent the Church was able to adapt itself to the changing atmosphere. In 1762 a pastor had been executed for the crime of preaching to a Protestant congregation, but the last Assembly of the Clergy, in 1788, while still demanding the exclusion of Protestants from public office, declared its sympathy for them as individuals with a warmth that would have scandalized previous generations. The Benedictine monastery of Saint Aubin, at Angers, was in possession of busts of Voltaire and Rousseau, and several of the local clergy belonged to masonic lodges. But there were obvious limits beyond which concessions could not be made.[35]

In his later book, *The Enlightenment* (1982), Hampson delves even deeper into the relationship between the writings of the *philosophes* and the outbreak of revolution.[36]

It is significant that Hampson dedicated *A Social History of the French Revolution*, 'To the memory of the late J.M. Thompson'. Thompson died seven years before Hampson's book was published, and on reflection it is clear that both men made an important contribution to the cause of 'soft' revisionism. Thompson endorsed the notion of 'pre-revolution', and also –

echoing Tocqueville – pointed to the 'continuities' (and 'disconti-nuities') at play in the period that followed on from 1789.

William Doyle was another 'Anglo' historian who added fire-power to the revisionist position. He was Professor of History at the University of Nottingham and also author of *The Old European Order 1660–1800*. Hampson was hardly a neutral onlooker – given his own sceptical attitude towards the Marxist line – but he, like others, recognised in Doyle a fellow traveller. He put it succinctly: 'W. Doyle in *Origins of the French Revolution* (1980) surveyed the controversy between Cobban and the last defenders of the Great Tradition. Without coming down on Cobban's side, which would have been difficult in view of the negative nature of the *Social Interpretation*, he mobilized all the evidence that cut the ground from beneath the feet of Lefebvre and Soboul.'[37]

Doyle's research led him to believe that things were far more complex than the Marxists had assumed, and that things had moved on since the era of Lefebvre. Kates puts the matter in perspective: 'In an article in the *Historical Journal* in 1984 ... William Doyle demonstrated that the market for venal office was more buoyant than Marxists and indeed many Revisionists had held. The price of some offices falls, but far more rise, and Doyle concludes in general that overall the price of office was rising; he ascribes this to the traditionalism of the Old Regime bourgeoisie, who were failing to give up their secular preference for status over profit.'[38]

R.R. Palmer in *The Age of the Democratic Revolution* (1959–64) broadened the scope of the debate. His thesis was that 1789 was but one part of a wider revolutionary 'event'. Palmer was so much an admirer of Lefebvre that he penned the introduc-tion to the great man's book, *The Coming of the French Revolution* (this 1947 work was originally published as *Quatre-Vingt-Neuf* in 1939, but it was quickly banned in Vichy France by the Occupation authorities). However, his writings did not go down too well with some post-Lefebvre Marxist historians. As Hampson put it: 'R.R. Palmer put the case for his Atlantic revolu-tion, which Soboul dismissed as a product of the cold war, designed to attach the French Revolution to democracy and to America, and to deny its connection with socialism and the Russian Revolution.'[39]

And finally we arrive at Richard Cobb, the English historian who defies all labels and pigeon-holes. He was a different type of revisionist, being neither as focused nor disciplined as, for example, Cobban. All the same, he put forward ideas and positions that, in the end, helped to dismantle the 'orthodox' viewpoint. His most famous works were *The Revolutionary Armies* (1961–63), *The Police and the People* (1970), and *Death in Paris 1795–1801* (1978). Hampson comments: 'Cobb, as he would be the first to agree, conforms to no pattern and follows his own course ... he confessed to "an almost constant urge to make fun of the revolutionary apostle".'[40]

The Police and the People became a classic of French social history, in which Cobb explores the nature of 'prison plots', 'popular violence', 'beggars and vagrants', 'the diseases of the poor' and many other significant societal issues. He pays tribute to historians of the Revolution who have gone before him – Soboul, Rudé, Hampson – and throughout his work pays close attention to the sources. 'For Paris, we have used the papers of the *commissaries de police* for 1793 and the year II', he says in Chapter 2 Part 3, as if giving the reader a running commentary.[41]

As is obvious, Cobb had diverse and eclectic interests. But there were interesting strands running through his work: a fascination with ordinary people, demography, town and country, gender, and popular protest. Like Soboul, he was interested in the *sans-culotte* movement, and he was not afraid to make criticisms of Soboul's work. As Parker puts it: 'He was quick to spot divergences between the detailed picture and the Marxist view of class struggle. But his work has been so subtle and sympathetic to his subjects that he may be interpreted as showing the complexity of active social movements within the revolutionary process.'[42] Cobb was writing in 1970, but in his style and approach he presages social historians of today.

The significance of 'soft' revisionism is that it marked a break with the 'Great Tradition' or 'classical' tradition. Until the post-war period, the majority of historians, in their varying ways, had celebrated, applauded and 'played up' the meaning of 1789. Of course, there was the odd exception, but on the whole it was viewed as a 'good thing' and a 'French thing'. However, with Cobban and his co-revisionists came a challenge. To put it another way:

> By 1939 ... the Great Tradition had things very much its own way.
> The few discordant voices – not merely Tocqueville and Taine, but a
> number of more or less popular, more or less royalist historians –
> could be safely disregarded. Since the tradition had come to be iden-
> tified with what was regarded as Marxism, to challenge it was to
> confess oneself both reactionary and unpatriotic. The debate on the
> French Revolution seemed to have reached a conclusion and there
> was something so splendidly definitive about Lefebvre's *Coming of
> the French Revolution* that few were disposed to express any doubts
> about the quality of the emperor's tailoring.[43]

It was not as if the revisionists were denigrating the significance of
1789 in a wholesale or irreverent manner.[44] Rather, with great
subtlety, they seemed to be muddying the waters. Perhaps the shift
from 'feudal' to 'bourgeois' society was not as marked as some repre-
sentatives of the Great Tradition had assumed? Perhaps the
Revolution was not about 'class struggle' after all? Perhaps France
was not alone in entering into a period of revolution? In a way it is
surprising that the Great Tradition had survived for so long intact. Of
course, it had undergone its transformations and reinventions, but
for the most part – and for over a century and a half – it had reigned
supreme, almost monolithically. Surely, a raft of able historians, with
an ever-expanding range of sources at their fingertips, should have
questioned the validity of successive orthodoxies before Cobban did
in the 1960s? Obviously not.

As it turned out, 'soft revisionism' was not just a 'blip', an isolated
exercise in scare-mongering and scepticism. Rather, it was the beginning of something more, and actually encouraged others to take an
even more forceful offensive, hence the arrival of 'hard revisionism'.

Notes

1 A. Cobban, *The Social Interpretation of the French Revolution* (London,
1964), p. 89.
2 G. Lewis, *The French Revolution* (London, 1993), p. 72. N. Hampson, 'The
French Revolution and its Historians', in G. Best (ed.), *The Permanent
Revolution* (London, 1988), p. 228.
3 Marcel Reinhard also explained the Revolution in 'social' terms. Like Aulard
he was another Sorbonne professor. In 1969 he published *La chute de la
royauté: 10 août 1792* (Paris, 1969).

4 G. Kates, *The French Revolution* (London, 1998), p. 4.
5 Lewis, *Revolution*, p. 72.
6 Cobban, *Interpretation*, p. 86.
7 Ibid., p. 89.
8 See C. Jones, 'Bourgeois Revolution Revivified' in Kates, *Revolution*, pp. 160–1, 165.
9 Lewis, *Revolution*, p. 72.
10 Cobban, *Interpretation*, p. 81.
11 See J. McManners, *The French Revolution and the Church* (London, 1969) and his other works too.
12 *Economic History Review* 15 (1962–63).
13 See J. Egret, *The French Pre-Revolution* (Chicago, 1977).
14 See Cobban, *Interpretation*.
15 Ibid., pp. 9–10.
16 Ibid., pp. 10–11.
17 See Lewis, *Revolution*, p. 72.
18 Cobban, *Interpretation*, pp. 21–2.
19 Ibid., pp. 22–3.
20 Ibid., pp. 26–7.
21 Ibid., pp. 66–7.
22 C. Lucas, 'Nobles, Bourgeois, and the Origins of the French Revolution' in Kates, *Revolution*, pp. 45–6.
23 Cobban, *Interpretation*, p. 67
24 A. Cobban, *Aspects of the French Revolution* (London, 1971), pp. 271–2.
25 Jones, 'Bourgeois Revolution', p. 159.
26 Kates, *Revolution*, p. 5.
27 Jones, 'Bourgeois Revolution', pp. 162–3.
28 Quoted in Jones, 'Bourgeois Revolution', p. 159.
29 Cobban, *Social Interpretation*, p. 55.
30 Kates, *Revolution*, p. 4. *Anatomy of Revolution* was first published in 1938 and revised in 1952.
31 Cobban, *Aspects*, p. 270.
32 Hampson, 'Revolution and Historians', pp. 211–12.
33 See W. Doyle, *Origins of the French Revolution* (Oxford, 1985), p. 15. This is a very helpful description.
34 Kates, *Revolution*, pp. 16, 17.
35 N. Hampson, *A Social History of the French Revolution* (London, 2000), p. 31.
36 In two other important works, *The Life and Opinions of Maximilien Robespierre* (Oxford, 1974) and *Danton* (London, 1978), Hampson developed key ideas.
37 Hampson, 'French Revolution', p. 232.
38 Jones, 'Bourgeois Revolution', p. 170.
39 Hampson, 'French Revolution', p. 230.
40 Hampson, 'French Revolution', p. 229.
41 R. Cobb, *The Police and the People* (Oxford, 1970), p. 207.
42 N. Parker, *Portrayals of Revolution* (Hemel Hempstead, 1990), p. 206.
43 Hampson, 'French Revolution', p. 226.
44 See Cobban, *Aspects*.

8

'Hard revisionism'

Today the historiography of the Revolution is hampered, even more than by political ideology, by mental laziness and pious rehashing.[1]

'Hard revisionism' went even further than 'soft revisionism'. It postulated not only that the Marxist interpretation was misinformed, but also that any theory of the Revolution based on social factors was inherently faulty. As such, 'hard revisionists' put the emphasis on politics and other factors less easy to categorise. They ensured that the work of Cobban, Taylor and others was not simply regarded as a 'blip'. They consolidated, but also enhanced, the revisionist offensive.

The central figure in 'hard revisionism' has been François Furet. With Denis Richet he penned *The French Revolution* (1970), and he was sole author of *Interpreting the French Revolution* (1981) and *Revolutionary France 1770–1880* (1992). Furet was influenced heavily by Tocqueville, and in turn, Furet's ideas were reinforced by the American historian Keith Baker and other revisionist historians. Before his death in 1997, *History Today* argued that Furet had 'a good claim to be considered the leading living historian of the French Revolution'.[2] Reviews of his books have been fulsome. Of *The French Revolution 1770–1814*, Patrice Higonnet of Harvard University wrote: 'This book is the best – and especially the best written – history of French politics during these years that I know. Conceived in the analytical tradition of Constant and Tocqueville, written in the narrative tradition of Guizot and Quinet, Furet's elegant pages are subtle, imaginative, learned and convincing.'[3]

In 1997 Furet was elected to the Académie Française. 'There

is no American equivalent to the Academie', said a University of Chicago spokesman. 'Furet, the Raymond W. and Martha Hilpert Gruner Distinguished Service Professor in Social Thought at the University, helped redefine the interpretation of the French Revolution through his many books ... In writing about Furet's election, the Paris newspaper *Le Figaro* called him "a revolution-ary of the Revolution". According to the newspaper, "One could even say that there is a Furetian school."'[4] Furet's pedigree and academic record is particularly impressive when one considers that his work on the Revolution has been controversial and very much out of line with what had gone before.

This chapter explains the main tenets of 'hard revisionism' via an examination of Furet's work. The main issues we need to consider are these: What was Furet's peculiar contribution to the historiography of the Revolution? What are the main themes and ideas in his work? How did he 'revise' the 'soft revisionists'? And who followed in his wake?

Furet's ideas on the Revolution cannot be separated from his own personal background. He was an ex-Marxist and wrote much of his history in the 1970s, 1980s and 1990s, as the fortunes of French Communist Party entered into almost terminal decline and became something of an irrelevance to modern French poli-tics. In *Interpreting the French Revolution*, he was very aware of this context:

> I am writing these lines in the spring of 1977, at a time when the criticism of Soviet totalitarianism, and more generally of all power claiming its source in Marxism, is no longer the monopoly, or near monopoly, of right-wing thought and has become a central theme in the reflections of the Left. What is important here, in referring to the historically related entities of Right and Left, is not that the crit-icism from the Left, which has occupied a culturally dominant position in France since the end of the Second World War, carries more weight than criticism from the Right. Much more important is that in indicting the U.S.S.R. or China the Right has no need to adjust any part of its heritage and can simply stay within the bounds of counter-revolutionary thought. The Left, on the other hand, must face up to facts that compromise its beliefs, which are as old as those of the Right. That is why, for so long, the Left was loath to face up to such facts, and why, even today, it would often rather patch up

the edifice of its convictions than look into the history of its tragedies. That will not matter in the long run. What does matter is that a left-wing culture, once it has made up its mind to think about the facts – namely, the disastrous experience of twentieth-century communism – in terms of its own values, has come to take a critical view of its own ideology, interpretations, hopes and rationalisations. It is in left-wing culture that the sense of distance between history and the Revolution is taking root, precisely because it was the Left that believed that all of history was contained in the promises of the Revolution.[5]

This background explains to a large extent Furet's derogatory attitude towards Marxist historians of the Revolution:

> It has long been fashionable among people of my generation, who were brought up under the double influence of existentialism and Marxism, to stress that the historian is rooted in his own times, his own choices and his own constraints. By now the continued harping on those truisms – however useful they may have been for combating the positivist illusion that 'objectivity' is possible – is liable to perpetuate professions of faith and polemics that have had their day ... Surely, it is time to strip it [revolutionary historiography] of the elementary significations it has bequeathed to its heirs, and to restore to it another *primum movens* of the historian, namely, intellectual curiosity and the free search for knowledge about the past. Moreover, a time will come when the political beliefs that have sustained the disputes within our societies over the last two centuries will seem as surprising to men as the inexhaustible variety and violence of the religious conflicts in Europe between the fifteenth and the seventeenth century seem to us. The very fact that the study of the French Revolution could become a political arena will probably be seen as an explanatory factor and as a psychological commitment of a bygone age.[6]

Furet makes an undeniably fair point, arguing in cogent terms for a 'free' and 'open' historiographical field. Yet, weighed down by his own, obvious prejudices (his disgruntlement with the Parti Communiste Français (PCF) and the left in general), is he not as 'rooted in his own times' as the Marxist writers he clearly wishes to demonise?

There was also a sense in which Furet was tired of the 'traditional' arguments and fatigued by the typecasting that went on in French historiographical circles. 'The historian of the French

Revolution ... must produce more than proof of competence', he argues.

> He must show his colours. He must state from the outset where he comes from, what he thinks and what he is looking for; what he writes about the French Revolution is assigned a meaning and label even before he starts working: the writing is taken as his opinion, a form of judgment that is not required when dealing with the Merovingians but indispensable when it comes to treating 1789 or 1793. As soon as the historian states that opinion, the matter is settled; he is labelled a royalist, a liberal or a Jacobin. Once he has given the password his history has a specific meaning, a determined place and a claim to legitimacy.[7]

Again, it is difficult to disagree with the main thrust of Furet's argument. It is this 'system' that Furet, almost subconsciously and subversively, wished to change and revolutionise.

When one comes to assess the significance of Furet as a historian of the Revolution, it is impossible to ignore the matter of his nationality. In a sense it was fair enough for Cobban and Taylor to question the 'traditional' interpretation of the Revolution. Cobban was British and Taylor American, and thus, in the eyes of many (French) commentators, their naivety and 'ignorance' could be understood, if not actually forgiven. But the case of Furet was different. As Kates puts it,

> No matter what is written about the French Revolution in England or the United States, it is really only France that counts. Revisionists would thus remain an iconoclastic minority until they could mount a beachhead in France. That occurred dramatically with the 1978 publication of François Furet's *Penser la Révolution française* (translated into English as *Interpreting the Revolution*). Despite its turgid prose, the absence of new archival material and an idiosyncratic structure, no other book has shaped the research agenda for French Revolutionary scholarship in the 1980s and 1990s more than this one.[8]

What Kates hints at is actually quite significant. *Penser la Révolution française* was not another 'general narrative' of the Revolution – far from it. It was an odd assortment of essay-style prose, with four slightly disjointed chapters straddling two main sections. But this did not pose a problem for Furet because the task that he had set himself was to 'conceptualise' the Revolution rather than 'narrate' it. That said, in his later book, *Revolutionary France 1770–1880*, he did attempt a standard, textbook-style approach, with ten chapters chronicling the story of France from the *Ancien Régime* up to 1880 and the establishment of the Third Republic.

What is interesting is that Furet's ideas came to dominate the Annales school of historical thought. This school had emerged in the late 1920s under the leadership of Lucien Febvre and Marc Bloch. In the words of Slavin, *Annalistes* 'rejected the history of events and the politics of states ... [a] traditional history, limited as it was to political, military, and diplomatic events'. In its place arrived a '"New History" [which] took the whole of society for its oyster and began to examine *mentalités* and feelings of not only the elite groups or ruling classes. History "from below" became another of its concerns ... The *Annalistes* have been criticized for excluding people from their studies in favour of impersonal forces.'[9] *Penser la Révolution française* certainly fitted the Annales 'model'. One of the consequences, or symptoms, of Furet's self-identification with Annales was his aversion to certain *kinds* of revolutionary history:

> It is perhaps inevitable that any history of the French Revolution should be, up to a point, a commemoration. It can be a royalist commemoration, where one weeps over the misfortunes of the king and lost legitimacy. We have also seen 'bourgeois' commemorations, which celebrate the founding of a national contract. Or it can be a revolutionary commemoration, which emphasises the dynamism of the founding event and its promises for the future. From that point of view, any historiography of the French Revolution can legitimately be related to the evolution of the political and social circumstances of the nineteenth and twentieth centuries. The result is rather odd, a kind of residual history that at each stage derives its distinct character from the part that the present plays in the different interpretations of the past. Such an exercise is undeniably useful, even salutary, for it makes us aware of the ambiguity in which historical questions are rooted and of the ways in which they become entangled in current issues. But lest it lead to complete historical relativism, to a concept of history as subservient to the demands of society, an illusory anchor amidst uncontrollable drift, it must do more than simply state the role of the present in the history of the Revolution; it must also be accom-

panied by an expertise, as precise as possible, of the constraints imposed by our own present.[10]

This is how Furet justifies his 'new' kind of historical approach. Not only was it anti- and non-Marxist in character; it also stood in opposition to routine 'commemorative history'.

Ostensibly, Furet shares the position developed by Cobban. Doyle comments: 'Now at last Cobban received some praise in France for showing how few links the bourgeois revolutionaries of 1789 had with capitalism. Like Taylor, Furet concluded that nobles and bourgeois were economically members of the same class, and that the essence of their wealth was proprietary.'[11] As such, Furet was extremely wary of what he called the 'revolutionary catechism'[12] – in essence, the 'unassailable' and 'unchallengeable' Marxist interpretation which had managed to turn the notion of 'bourgeois revolution' into a seemingly unquestionable historical truth. He also agreed on specific aspects of 'soft' revisionism, most notably the belief that the middle and upper classes were not totally distinct as social groupings in eighteenth-century France, and actually merged and overlapped in key places. But in another sense it could be argued that Furet revolutionised Cobban's position in just as radical a manner as Cobban had previously remoulded the Marxist position. As Kates puts it, 'he did much more than translate Cobbanite Revisionism for a French audience'.[13] For a start, Furet viewed the Revolution through a political and ideological lens. Unlike the 'soft' revisionists who, although they disagreed with the Marxist line, still proffered a socially-orientated interpretation, Furet could not compromise. Thus, his hardline interpretation plays down, and actually denigrates, the social and economic dimension – hence the term, 'hard revisionism'.

Reading *Revolutionary France 1770–1880* – here Furet *does* try to 'tell the story' of the Revolution in a conventional manner – one is struck by the emphasis that is placed on political narrative, on the fascination with 'high' politics and the corridors of power:

> With the convening of the notables, the French monarchy had entered into the machinery of consultation: a strong government, a definite policy might have found support in that. But a weak and

indecisive government risked exposing its isolation and hastening its own downfall; a single breach in the wall and a rout would ensue. Calonne's little artifice thus unleashed one of the most gigantic crashes in history. It inaugurated an acceleration of events in which the historian can with hindsight read the preface to a revolution.[14]

And later:

> The year 1788 ... saw the culmination of the old struggle which had begun after Louis XIV's death, between absolutist administration and *parlementaire* resistance. But it soon revealed to what extent the inequality of political forces had grown since Louis XVI's accession. Between a solitary and discredited monarchy, with nothing to offer but vague inclinations, and the great liberating watchword of the Estates-General, uniting all ambitions, public feeling did not hesitate.[15]

Furet even gave new life to the age-old (and slightly discredited) school of thought which said that the Enlightenment paved the way for revolution in a fairly direct manner:

> The society which the monarchy had fragmented was united by the culture of the century: public opinion was burgeoning in the twilight of the court and in the birth of a formidable power – which would last until universal suffrage was achieved – the omnipotence of Paris. The nobles of both Versailles and the capital read the same books as the cultured bourgeoisie, discussed Descartes and Newton, wept over the misfortunes of Prévost's *Manon Lescaut*, enjoyed Voltaire's *Lettres philosophiques*, d'Alembert's *Encyclopédie* or Rousseau's *Nouvelle Heloise*. The monarchy, the orders, the guilds, had separated the elites by isolating them in rival strongholds. In contrast, ideas gave them a meeting-point, with special privileged place: the salons, academies, Freemasons' lodges, societies, cafes and theatres had woven an enlightened community which combined breeding, wealth and talent, and whose kings were the writers. An unstable and seductive combination of intelligence and rank, wit and snobbery, this world was capable of criticizing everything including and not least itself; it was unwittingly presiding over a tremendous reshaping of ideas and values. As if by chance, the ennobled nobility, in the legal profession and particularly in finance, played a vital part. They threw a bridge between the world from which they had come and the one in which they had arrived; an additional testimony to the strategic importance of that graveyard area of society, groping – with that slightly masochistic irony born of a dual awareness of its strangeness and its success – for something which resembled neither

of those worlds. The new intellectual realm was the workshop where the notion of *ancien régime* would be forged, although it did not employ that term before the Revolution. What characterized it in the political field, quite apart from its philosophical and literary brilliance, was in fact the scale and the forcefulness of the condemnation it brought to bear on contemporary life – including the Church and religion. There was a violently anticlerical and anti-Catholic side to the philosophy of the French Enlightenment which had no equivalent in European thought.[16]

This kind of analysis is useful but, in Furet's work, it does tend to take the place of a more sociological explanation of events. This of course helps to define the man and his historiographical style. Furet certainly does not get excited by the role of the 'bourgeoisie'. In fact, like Taylor, he had a problem with the term itself on account of its vagueness and Marxist heritage (though this did not stop the index to *Revolutionary France 1770–1880* including several dozen references to the word!).[17] Thus, in Furet we see not just Cobban's heir, but also a new *ultra-radical* revisionism. That said, we should not try to pigeon-hole Furet. He was certainly an 'anti-Marxist' and 'revisionist', that much is for certain. But can we attach a more 'positive' label to him? His identification with the Annales school makes this task a difficult one, for the *Annalistes* thrived on their independence and 'new' approaches to the subject. It is curious, for instance, that Comninel calls him a 'liberal', while Kates describes him as a 'conservative'.[18]

Furet was a thinker who dealt almost exclusively in political and ideological perspectives, but even this statement serves to underestimate his significance. For, in line with the methodology of Annales, he developed a strong interest in the cultural, linguistic and psychological basis of the Revolution – in particular, the Enlightenment and its discourse. Kates sums up Furet's significance: 'By studying more carefully the meaning of revolutionary rhetoric, historians could recapture the profound ideological change that occurred in how Frenchmen thought about politics. Furet ignited new interest in the cultural history of the Revolution, which diminished into an isolated corner by the mid-1970s.'[19]

The uniqueness (and newsworthiness) of Furet's position was

enhanced by his assertion that the Revolution had finally 'come to an end'. He argued that 'an act of reconciliation was needed' on the historiographical and political fronts, so that France could move on and consolidate her democratic achievements.[20] It was a radical step for a distinguished historian of the Revolution to make such a statement, particularly when the country at large had, in various ways, shown itself to be obsessed by the Revolution and its memory throughout the nineteenth and twentieth centuries. In 1978 Furet published an essay entitled, 'The French Revolution is over'. A decade later, Hampson, a 'soft' revisionist who would have had an interest in promoting Furet's ideas, delivered his verdict on the final page of *The Permanent Revolution: The French Revolution and its Legacy 1789–1989*. He declared: 'Furet is probably right: it *is* over and its bicentenary is as good an occasion as any to celebrate its demise as theology and its reincarnation as history.'[21]

Furet's thesis gained significant coverage in academic circles, but even so, it is not quite clear *when* he judged the Revolution to have 'finished':

> One could ... envisage a much longer history of the French Revolution, extending even farther downstream, and ending not before the late nineteenth or early twentieth century. For the entire history of nineteenth-century France can be seen as a struggle between Revolution and Restoration, passing through various episodes in 1815, 1830, 1848, 1851, 1870, then Commune and 16 May 1877. Only the victory of the republicans over the monarchists at the beginning of the Third Republic marked the definitive victory of the Revolution in the French countryside.[22]

At other junctures he infers that the Revolution 'ended' with *either* the collapse of Napoleon's empire or with the Bicentenary celebrations of 1989 (a claim that Hampson picks up on above). He also floats the idea that, with the Liberation in 1944 and the demise of Vichy, a new democratic and republican consensus emerged in the immediate post-war years. In this way he makes the case for 1945 (or around that date) as the point at which the Revolution arrives at (final) closure. This line of argument has gained important adherents, including Comninel.[23]

Beyond these 'headline' positions there were other interesting and important dimensions to *Furetism*. In his work Furet aims a discernible nod in the direction of Tocqueville. In Chapter 4 we examined and explored the work of Tocqueville, paying particular attention to his notion of 'continuities'. A century and a quarter later, Furet resuscitated this idea and identified significant commonalities in, and connections between, the *Ancien Régime*, the early revolutionary period, the Terror and Napoleon's regime.[24]

Most of Furet's chapter on Tocqueville is spent describing and explaining his work. He is an admirer ('*L'Ancien Régime et la Révolution* is written in an extremely brilliant and compact style'),[25] but he also identifies 'problems' in Tocqueville's analysis, most notably 'historical accuracy' and 'chronology and causes'.[26] On the whole, however, Furet is drawn to Tocqueville. This is probably because he recognised in the latter a kindred spirit. It is especially noticeable how Furet admired Tocqueville's method:

> Tocqueville's attachment to history did not spring from a love of the past but from his sensitivity to the present. He was not of that breed of historians who wander in the past, seeking the poetry of bygone ages or the diversions afforded by scholarship; he was totally committed to a different kind of historical curiosity, in which an examination of the present leads to the search for filiations. Unlike his contemporary Michelet, he was free of the obsessive passion for the past, the lugubrious and sublime fanaticism of a haunter of graveyards. The object of the lifelong search that gave his intellectual work its penetrating insight and its coherence was to find the meaning of his own time. He began his quest not in time, but in space, using geography as a kind of comparative history. To test his inspired reversal of the traditional hypothesis, he went to study the United States, not in order to recapture the childhood of Europe, but to gain a sense of its future. The history of Europe was but a second voyage for him, closely related to the first and subjected to the set of hypotheses that had resulted from sounding out the present ... History for him was not a resurrection of the past, even less a description or a narrative, it was a set of materials to be organised and interpreted.[27]

Perhaps Furet was conscious of this when he wrote this passage, but in describing Tocqueville the historian, he was also indulging in a spot of self-analysis. For, like the author of *The Old Regime and the French Revolution*, Furet was interested in comprehending and understanding, rather than simply narrating or describing.

As to the core of what Tocqueville actually said – as against his technique as a historian – there is no doubt that Furet saw an overlap with the argument he himself was advancing. We can say that both men conceptualised the Revolution as a staging post in France's history, but they also saw it as a process that was neither isolated nor out of kilter with events that came before, or would come later. Quoting Tocqueville, Furet comments:

> So the Revolution did not create a new people, nor a new France: 'It regulated, coordinated, and put into law the effects of a great cause but it was not itself that cause.' It was the end result of long-term trends in Ancien-Regime society, far more than a radical transformation of France and the French. These trends toward democracy, which Tocqueville analyses according to their impact on civil society, on attitudes, on government and on ideology, formed a kind of common rootstock for both the old and the new regime, and the Revolution simply appears as one stage in the development of their effects – a stage to which Tocqueville does not attribute a specific character. In his view, the continuity of French history has wiped out the traces of its discontinuities.[28]

Both men had their attitude towards the Revolution shaped by external events (in the case of Furet, his fall-out with communism; in the case of Tocqueville, his aristocratic background and fear of sudden revolutionary change). And because of their non-narrative style, and their emphasis on 'continuities', at times Furet sounds distinctly like Tocqueville and Tocqueville like Furet.

On the Terror, Furet does not pull his punches. He characterises it as 'an integral part of revolutionary ideology' and argues that it was not the product of 'circumstances'; rather, it 'gave its own meaning to "circumstances" that were largely of its own making'.[29] He also uses the Terror to buttress his attack on Marxist historians:

> In 1920, Mathiez justified Bolshevik violence by the French precedent, in the name of comparable circumstances. Today the Gulag is leading to a rethinking of the Terror precisely because the two undertakings are seen as identical. The two revolutions remain connected; but while fifty years ago they were systematically

absolved on the basis of excuses related to 'circumstances', that is, external phenomena that had nothing to do with the nature of the two revolutions, they are today, by contrast, accused of being, consubstantially, systems of meticulous constraint over men's bodies and minds.[30]

Returning to Furet and his personal conceptualisation of the Revolution, there is no doubt that his distinctiveness as a historian rests, partly at least, on his broad-ranging schema, on his belief that the Revolution, although fundamentally significant as an event, should not be decontextualised. Thus, according to Kates, 'Just as Furet interpreted the early years of the Revolution as a kind of prologue to the Terror, so he viewed the Napoleonic Empire as its epilogue. Napoleon did not so much turn against the Revolution as consolidate its radical principles.'[31] Moreover, Furet sees the Revolution as a uniquely *French* event, and also 'represents' it in an interesting and provocative manner, as Parker indicates.[32]

Furet may have been the 'headline act', but in his wake came other hard revisionists. We have already mentioned two: Keith Baker and Denis Richet. Baker wrote *The French Revolution and the Creation of Modern Political Culture* (1987) and *Interpreting the French Revolution* (1990). The fact that the first book focused on 'culture' and the second had an identical title to Furet's main work on the Revolution is significant. 'Culture' was the new battleground and Furet was, and would stay, a key reference point.

Baker is an American academic who was based at the University of Chicago and is now working at Stanford University, where he is the J.E. Wallace Sterling Professor in Humanities, professor of history and director of the Humanities Centre. He has co-edited the *Journal of Modern History*. One media article says, 'Baker's research on the cultural and political origins of the French Revolution has made important contributions to the development of a new understanding of that event and of its significance for the creation of modern politics.'[33] This puts his contribution into perspective. And whereas Furet was a lapsed Communist, with a very discernible axe to grind, Baker was a historian who had spent his formative years in Britain (he gained his BA and MA at the University of Cambridge, his PhD from

University College London, and also studied at the Institute for Historical Research, London). Thus, neither man was a 'typical' historian of the Revolution. Both, in fact, were subject to (different) outside influences.

In general terms, Baker added depth to the revisionist cause. He introduced Furet to the American scene and the two historians focused on similar areas and themes in their research (the significance of the Abbé Sieyès, the enlightened pamphleteer, for example).[34] According to Jack Censer, there was a significant overlap:

> Furet's ability, his charisma, his authority in France as head of the history section of the École Pratique des Hautes Études, his Anglophone connections – all pushed his theory to the forefront. The simultaneous decline of the traditional university in France, which housed most of the Marxist school historians, helped clear the field for him. Keith Baker, Furet's most eminent ally in the United States, developed a theory, evidently modeled after J.G.A. Pocock's conception of the working of political theory, which also embraced the world of language. For Baker, three competing discourses circulated in the second half of the eighteenth century. The language of will promised rights to the majority while other loci on justice and equality also played important roles before 1789.[35]

It was as if Baker and Furet were trying to revivify the traditional interpretation of the Revolution which put great store on the Enlightenment. Censer went on:

> Furet and Baker primarily sought explanations in ideas and discourses ... Some of Baker's own recent work highlights the autonomy of ideas and leaves out social matters. Likewise, some of Furet's acolytes have also travelled this route. One must insist, moreover, that this approach is the most recognizable, coherent method available ... Important studies of this genre continue to emerge such as Ran Halevi's investigation of the political education of Louis XVI.[36]

The talk of 'acolytes' is interesting, for Furet had an ability to influence others.

Richet was an apostle of Furet and another ex-Communist who had sought refuge in the revisionist camp. Like Furet he had worked at the Ecole des Hautes Etudes en Sciences Sociales in Paris and published widely, in journals such as *La Revue*

Historique and *Les Annales*. Like Furet too, he assigned a key role to Enlightenment ideas. He claimed that they were particularly attractive to 'men of property' who, otherwise, would have felt alienated from the state. The Richet-Furet collaboration gave rise to more debate. One commentator argued that with *The French Revolution* (1970) emerged a new 'neo-liberal' school of historians who emphasised the libertarian over the egalitarian and who portrayed the Terror as a precursor of Soviet Gulag.[37] Richet and Furet attacked left-wing historians like Guérin for their 'reactionary' ideas and their 'golden age' nostalgia, but gave ground on occasions (for example, they agreed with Soboul on the popular origins of the Terror).[38]

Lynn Hunt is a historian who places the primary emphasis on culture. It has been argued that her book, *Politics, Culture and Class in the French Revolution* (1984), is representative of the 'new socio-cultural history', and that it re-frames 'the debate on the French Revolution, shifting the discussion from the Revolution's role in wider, extrinsic processes (such as modernization, capitalist development, and the rise of twentieth-century totalitarian regimes) to its central political significance: the discovery of the potential of political action to consciously transform society by moulding character, culture, and social relations.'[39]

Reviewers also noted the significance of her work, though they did not shirk from criticising her where necessary. William Brustein stated: 'Rebutting the standard Marxist view of the revolutionary political class, Hunt argues that this class was defined as much by its cultural position and relationships as by its types of occupations.'[40] For Ran Halévi, 'Lynn Hunt's ... book is written from the viewpoint of th[e] historiographic shift, initiated ... by François Furet. The "return to the event" ... has little to do with the "revival of narrative" ... The emergence of a new political culture and its visual, symbolic, rhetorical, and iconographic expression is the object of Lynn Hunt's analysis.'[41] Norman Hampson, a fellow revisionist, declared: 'The unwary should be warned that she understands politics in a sociological sense as "political culture", as a matter of responses to symbols, rather than in terms of specific political activity.'[42] This was an accurate assessment. According to Simon Schama.

Hunt substitutes process for structure, language for class, symbol for ideology, and form for content in her stimulating endeavor to 'uncover the rules of political behavior' of revolutionary culture. Above all she is concerned to restore to the French revolution its sense of spontaneous self-invention depleted by not only Marxist but also by Tocquevillian and 'modernization' models of assigned significance ... In her understandable zeal to free revolutionary language and conduct from the curse of structural predictability, she exaggerates ... somewhat the degree to which their new vocabulary had to be coined de novo.[43]

And George V. Taylor, Cobban's accomplice in the early attacks on the Marxist interpretation of the Revolution, added: 'Hunt proposes that we consider the French Revolution not as a stage on the march from feudal to bourgeois society, or from old regime monarchy to the modern bureaucratic state, but as a new political culture ... What the members of the new political class had in common was an attachment to certain values.'[44]

Talk of the 'common cultural positions' of the 'new political class' is trademark stuff, entirely representative of 'hard' revisionism in action. Hunt has also authored Liberty, Equality, Fraternity: Exploring the French Revolution (2001), a textbook which comes with an interactive CD. This was an experimental project, but one that enabled Hunt to develop her ideas about culture and cultural history.

With Jack Censer she produced Imaging the French Revolution: Depictions of the French Revolutionary Crowd. This was another multi-media project. 'The usefulness of cd-rom and the World Wide Web for pedagogical and archival functions is now well established', announced the two authors. 'Historians can find a wealth of digital representations of texts, pictures, film clips, and music for use in their classrooms, and many use electronic forms of periodicals, on-line text searching tools, or other kinds of on-line data collections for their research.'[45] Censer and Hunt were also intent on changing the way that historians looked at history, the French Revolution in particular:

The world of scholarship does not usually move at a lightning pace, but the study of French revolutionary imagery may prove to be an exception to that rule. It is only in the last twenty years that scholars have shown much interest in the cartoons and political prints of the

French Revolution. Most art historians considered politicization, terror, and constant warfare incompatible with the production of great art, and in any case, they did not consider prints or cartoons as fine art. Historians rarely considered visual culture part of their regular repertoire of possible sources; at best, paintings or prints served as illustrations of points established through text-based research. In the last twenty years, this situation has changed dramatically. The fact that we could find so many collaborators already distinguished for their contributions to this field is a sign of how remarkable the change has been. But historians and art historians have all been laboring in our individual vineyards in isolation from each other. What we as a group have gained from the scholarly collaboration is not so much definitive answers as newly pertinent questions.[46]

This is an important statement, justifying and at the same time explaining the essence of the 'new approach'. Hunt may be correct in saying that the 'world of scholarship does not usually move at a lightning pace', but at the same time we should recognise the advances made. What would Carlyle have thought of the 'study of French revolutionary imagery'? And how would Michelet have related to 'art historians'?

Colin Lucas, Donald Sutherland and Michel Vovelle should also be mentioned as historians who have made a contribution to 'hard' revisionism as a school of revolutionary historiography. However, it is Furet – pioneer and radical – who stands head and shoulders above everyone, the 'Pope of Revisionism', as one commentator labelled him. Furet's achievement was to build on Cobban's ideas, stay loyal to the main tenets of 'soft' revisionism, but to create something new, bolder, and even more distinctive. When he died in 1997, the University of Chicago – his erstwhile employers – broadcast a simple but moving obituary on its website: 'François Furet, one of the world's leading authorities on the French Revolution, died July 12 in Toulouse, France ... Furet, one of France's leading scholars, helped redefine the interpretation of the French Revolution through his many books ... "He was responsible, more than anyone else, for the revival of liberal thinking in France," said Nathan Tarcov, Chairman of the Committee on Social Thought.'[47] It was a fitting and fulsome tribute. Furet's death left a void in revisionist circles. But the Bicentenary of the Revolution, celebrated in 1989, was still fresh in people's memories. It had generated an array of new historical studies, and provoked much debate and discussion in so doing.

Notes

1 F. Furet, *Interpreting the French Revolution* (Cambridge, 1981), p. 10.
2 www.historytoday.com.
3 A review used on the cover of the book.
4 www-news.uchicago.edu/releases/97/970327.furet.shtml.
5 Furet, *Interpreting*, p. 11 – my italics.
6 Ibid., p. 10.
7 Ibid., p. 1.
8 G. Kates, *The French Revolution* (London, 1998), p. 5.
9 Morris Slavin, 'The French Historical Revolution: The Annales School, 1929–89', *The Historian* (Autumn 1991), v54 n1, pp. 112–13.
10 Furet, *Interpreting*, p. 83.
11 W. Doyle, *Origins of the French Revolution* (Oxford, 1985), pp. 19–20.
12 Furet, *Interpreting*, pp. 81–131.
13 Kates, *Revolution*, pp. 5–6.
14 F. Furet, *Revolutionary France 1770–1880* (Oxford, 1999), p. 41.
15 Ibid., p. 43.
16 Ibid., p. 14.
17 Furet, *Revolutionary France*, pp. 622–30.
18 See G. Comninel, *Rethinking the French Revolution* (London, 1987), p. 28, and Kates, *Revolution*, p. 7.
19 Kates, *Revolution*, p. 6.
20 G. Lewis, *The French Revolution: Rethinking the Debate* (London, 1993), p. 112.
21 N. Hampson, 'The French Revolution and its Historians' in G. Best (ed.), *The Permanent Revolution* (London, 1989), p. 234.
22 Furet, *Interpreting*, p. 4.
23 Comninel, *Rethinking*, p. 114.
24 Hampson, 'Revolutions and Historians', p. 233.
25 Furet, *Interpreting*, p. 140.
26 Ibid., pp. 142–5.
27 Ibid., pp. 132–3.
28 Ibid., p. 135.
29 Ibid., p. 62.
30 Ibid., p. 12.
31 Kates, *Revolution*, p. 6.
32 N. Parker, *Portrayals of Revolution* (Hemel Hempstead, 1990), pp. 210–18.
33 http://news-service.stanford.edu/news/2000/january19/baker-119.html.
34 Kates, *Revolution*, p. 7.
35 Jack R. Censer, 'Amalgamating the Social in the French Revolution – Social History And Standard Topics', *Journal of Social History* (Fall 2003).

36 Ibid.
37 http://chnm.gmu.edu/declaration/marien.html.
38 F. Furet & D. Richet, *The French Revolution* (London, 1970), pp. 183–6.
39 Description on www.amazon.com.
40 *Contemporary Sociology* 14.6 (November 1985): 754–5. JSTOR.
41 *The Journal of Modern History* 60.1 (March 1988): 159–62. JSTOR.
42 Norman Hampson, *Eighteenth-Century Studies* 19.2 (Winter 1985–1986): 297–300. JSTOR.
43 *The American Historical Review* 93.2 (April 1988): 427–9. JSTOR.
44 *Journal of Interdisciplinary History* 16.4 (Spring 1986): 734–6. JSTOR.
45 J. Censer & L. Hunt., 'Imaging the French Revolution: Depictions of the French Revolutionary Crowd', *The American Historical Review*, Vol. 100, No. 1 (February 2005) (www.historycooperative.org/journals/ahr/110.1/censer.html).
46 Ibid.
47 http://chronicle.uchicago.edu/970925/furet.shtml.

9

Bicentenary re-evaluations

'If I wanted a quiet life, obviously, I shouldn't have written *Citizens*.'[1]

This final section deals with the 200th Anniversary of the Revolution in 1989. Here we must ask ourselves a range of questions: How should we characterise the Bicentenary as an 'event'? In general terms, how did it impact on the academic community? Which major studies emerged and what significance did they have? And finally, what kind of themes emerged in the literature that appeared around this time? If we are to get a clear picture of the Bicentenary as a landmark in French history, and in the story of revolutionary historiography, these are important issues to deal with. Keith Baker, an apostle of the new historiography, suggested that, purely by accident, the Bicentenary had come around at a time when, 'longstanding historiographical interpretations of the events it celebrates have collapsed'.[2] As if for good measure, he added that political and cultural approaches to the Revolution were now 'dominant'.[3]

Few anniversaries in French history have been celebrated with as much pomp and ceremony as the Bicentenary of the Revolution. One only has to examine the grandiosity of the Grande Arche in Paris to appreciate this. It was 'opened' officially at La Défense on Bastille Day, 1989. A Danish architect, Johan Otto von Spreckelsen, had been responsible for the design. We know that President Mitterrand – the politician who commissioned the work – monitored the project closely and was delighted with the outcome.[4]

But commemorations of the Revolution were nothing new. In 1880 Jules Ferry, one of the Third Republic's most celebrated politicians, had proposed an *exposition*,

> with three political goals of 'reconciliation, rehabilitation, and imperial supremacy' in mind. The *exposition* would portray the Third Republic in a prestigious light, restoring pride and confidence in the flagging government. It would boost the economy, bolster the metal industry with the erection of immense pavilions, and create new job opportunities for workers. Political and social differences would be suspended for the duration of the fair.[5]

Hosting an *exposition*, or international fair, also gave the Republican authorities an excuse to do something a little more grandiose, hence Alexandre-Gustave Eiffel's commission to design a monument to the Revolution, and to the reforming efforts of the Third Republic, in the middle of Paris. What emerged was a '984 foot (300 meter) open-lattice wrought iron tower'.[6] A hundred years later, the celebrations were no less epic. The Arche was the most visible symbol of the Bicentenary. The fact that France's president in 1989 was a Socialist was acutely significant. Mitterrand had been elected to office in 1981. Then, he had made great play of the fact that his election victory was a milestone in the history of a country that had been for so long dominated, politically, by the conservative right – hence the notion of *l'alternance*, of France in 1981 making a giant political leap.

In 1989 Mitterrand was no less conscious of history and the political symbolism of the moment. He had long anticipated the Bicentenary and was determined to celebrate it, not just as a dry and dusty 'historical event' – as an unknowing tourist, or an apolitical French person, might – but as a landmark with profound social and philosophical overtones. Of course Mitterrand had his selfish political objectives. The government, over which he presided, 1981–95, was one that self-consciously aligned itself with the revolutionary legacy of the 'rights of man' and the triptych, *'liberté, egalité, fraternité'*. Thus, in a somewhat immodest manner, he sought to place his regime wholly and squarely in the tradition of 1789. In architecture, the President commissioned the Arch and the Pyramid outside the Louvre. He also hosted a G7 meeting on the banks of the Seine 'at the height of the French Revolution bicentenary celebrations'.[7] This was a gigantic political stunt to pull off, but it was choreographed superbly.

Away from Mitterrand and the Socialists, there were other Bicentenary initiatives. In cinema, *La Révolution française*, a 'two-film' production, hit the big screen, focusing on 'The Years Of Light' (1789–92), the beginnings of the revolutionary movement and the overthrow of the monarchy, and 'The Terrible Years', which chronicled the struggle for power between Robespierre and Danton. As one reviewer put it, 'The films, in particular the second episode, do not pull any punches and portray the Revolution in a realistic, if not flattering, light.'[8] Further, the Grand Palais in Paris staged a special exhibition on the theme, 'The French Revolution and Europe: 1789–99'. Naturally, this exploration of the Revolution focused on its successes and achievements. Interestingly too, in scope and depth, France's bicentenary celebrations outweighed and outshone the various anniversary celebrations of the Revolution of 1688 in England.

However, there was also controversy. Margaret Thatcher, the British prime minister, caused a stir when she lectured the French on television about their Revolution, and actually tried to minimise its importance in comparison to the 'birth of democracy' in ancient Greece. In a patronising tone, she also implied that Britain did not require a revolution in 1789 because 'we, of course, had the Magna Carta'. There was some embarrassment too when the British Museum put on a special exhibition entitled 'The Shadow of the Guillotine: Britain and the French Revolution'. This explored the British response to 1789, but also wider aspects of the Anglo-French relationship. One British writer offered an honest appraisal of the exhibition:

> The image is created of the Revolution as an alien and violent, senseless and destructive event. Reason gone mad. This is what the exhibition dwells upon ... We get no sense of the way in which the rest of Europe saw the Revolution, or of how the Revolution saw itself ... The emphasis was almost entirely negative. The French are reported to be angry about this; but it is we who should be upset. For the exhibition forces us to face up to some of the uglier aspects of our attitudes to France and Europe.[9]

In France, too, there was controversy when the authorities in the Vendée refused to join in the Bicentenary celebrations. Their argument was that for the West of France the Revolution brought civil war and genocide, and that it would not be appropriate to commemorate such an event. 'At the recent bicentenary celebrated by the intruders, not a mention was made of the dead. Not a mention was made of the genocide', commented one writer with obvious sympathies for the Vendéans in 1995.

> It was the people themselves who remembered. For that is what the intruders did not take into account: memory. The people still tell the tale, vividly, with pain. But their pain is not that only of victims. It is a glowing, rich thing, a thing that paradoxically enabled them to survive. Paradoxically, it united them in a way that could never otherwise have been possible. At least half of the people of that secret, remote and beautiful land died during that hideous time, but their memory is still there.

And, even more alarming, she went on:

> Many people in Vendée who keep the memory in their hearts refuse to vote at all in general elections, considering that the soul of the republic itself is soiled and flawed. They find it bitter indeed that the 1989 bicentenary ignored them completely. There are some who would sanctify all the Chouans, would make of them impossibly perfect heroes. For them, the 'Bleus', the republicans, were devils without any redeeming features. But it is remarkable how many in Vendée do not hate. They only wish to remember.[10]

The academic world was no less affected by the 1989 celebrations. For historians, the Bicentenary was the ideal 'peg' on which to hang their new interpretations. In this section we consider studies published in 1989, but also during the periods immediately before and after the 200th Anniversary, 1987–89 and 1989–91. There was a reservoir of new monographs, edited volumes and textbooks. Of course, it was the ultimate marketing opportunity. Take, for example, the Andrew Browning Lectures of 1989 entitled 'Rewriting the French Revolution'. 'Composed to mark the bicentenary of the French Revolution', wrote one reviewer:

> and recast as richly documented essays, these lectures provide a range of interpretive synthesis ideal for use by advanced undergrad-

uates and graduate students seeking an introduction to the current historiography of the Revolution ... Essays by Robert Darnton, François Furet, Norman Hampson, and Michael Vovelle deal with the intellectual and ideological dimensions of the revolutionary age ... These essays serve the field well by digesting a superabundance of recent research and pointing it toward some new conclusions.[11]

This was typical of the Bicentenary-induced hype that enveloped new publications in and around 1989.

The landmark gave historians the opportunity to revisit old debates. 'The primary political meaning of "revolution" remains profoundly controversial', wrote Eric Hobsbawm, 'as the historiography of the subject demonstrates, and as the debates surrounding the bicentenary of the French Revolution of 1789 demonstrate even more unmistakably.' He went on to talk about the 'intellectual war' that had broken out between pro- and anti-Bicentenary 'celebrators', and argued:

As is quite evident from the pre-bicentenary debates in France, the traditional opponents of 1789 have been reinforced by the opponents of 1917; by reactionaries who would not disclaim that label, by liberals who certainly would. Yet the antirevolutionary attempt to demote the revolution, or shunt it onto a sidetrack of French historical development, has also failed, since, if it had succeeded, it would no longer need to be seriously argued. Indeed, the mere project of trying to prove that the French Revolution is not an altogether major event in modern history must strike non-Frenchmen as brave and quixotic – that is, as absurd.[12]

As Hobsbawm infers, historians were becoming fascinated anew by the idea of 'revolution'. The fact that the Bicentenary coincided with the fall of the Berlin Wall and anti-Communist revolution throughout Eastern Europe was incredibly poignant – and did nothing to dampen down interest in 1789.

But, without decrying the new histories that emerged to coincide with the Bicentenary, they were very much a hotch-potch. Forrest, writing six years later in 1995, puts it well:

It would be difficult to claim that the Bicentenary has created any new interpretation or established any new orthodoxy. Public celebrations of its kind seldom do. But the work of historians in the 1980s, much of it published in and around the period of the Bicentenary, has moved on from some of the old debates and obsessions of the previous generation ... The academic treatment of the Revolution is much healthier in the 1990s for being more open, arguably more confused, certainly less entrenched in rival encampments.[13]

That said, the debate between 'orthodox' historians and revisionists continued unabated, even though some onlookers were beginning to view it as a distraction. In some ways, the Bicentenary put the debate in the spotlight once again. Michel Vovelle, Sorbonne professor of the Revolution, helped fuel the fire by contributing to a special edition of French Historical Studies devoted to the historiographical debate. While the revisionist William Doyle was invited to comment on the traditional Marxist account, Vovelle – an arch-enemy of Furet – reflected on the revisionist position.

In his piece, Vovelle made many good and sensible points about the nature of revisionism: for example, that there was no one single revisionist line. But he was also slightly mocking of Furet – reminding readers that the media had crowned him 'King of the Bicentennial', and that a Spanish newspaper had published a story about him, and the historiographical debate, under the headline: 'I've won!'. Vovelle was also intrigued by the apparent 'softening' of Furet's message at the time of the Bicentenary, and the fact that Furet had even found something positive to say about the Revolution.[14]

The book that seemed to epitomise the new climate – not least because it was so difficult to classify – was Citizens by Simon Schama. Published in the year of the Bicentenary, and then reissued in 1990, it seemed to break all the rules. It was written in a grand, epic narrative style, and focused on the lives of ordinary people as much as key political figures. This extract, from Schama's chapter on 1791–2, is representative:

> Someone asked the young army engineer Rouget de Lisle, who had made a minor reputation in Paris as a composer, if he could not produce a song that would send the armies off to the frontier with a patriotic march ... Rouget de Lisle had some experience in this work. The son of a Franche-Comté family of minor gentry, he had won a scholarship to the military engineering academy at Mezieres, where he had met both Lazare Carnot and Prieur de la Cote d'Or. Though able enough as a sapper, he had taken time off from

constructing bridges and artillery carriages to compose airs in the jaunty style that sold well in Paris.

Schama goes on:

> After five years of part-time composing he decided to try his luck in the capital, where he made friends with Grétry. His style became more serious; a 'Hymn to Liberty' was produced ... From this rather humdrum mix of talents, the musical engineer some-how came up with the 'Chant de Guerre de l'Armée du Rhin' (Song of the Rhine Army). Energised by the sense of coming battle and forti-fied by champagne, Rouget de Lisle worked through the night of the fifteenth-sixteenth of April, flourishing the score before Oietrich in the morning ... The song that, under the name 'La Marseillaise', was to survive when all the works of Pleyel, Gossec, Mehul and Gretry combined were forgotten was an astonishing invention, the nearest thing to a speech of Pierre Vergniaud's set to rhyme and music, a tune and a rhythm to set the pulse racing and the blood coursing. When Oietrich's wife and Gossec had scored in the harmonics for a military band, it opened into a great swelling anthem of patriotic communion. Nothing like the 'Marseillaise' has ever been written that comes so near to expressing the comradeship of citizens in arms and nothing ever will.[15]

Here we see the author linking the humdrum (de Lisle's personal background) with the genuinely profound (the mystical power of what was to become the national anthem).

Schama is critical of the Republic and the Terror. He talks about the 'absurdly indiscriminate' arrests and the 'relentless normality' of the guillotine.[16] Not surprisingly, his approach and opinions were deemed controversial. He himself admitted:

> Any book tactless enough to offer a critical view of the French Revolution in the year of the Bicentennial was bound to attract its fair share of criticism. But steeled as I was for the controversy I was nonetheless taken aback by the eagerness with which the book was seized as a bludgeon by the warring parties of revolutionary history to beat each other (and me) over the head. 'What did you expect?' said a historian friend. 'History isn't just a stroll down memory lane.' How right he was![17]

In effect, Schama had dared to be different and, notwithstanding some excellent reviews, he had paid the price. He also broached the subject of his own method: 'For some professional historians the wholehearted adoption of narrative seemed also to be another serious failing, at odds not only with conventions of analytical history, but completely unsuited to scholarly argument. But there were many others who generously welcomed a return to narrative as a way to recapture a general readership alienated by the conventions of academic history.'[18] Here, in a way, Schama was reverting to the style of some of the early historians of the Revolution. Time, though, had moved on, and his 'descriptive', 'narrative' style was now viewed as odd and anachronistic.

However, the fact was that the book succeeded in bringing the event to life. It had become that rare thing – a popular history book. In this sense, it was one of the first in a long line of 'populist' and 'popularising' modern histories. Where Schama went, so did David Starkey and Andrew Roberts. In fact, the rumour was that *Citizens* had achieved 'half-million sales' – something that Schama himself hotly denied.[19] Perhaps his critics were motivated by envy and jealousy as much as anything else.

Away from *Citizens*, which as a book was almost impossible to pigeon-hole, there were some discernible patterns: the fall of Communism in the late 1980s meant that there was an anti-Marxist tone to some studies; there was also a new emphasis on cultural history; and some interpretations even questioned the importance of the Revolution altogether, albeit in the most general of terms. In some respects, therefore, the influence of hard revisionism could still be felt, for all these tendencies could be detected in Furet and the *Furetistes* as well. For us the key questions are these: Why did the Bicentenary inspire such a collection of new histories? How far had the historiography of the Revolution travelled since 1789? Was there anything new to say about the Revolution?

In 1995 Gwynne Lewis wrote: 'If the Marxist paradigm of a revolution moving France from feudalism to capitalism is for all purposes dead, so interest in the classic "revisionist" arguments about the causes of 1789 has also fallen away. In a sense that is because there was no longer a debate to pursue, so completely has the historiographical landscape shifted.'[20] A book published in 1987 and reissued in 1990 seemed to both confirm and refute this argument in the unique synthesis it offered to readers.

George C. Comninel's study, *Rethinking the French*

Revolution: Marxism and the Revisionist Challenge, started life as a doctoral dissertation, presented to the Graduate Programme in Social and Political Thought at York University, Toronto. Comninel studied under George Rudé and went on to become Assistant Professor in Political Science at York. Approaching the Revolution from the left, Comninel was realistic enough to admit that the traditional Marxist interpretation had its deficiencies. But, at the same time, he was clear that the debate between Marxist and revisionist historians was a relevant and interesting one.

In his introduction, Comninel explains how a new examination of the French middle classes was required, precisely because a plethora of Marxist historians had based their ideas *totally* on the notion of a distinct, homogenous, and upwardly-mobile middle class. And in Comninel's view, this had not been *proven* to be the case. 'This book was first inspired by a desire to understand precisely how a revolution emerges from class society', he wrote. 'Like so many others, my interest in the French Revolution had been originally directed towards understanding the social radicalism of the popular movement, for which the social interpretation of the Revolution as a bourgeois revolution seemed to provide a lucid and logically necessary backdrop.' He went on:

> It was striking, however, that while the history of the popular movement had been set out in great social and political detail, there was nowhere to be found a comparably detailed account of the bourgeoisie, their interests as a rising capitalist class, and the political dynamics of their revolutionary career. Indeed, when the snippets of evidence offered in demonstration of the emergence of a capitalism were actually pinned down, one was left with the unmistakable impression that the strength of the *theory* of bourgeois revolution, its *history* was marked by looseness and vague allusions. Most troubling was the fact that the strongest evidence with regard to the social and political interests of the bourgeoisie seemed to be that offered by Alfred Cobban in his polemically charged attack upon the Marxist position. Approaching, then, the Revolution from a Marxist theoretical perspective that was virtually predicated upon the existence of bourgeois revolution, it came at first as something of a shock to discover just how much of a case against it had been made by revisionist historians in Cobban's wake.[21]

For someone approaching 1789 'from a Marxist theoretical perspective' – as Comninel acknowledged that he was – this was a major statement. Over the course of the twentieth century, Marxist historians had developed ideas about 1789; and in the post-war period they had seen them rebuffed by a cohort of determined revisionist historians. Now, Comninel seemed to be admitting that there might be serious flaws in the Marxist position. As if entering a confessional, he stated:

> It must now be accepted that the long-standing claims to historical validity of the Marxist interpretation of the French Revolution have been exploded. Granting this, but also upholding a commitment to understanding the role of class relations in historical development, the primary purposes of this work will be: to argue that, despite his incisive criticism of the ideology of political economy, it was Marx's own *uncritical* appropriation of bourgeois-liberal materialist history that introduced distortions into Marxist history; to demonstrate, however, that the method of historical social analysis which Marx actually created is *not* implicated in these distortions; and, finally, to consider both the nature and practice of this method itself – historical materialism – as the necessary foundation for a new interpretation of the French Revolution as an event in the historical development of class society. In order to justify this contentious line of argument, the responses which already have been made to the revisionist challenge by other Marxists will be examined to reveal the sources and extent of their weaknesses. Perhaps the central point of this work will be that the theory of bourgeois revolution did not originate with Marx, and in fact is not even consistent with the original social thought which Marx did develop.[22]

Here Comninel appears to be retreating slightly from his original, slightly bold position. His argument seems to be that whatever conclusions he reaches, he will not be undermining Marx *per se*, but this is the way that some later historians interpreted his work. Comninel's mentor, Rudé, also published a new work to coincide with the 200th anniversary, *The French Revolution: Its Causes, its History, and its Legacy*.

If Comninel, Rudé and others were intent on revisiting old, slightly worn debates, albeit with a fresh eye, other historians saw in the Bicentenary an opportunity to look at the Revolution from totally new perspectives. Prior to the 1980s the cultural dimension to the Revolution had been rather neglected. But, with the Bicentenary on the near horizon, things began to change. Instead of confining themselves to straight politics or political history, historians started to dabble in the 'murky waters' of *political culture* and *cultural history*. Several factors encouraged them to diversify: the end of the Cold War, the fall of Communism and the impact of postmodernism, to name but three. Those commentators with an open mind argued that historians had every right to move into these new areas. Others, though, dismissed 'cultural history' as a nebulous and slightly ambiguous field of study.

Some commentators viewed the work of François Furet and Mona Ozouf – *A Critical Dictionary of the French Revolution* – as the most important academic study to be published in 1989. Schama certainly agreed. He described it as a,

> spectacular collection of essays covering virtually every aspect of the French Revolution, written by the most powerful minds currently working on its history. As a whole, the book provides a stunning vindication of the centrality of politics to the lasting significance of the event. Some of the essays – Furet on Quinet, Higonnet on the Sans-culottes, Ozouf on Revolutionary Religion – are miniature masterpieces. The bicentennial is unlikely to produce any other work that serves up so rich and nourishing an intellectual feast.[23]

At the same time, Kates claimed that the dictionary now defined the revisionist approach, and that, in its wake, the revisionist interpretation had evolved into the 'orthodoxy'.[24] These were significant verdicts.

Furet's ideas were still very much in circulation, in the *Dictionary* and in the work of others. 'Hard' revisionism was also alive and kicking in a more general sense. Keith Baker marked the Bicentenary with two major studies. Significantly, both had the phrase 'Political Culture' in their title.[25] Throughout, Baker's concerns revolve around the nature of political discourse and the language and political strategies of the *Ancien Régime*. Jacques Guilhaumou took Baker's work a step further. He examined the nature of political language in the first three years of the Revolution.[26] Meantime, Forsyth produced a new work on the ideas of the Abbé Sieyès – proof, in Hampson's eyes at least, of the 'new interest' in politics and the political.[27]

Alongside this interest in political culture there was a notice-able shift towards examining culture in a broader sense. Emmet Kennedy led the way with a wide-ranging cultural history of the Revolution. His way of interpreting the Revolution bore little resemblance to that of traditional historians, to the Marxists and revisionists who had dominated the historiography of the Revolution during the twentieth century. Instead, as a historian of ideas and culture, he sought to open up a new window on the subject, to leave aside politics, economics and class and to high-light the Revolution's 'lasting impact on French culture'.[28] Thus, the debate about 1789 was broadened out and given a new trajec-tory. In essence, Kennedy argued that in key spheres – education, theatre and fine art, to name but three – the Revolution had a dramatic effect. He coins the phrase 'revolutionary vandalism',[29] and goes on to argue that the attack on culture was intrinsic to the early phase of the revolution:

> The attack on the cultural corporations of the old regime began before the attack on the king, largely because, like the church, the corporations had fewer defenses than the crown, which had the courts, police, and army. The academies, the church, and the theaters had been exposed to ridicule before 1789. The Chapelier laws of 1791 dissolved such economic and cultural corporations as guilds and privileged theaters, withdrawing all protection from them. With the regicide of January 1793, all royal protection vanished.[30]

This offensive against the cultural bastions and icons of the *Ancien Régime* was paralleled by a concerted effort to create something new and radical:

> The ... liquidation [of pre-1789 culture] left a vacuum, which the Terror and the Directory strove to replace with republican schools and pedagogy, secular festivals, a civic and patriotic religion, a subsi-dized press, and republican music ... The revolutionaries employed music, art, and theater to persuade a vacillating public of the right-ness of the revolutionary cause and the villainy of counterrevolution. Since the time of Condillac and Diderot creative artists and their patrons had been aware that the average person depended on the aural and visual senses for ideas. For the Revolution to succeed, a similar revolution in human outlook had to take place, one brought about with the help of the arts.[31]

Perhaps the 'old' historians of the Revolution had missed a trick. What Kennedy's analysis demonstrates is that in the 1790s culture was viewed as *political* as politics itself, hence the almost immediate efforts to substitute one culture for another (for example, Dechristianisation). Here also we can see the beginnings a 'pre-totalitarian' mentality, one that placed an enormous premium on the manufacture of a 'single will'. Ozouf contributed in this sphere as well, with an in-depth study of revolutionary festivals.[32]

The Bicentenary gave rise to a host of new general histories. In terms of reference, pride of place must go to the Furet-Ozouf work and C. Jones', *The Longman Companion to the French Revolution*.[33] The general texts spawned by the Bicentenary also included works by Doyle, Bosher, Blanning, Petrey, and Forrest and Jones.[34] More provocative perhaps were S. Desan's *Reclaiming the Sacred*, F. Feher's *The French Revolution and the Birth of Modernity*, J.-P. Hirsch's *L'imbroglio revolutionnaire*, and René Sédillot's *Le Coût de la Révolution française*. The *Ancien Régime* also came in for treatment. P.R. Campbell's *The Ancien Régime in France* was a very general study, while Robert D. Harris, *Necker and the Revolution of 1789*, and Robert Griffiths, *Le Centre perdu: Malouet et les 'monarchiens' dans la Révolution française*, dealt with important aspects of pre-1789 France.

These general histories were supplemented by a range of more specialist works. There was significant interest in the military dimension to the Revolution. Alan Forrest produced a pair of books: *Conscripts and Deserters* and *Soldiers of the French Revolution*.[35] Jean-Paul Bertaud, *The Army of the French Revolution: From Citizen-Soldiers to Instruments of Power,* and Richard Cobb, *The People's Armies*, supplemented this. And Yves Benot, *La Révolution française et la fin des colonies*, explored the world beyond mainland France.[36]

Social and economic topics drew their fair share of attention, too. F. Hincker and Florin Aftalion produced studies of the economy.[37] The peasantry in the Revolution was also well covered, with both Peter Jones and Snatoli Ado publishing in-depth works.[38] Meanwhile, Norman Hampson added to his portfolio of biographies. In 1991 St Just was his subject, whereas in 1974 it had been Robespierre, and in 1988 Danton. Further, the Bicentenary gave rise to major works on religion by Ralph Gibson, and on the press by Hugh Gough and J.D. Popkin.[39] In *French Historical Studies*, the reviewer of Popkin's book explained the broader significance of the work:

> The outpouring of new scholarly ideas inspired by the bicentennial has renewed practically every subspeciality in the domain of French revolutionary studies, and the history of the revolutionary press has been among those most affected ... Long treated as a modest supplement to the political history of the Revolution, the study of the revolutionary press now appears as a critical bridge between the culture of the revolution, one of the branches that has grown the most in the hothouse of the bicentennial celebrations, and the realm of high politics.[40]

This was a significant testimony and situated new research on the newspapers of the 1790s in its true context.

Arguably, though, the major growth area was in the study of women. Revisionism meant that the key tenets of the revolution-ary canon were being challenged – especially the role of class and economics – and so it was natural also to question the notion that the Revolution was all about men. According to Karen Offen, 'The Bicentenary of the French Revolution ... stimulated exten-sive reexamination of women's relationship to the Revolution.'[41] In a sense, this was no surprise, for the period 1970–1990 had witnessed a general upsurge in academic interest in women and gender. Offen continued: 'In the time of the French Revolution, women's actions often took on a highly politicized form and even the most private acts could be interpreted as having public signifi-cance. Questions of women's agency and women's activism in revolutionary events are readily acknowledged as important.'[42] So, no longer would the study of women in the Revolution be confined to Marie Antoinette and the myth-making surrounding her exclamation: 'Let them eat cake!'

Lynn Hunt, Jane Abray, Barrie Rose and Olwen Hufton have all made significant contributions to the (new) study of women in the Revolution. 'Research into the role played by women during the era of the French Revolution has come of age quite quickly', argues Peter Jones.

If, in the 1960s, all competent scholars were familiar with specific moments of female participation, there was no general awareness of the interconnections between these episodes; least of all of the potential for a fully gendered account of the Revolutionary climacteric. Even the pioneer work on the crowd undertaken by George Rudé did not really draw out the significance of female political activism. For example, his memorable portrait of Constance Evrard, the cook and Cordeliers militant caught up in the Champ de Mars affair (July 17, 1791), was drawn merely to illustrate the developing radicalism of 'many ordinary Parisians'. In the 1960s and early 1970s, that is to say, social class rather than gender seemed to be the obvious line of enquiry to pursue.

He continues:

> Of course, it is also true that the post-war generation of French historians consisted overwhelmingly of men. This situation no longer obtains. Changes in the gender balance of the profession, combined with the retreat of class-bound social history have facilitated the establishment of new research agendas. Women's history was an early beneficiary of these shifts, and the parallel growth of the women's movement ensured that it rapidly acquired academic breathing space. The question which students of the *ancien régime* and the Revolution need to address is whether gender can, indeed, be construed as a 'founding category' for the purposes of analysis. After all, a sceptic might argue that women now occupy a place in Revolutionary historiography out of all proportion to the place they occupied in the Revolution proper.[43]

At this point it is worth focusing on the contribution of two particular writers: Joan B. Landes and Marilyn Yalom. In her 1988 work, *Women and the Public Sphere in the Age of the French Revolution*, Landes – a US-based academic – examines the role of women in the 'absolutist' Old Regime and also in the 'bourgeois' Revolution. She sets this against developments in the realm of political ideas, looking at Rousseau, Montesquieu, Condorcet, Wollstonecraft and others.

The book is inter-disciplinary in the sense that it broaches a number of subject areas including history, politics, political theory and gender studies. It also dwells on the linguistic, cultural and symbolic dimension to gender relations both before and after the Revolution. Landes' conclusions are anything but straightforward. 'Elite women', she argues, had significant influence under the Old Regime; one consequence of the Revolution, she asserts, was the emergence of a 'male bourgeois sphere'. Throughout, Landes is sceptical about the Revolution and its effects. She cannot deny its general significance as a watershed, and as a landmark in the history of feminism, but she maintains that, 'women failed to achieve political emancipation'[44] as a result of the Revolution. Jack R. Censer, writing in *French Historical Studies*, called Landes' thesis an 'explosive' one.[45]

Writing five years later in 1993, Marilyn Yalom – senior scholar at the Institute for Women and Gender at Stanford University – took a different approach in *Blood Sisters: The French Revolution in Women's Memory*, examining a variety of female writings on the Revolution. She analyses a kaleidoscope of writers: from the ordinary women of the Vendée to the duchesses in the capital and those, like Germaine de Staël, who eventually had to flee abroad into exile. Her aim is to reconstruct the lives – the hopes and fears – of a cross-section of French women in the late eighteenth century.

One of the major themes in Yalom's study – as it is in Landes' – is the negative effect of the Revolution on women. In the Vendée:

> The peasant Renée Bordereau, masquerading as a man, fought fiercely in the royalist army to avenge forty-two members of her family who, according to her story, had been killed by the republicans. In time she became known as the Vendean Joan of Arc. Françoise Després, a woman of humble origins with an education 'beyond her station', served the royal army as messenger, provisioner, and even troop leader. With one eye missing, she was often recognised and imprisoned, and, on more than one occasion, came within a hair's breadth of the guillotine. Louise Barbier, an innkeeper's daughter, fled her native Cholet with her older sister and younger brother after that large textile town had been burned and its inhabitants expelled.[46]

In essence, Yalom argues that the Revolution brought hardship and suffering to many women. In her final chapter, she explains: 'Almost all the women memoirists [covered in this book] echoed Mme Vallon's assessment of the Revolution as "an execrable word that should be written only in blood".'[47] Yalom's thesis is interesting because it takes account of women of all classes and from many geographical areas. In giving a voice to many ordinary (and forgotten) women, she is engaging in 'history from below'. There is also an emphasis on identity and shared memory.

Sometimes it is easy to forget that the Revolution gave birth to a *Declaration of the Rights of Woman*.

In recent years, certainly, historians have been keen to see the Revolution in perspective, and to question the notion that it symbolised progress and liberation. Perhaps the 'gendering' of the French Revolution was inevitable, but it is no coincidence that this process eventually took place during the years when 'hard' revisionism held sway.

Bicentenary historians also turned the spotlight on the big cities and the provinces. C. Hesse and M. Fitzsimmons both wrote about Paris. The former was interested in the publishing industry in the 1790s, the latter in the capital's order of barristers.[48] Lyon, Toulon and Lille also acquired new historians: respectively, W.D. Edmonds, Malcolm Crook and Gail Bossenga.[49] There was a more general interest in the Revolution in the regions. Paul Hanson focused on 'provincial politics' in the revolutionary decade, while Chomel and Gobry put the spotlight on the Dauphine and the Nord respectively.[50]

A decade on from the Bicentenary, Peter McPhee produced a volume of research on rural southern France. According to Denise Z. Davidson of Georgia State University, this was a praise-worthy volume and also – reading between the lines – almost the epitome of the 'local study'. She commented:

> The Corbières, a remote region in southwestern France located between Carcassonne, Narbonne, Perpignan, and Quillan, has consis-tently been and continues to be one of France's least populated – and least studied – regions. In the eighteenth century, the Corbières housed wool and tanning industries and an agricultural sector that included sheep and goats, grain, and some vineyards. By the early nineteenth century, the region's rocky hillsides were largely denuded of their oak and other trees, which in turn caused erosion and flooding in the valleys as the soil and stones formerly on the mountains blocked rivers and streams. At the heart of these changes was the deforestation of garrigues, pastures and forests that had been used as common lands, despite their technically belonging to local seigneurs, many of whom were absentee landlords. The herds

of sheep and goats dwindled as their food sources disappeared, and the result was a turn to mono-agriculture with a focus on wine production over all other crops. Peter McPhee's study of the Corbières during and after the Revolution explores the causes of this environmental transformation, and in the process provides a rich analysis of political, economic, and social trends in the region. He also links these trends to an infamous event: the murder of two local nobles by disgruntled villagers in August 1830.[51]

In reality, these histories were doing nothing more than reinvigorating an old tradition. They were nothing new.

The big cities have had a long-standing fascination for historians. *The Parisian Sans-Culottes and the French Revolution*, by Albert Soboul, is one of the most famous local studies (it appeared in 1964, an abridgement of his doctoral thesis). Over the course of six chapters, Soboul tries to unmask the 'typical' *sans-culotte*, examining his mentality and socio-political attitudes, and also his daily routine (and even goes so far as to investigate the 'family budget' of a *sans-culotte* household).[52] All this is set against the background of political goings-on in the capital.

Soboul's analysis is comprehensive and meticulous. He dissects the faction in minute detail. He also seeks a justification for his work in the omissions of others:

> Every historian of the Revolution has insisted upon the part played by the popular classes in the towns, particularly in Paris ... No historian has ignored this extremely important contribution. The people are the principal actors in Michelet's *Histoire de la Révolution française*. Not the sans-culottes, but *le Peuple*, a word which is neither defined nor analysed; it is as if the nation in its entirety had been moulded into one mythical person. But whether the part played by the 'people' of Paris in the fluctuating course of the Revolution has been fully appreciated is still open to question.[53]

Hence the rationale for his study – and it should be noted that Soboul is extremely conscious of what has gone before in terms of historiography.

Nine years on from Soboul's study came Michael L. Kennedy's work on the Jacobin Club of Marseilles. It was billed as, 'the first history in English of the most active and most powerful revolutionary society in southern France – the Jacobin Club of the Rue Thubaneau'.[54] Kennedy paints a vivid picture of the city in 1789: 'An urban working class proletariat, properly speaking, did not exist in Marseilles in 1789. Rather, the working classes consisted, by and large, of artisans belonging to corporations or guilds.'[55]

These are significant pointers but – as with Soboul – what is fascinating is the author's motivation. Kennedy states: 'The development of Jacobin societies remains one of the most interesting and important aspects of the French Revolution. Hundreds of books and articles have appeared, analysing their political actions, doctrines, organisation and personnel. Most major popular societies of France, and many of the smaller ones, have had their historians. Yet, despite its significant role during the Revolution, the Society of the Rue Thubaneau has been neglected.'[56] Over two centuries, the capital, and the story of the capital during the Revolution, has tended to dominate. Perhaps, in the last decades of the twentieth century, historians have started to restore the balance between Paris-centric histories and non-Paris-centric histories.

Charles Tilly's path-breaking study of the Vendée was published in the same year as Soboul's work on the *sans-culottes*. But unlike Soboul, and Kennedy, Tilly's concern was not the Revolution but the Counter-Revolution, and one key aspect of the Counter-Revolution: namely, the revolt of the Vendée in 1793. Interestingly, what was radical about Tilly's work was not the fact that he had chosen to study the Counter-Revolution and the West rather than the Revolution and Paris, but *how* he chose to study the phenomenon of centre-periphery relations.

Instead of focusing on traditional explanations for the revolt in the West – loyalty to King and Crown, hardline Catholic ideology, or even the 'trigger' of the *levée en masse* – Tilly chose a new approach. As a lecturer in sociology at Harvard University, it was natural for him to seek another way of understanding the Vendée. The model he arrived at was a radical one. He chose to sub-divide the Vendée into strips of land and, with each, to assess the relationship between type of economy, attitude to the 'new bourgeoisie' and role in the revolt. He also wove in a special 'occupational classification scheme'.

Tilly arrived at some general conclusions regarding the nature of the revolt – the areas that reacted most violently to the

Revolution were those where the local economy was least developed and vice-versa – but he also made a significant contribution to the historiography of the Revolution, most notably by introducing sociologists to the challenges of historical enquiry and making historians aware of the extra value of sociological analysis. The last line of his book reads: 'Sociologists have cut themselves off from a rich inheritance by forgetting the obvious: that all history is past social behaviour, that all archives are brimming with news on how men used to act, and how they are acting still.'[57] And for us, it is significant that it took a revolt far away from Paris to inspire such a socio-historical investigation.

The Bicentenary also gave fresh impetus to the 'anti-history'. The major figure here was Pierre Chaunu. According to Peter McPhee:

> While there have long been attempts to associate the Terror ideologically with twentieth-century totalitarianism, in 1983 a rather different link was posited by Pierre Chaunu: 'The Jacobin period can only appear today as the first act, the foundation stone of a long and bloody series stretching from 1792 to our own times, from Franco-French genocide in the Catholic west to the Soviet gulag, to the destruction caused by the Chinese cultural revolution to the Khmer Rouge genocide in Cambodia.' Chaunu's allegation was thus that the Revolution's link with totalitarianism was one of ideology as well as revolutionary practice – the genocidal repression in the Vendée in 1793–94.[58]

Reynald Secher was a PhD student working with Chaunu. His thesis, submitted in 1985, gave rise to two books. One was a study of his own village, La Chapelle-Basse-Mer, during the Revolution; the other was a more general study of the Vendée revolt, *Le Génocide franco-français*. Of course, the title of this study was highly contentious. Secher stated that the Vendée was not just a rebellion but an example of civil war, with the Paris authorities intent on eradicating the population of the Vendée. Reviewing the book, McPhee, took issue with the main argument: 'The claim of genocide gained Secher notoriety and certainly contributed to the commercial success of his book. It is based, however, on a radical misuse of the term and on dubious historical methodology ... For this reviewer, the civil war in the Vendée cannot be described as "one-sided mass killing"; nor is the evidence compelling that the Convention intended to exterminate the inhabitants of the Vendée per se.'[59]

Perhaps we should finish with Furet. As Chapter 8 demonstrated, he had been a major player in historiographical circles since the 1970s and had become, arguably, one of its most pre-eminent historians. In 1989 he asked a simple question: 'What exactly are we celebrating?' This was symptomatic of the new sceptical and questioning climate.

As it happened, the Bicentenary had a long-term as well as a short-term effect on the historiography of the Revolution. Throughout the 1990s and into the twenty-first century, new academic studies continued to appear. William Doyle has spoken of 'post-revisionism',[60] and maybe, together, the multitude of innovative studies that greeted the Bicentenary, and that also appeared in the wake of the event, do actually amount to a new school of revolutionary historiography.

Notes

1 *The Observer*, 31 December 1989.
2 *French History*, Vol. 3, No. 1 (Mar 1989), p. 130.
3 Ibid.
4 http://arthistory.heindorffhus.dk/frame-ArchitectureSpreckelsen.htm.
5 www.lib.umd.edu/ARCH/honr219f/1889pari.html.
6 www.engineering.com/content/ContentDisplay?contentId=41007001.
7 www.g8.fr/evian/english/navigation/ the_g8/previous_g8_summits_in_france /paris_-_1989.html.
8 www.musicfromthemovies.com/review.asp?ID=1229.
9 www.kent.ac.uk/secl/philosophy/ss/images.htm.
10 www.godspy.com/culture/Remembering-The-Vendee.cfm.
11 *The Historian*, Spring 1993.
12 E.J. Hobsbawm, 'The making of a "Bourgeois Revolution"', *Social Research* (Fall 2004).
13 A. Forrest, *The French Revolution* (Oxford, 1993), pp. 6–7.
14 'Reflections on the Revisionist Interpretation of the French Revolution', *French Historical Studies*, Vol. 16, No. 4 (Fall 1990), Special Edition, pp. 749–50.
15 S. Schama, *Citizens* (London, 1989), p. 598.
16 Ibid., pp. 625, 669.
17 *The Observer*, 31 December 1989.
18 Ibid.
19 Ibid.
20 G. Lewis, *The French Revolution* (London, 1993), pp. 6–7.

21 G. Comninel, *Rethinking the French Revolution* (London, 1987), p. 1.

22 Ibid., pp. 3–4.

23 www.hup.harvard.edu/reviews/FURCRI_R.html.

24 Book review by Gary Kates, *French Historical Studies*, Vol. 16, No. 3 (1990).

25 *Inventing the French Revolution: Essays on French Political Culture in the Eighteenth Century and, as editor, The French Revolution and the Creation of Modern Political Culture: The Political Culture of the Old Regime* (the first volume of papers from a major international symposia commemorating the Bicentenary).

26 See Jacques Guilhaumou, *L'avènement des porte-parole de la République (1789–1792): Essai de synthèse sur les langages de la Révolution française* (Lille, 1998).

27 Norman Hampson quoted in *French History*, Vol. 2, No. 3 (1988).

28 E. Kennedy, *A Cultural History of the French Revolution* (Yale, 1989), p. xvii.

29 Ibid., p. 3.

30 Ibid., p. 144.

31 Ibid., p. 235.

32 See M. Ozouf, *Festivals and the French Revolution* (Harvard, 1989).

33 Published 1989 and 1988, respectively.

34 See S. Petrey, *The French Revolution* (Texas, 1989); T. Blanning, *The French Revolution: Aristocrats v Bourgeoisie?* (London, 1987); J.F. Bosher, *The French Revolution* (New York, 1989) – which incorporated an in-depth analysis of the Old Regime; W. Doyle, *Oxford History of the French Revolution* (Oxford, 1989) – a thorough history of the revolutionary decade; and A. Forrest and P. Jones (eds), *Reshaping France* (Manchester, 1991).

35 Published 1989 and 1990, respectively.

36 Published 1988.

37 See F. Hincker, *La Révolution française et l'économie. Décollage ou catastrophe?* (Paris, 1989); F. Aftalion, *The French Revolution: an economic interpretation* (Cambridge, 1987).

38 See P. Jones, *The Peasantry in the French Revolution* (Cambridge, 1988), Snatoli Ado, *Les paysans et la Révolution française: le mouvement paysan en 1789–1794* (Paris, 1987).

39 The first two books were published 1989 and 1988 respectively. Gibson's book was *A Social History of French Catholicism*. See also H. Gough, *The Newspaper Press in the French Revolution* (Chicago, 1988) and J.D. Popkin, *Press, Revolution, and Social Identities in France, 1830–1835* (Illinois, 1988).

40 Book review, *French Historical Studies*, Vol. 16, No. 3 (1990), p. 664.

41 K. Offen, *French Historical Studies*, Vol. 16, No. 4 (1990), p. 909.

42 Ibid.

43 P. Jones, *The French Revolution in Social and Political Perspective* (London, 1996), p. 232.

44 J.B. Landes, *Women and the Public Sphere in the Age of the French Revolution* (London, 1988), p. 170.

45 Jack R. Censer, 'Revolutionary Historiography since the Bicentennial', *French Historical Studies*, Vol. 22, No. 1 (1999), p. 144.

46 M. Yalom, *Blood Sisters: The French Revolution in Women's Memory*

(London, 1995), p. 193.
47 Ibid., p. 238.
48 Published 1987 and 1991, respectively.
49 The Toulon book was published 1990; the Lille book 1991.
50 Published in 1989, 1988 and 1991, respectively.
51 Oxford and New York: Oxford University Press, 1999. xi + 272 pp. Maps, tables, figures, notes, bibliography, and index.
52 See Chapter 6.
53 A. Soboul, *The Parisian Sans-Culottes and the French Revolution 1793–4* (Oxford, 1964), p. 5.
54 M.L. Kennedy, *The Jacobin Club of Marseilles, 1790–1794* (London, 1973), p. 5.
55 Ibid., p. 8.
56 Ibid., p. xi.
57 C. Tilly, *The Vendée* (London, 1964), p. 342.
58 www.h-france.net/vol4reviews/mcphee3.html.
59 www.h-france.net/vol4reviews/mcphee3.html.
60 *See French Historical Studies*, Vol. 16, No. 4 (Fall 1990), Special Edition.

POSTSCRIPT

> All historians are individuals, and important ones ... History, for
> them, is more than a matter of intellectual curiosity; it is a statement
> about life.[1]

We are now almost two decades on from the Bicentenary. How
has the historiography of the Revolution evolved since then?
Significant studies have emerged in the period between the
Bicentenary and today, and they have grappled with pertinent
issues including politics, culture, the regions and women. The
200th Anniversary of the Revolution was certainly a catalyst. In
the years that followed, historians continued to work in new and
stimulating areas. Interestingly too, the work of French historians
came to predominate. It was as if they had been provoked by the
celebrations and the significance of the Bicentenary.

Political culture has absorbed scholars in the 1990s and
beyond. The title of Annie Jourdan's study, *La Révolution, une
exception française?* hints at its main objective: to explore the
array of recent studies on the Revolution and to evaluate its
uniqueness as an event.[2] Xavier Martin's book is a legal historian's examination of revolutionary discourse.[3] Patrice Gueniffey,
meanwhile, has produced an 'essay on revolutionary violence
1789–1794' (his words).[4] One reviewer commented:
'[Gueniffey's] new book aims to resolve one of the most important dilemmas about the revolution: whether its radicalisation
was caused by a pre-existing ideology or by circumstances. Every
specialist in the field knows that the commanding narrative
depends upon the notions that the revolutionaries improvised
their reaction to events and that ideology counted for very little.
Gueniffey wants to challenge this master plot.'[5] This is indeed a
key debate in need of resolution. It should also be noted that
Christine Peyrard and Jean-Pierre Jessenne have added to our
knowledge of the slightly neglected Directory, while the latter has
contributed an article on the political culture of France's rural
community to Baker's path-breaking study.[6]

Slightly more orthodox in their range and scope are Tim
Blanning's kaleidoscopic and eclectic collection of 17 articles on

the course of the Revolution and Peter McPhee's volume on the revolutionary decade, 'an excellent corrective to many recent "revisionist" texts, reasserting the importance of social dynamics before and during the Revolution and eschewing simplistic explanations of the Terror based solely on ideology or internal politics', according to Timothy Tackett.[7] Thus, in the post-Bicentenary years, the '"return to politics" [or] "political cultural approach" in American terminology' has remained strong.[8] And clearly, Furet would have approved.

The emphasis on culture in its broadest form has also been maintained, as if acknowledging the strides made in this area during the Bicentenary period. Serge Bianchi has explored two topics that might have alienated previous historians: the 'cultural revolution' of the Year II and 'revolutionary Christian names'.[9] Key works have also been published on 'high' culture. Roger Chartier asks: 'Do books make revolutions?' His provocative essay explores the significance of the written word in the pre-revolutionary years. After quoting Tocqueville, Taine and Mornet on the origins of the Revolution, Chartier comments:

> These three authors, each in his own way, understood the shaping of opinion in pre-Revolutionary France as a process of internalization, on the part of more and more readers as the century progressed, of ways of thinking proposed by the philosophical texts. Borne by the printed word, the new ideas conquered people's minds, moulded their ways of being, and elicited questions. If the French of the late eighteenth century fashioned the Revolution, it is because they had in turn been fashioned by books.[10]

This interesting conclusion is accompanied by a short statistical survey dealing with literacy rates, inventory contents and library stocks. We should also mention Laura Mason's book, *Singing the French Revolution*, and the collection of essays on theatre during the 1790s edited by Philippe Bourdin and Gérard Loubinoux.[11] The premise of both books is that, in the early years at least (consciously and/or subconsciously), the Revolution freed up French culture just as it tried to liberate the French economy.

The move towards more 'regional' history continued after 1989. Gwynne Lewis, *The Advent of Modern Capitalism in France* (1993), and Patrice Higonnet, *Goodness Beyond Virtue: Jacobins During the French Revolution* (1998), are representative. The former is an enquiry into the nature of the Cévennes region and the work of industrialist Pierre-François Tubeuf, while the latter is a local political history. For his part, Michel Biard has analysed the relationship between the capital and the provinces, making special reference to the 'dialectic' involved. His work has focused on the agents of Paris in the regions:

> Traditionally perceived as more agents of 'centralization' reinforced by the momentum of the 'Jacobin' state, the representatives on mission acted rather as cultural and political middle-men (except, of course in the areas affected by large-scale repression). While the provinces as seen by Paris were above all places where missions needed to be performed by delegates supposed to hasten the course of the Revolution, the individual geographical vision of each representative, their activity on the ground, their ability to deal with every subject under the sun turned them into singular 'centralisers'.[12]

Another French historian, Christine Peyrard, has been working on a similar theme. Her book on the Jacobins departs from the usual script. She analyses the political histories of six *départements* during the revolutionary period and tries to unravel the phenomenon of the 'Parisian extremists' in the rural west.[13] Furthermore, Jean-Clement Martin, a Vendeé specialist, has analysed the regional dimension to counter-revolution.[14]

Rebel Daughters: Women and the French Revolution is a collection of gender-related essays edited by Sara E. Melzer and Leslie W. Rabine. This is one of the many studies that build on the work (on women and the Revolution) surveyed in Chapter 9. In 1994, Barrie Rose explored the evolution of scholarly writing on women and the Revolution: from women 'knitting' and 'armed with murderous pikes, clubs and cutlasses' to the more 'active, participating, revolutionary woman'.[15] He argued that undeniably historians are now taking women far more seriously, as key actors in popular activism and organised politics.[16]

As Rose, among others, has shown, there are now a plethora of images of women as revolutionary 'actors'. Interestingly, Olwen Hufton has switched tack and investigated the phenomenon of 'counter-revolutionary women'. She resurrects and reconstructs a 'lost' history. 'The more one familiarizes oneself with the years 1796–1801', she says, 'the more apparent it becomes that the attempt by women to establish a pattern of religious worship, and an expression of community solidarity which simultaneously hallowed the structure of family life, was the most constructive force one can determine at work in society ... The state had intruded too far and women entered the public arena to push it back and won. It was one of the most resounding political statements to be made by the populace in the entire history of the Revolution.'[17] Given the focus previously – for the best part of two centuries in fact – on Paris, the Revolution and men, Hufton's work is a significant departure.

Finally, according to Jack R. Censer, we have now moved into the age of postmodern approaches to the French Revolution. He cites Antoine de Baecque's work, *Body Politic*, as a classic of this new genre.[18] With its emphases on language, the body, and also body language (in the context of the Tennis Court Oath, for example), this study moves into new and exciting areas.

So, we have arrived at the present day – after more than two centuries of historical research and writing. What general conclusions can we draw? The first thing to say is that how historians have interpreted the Revolution has *mattered*. France was proud of what she achieved in 1789. She was a pioneer; she was engaged in a war of ideas. The Revolution, therefore, was viewed as an achievement, a profound landmark in the history of European civilisation. It signalled a huge transformation, from feudalism to capitalism, from monarchy to republic, from 'medieval' France to 'modern' France. Whether for ideological or patriotic reasons, some historians did not want to believe that the Revolution was anything other than a turning point. This was the line put forward by historians who have become associated with the 'Great Tradition' or 'classical' tradition.

Thus, when revisionists – 'soft' and 'hard' – began to question the meaning of 1789, some historians took umbrage. It was 'disrespectful', almost 'sacrilegious', to question the Revolution's importance. The fact that Anglo-American historians took the lead in trying to undermine its innate significance added to the controversy. Some, too, like Furet were ex-Communists with an American training. Historiography also mattered because France – always keen to portray herself as a highly literate and educated nation – cared about ideas, and historical interpretations. In specific periods of French history, historians had been important and celebrated figures, and also viewed as such. All this pointed to the fact that the Revolution mattered, and so did the way that it was written about and interpreted. And of course it *still* matters.

What commentators have said about the Revolution is interesting, but why they said it is probably even more so. Here a number of factors come into play. For onlookers and observers in the 1790s it was shock, exhilaration and fear that motivated them. Individuals like Burke, Wollstonecraft, Paine and de Maistre had been affected (in the case of the latter, actually dislocated) by the experience of revolution. For the early liberal writers it was hope – the hope that memories of the Terror and Napoleon would subside and, one day, some day, real liberty would win through. The idealists and romantics of the mid-nineteenth century were inspired by epic visions. France was in the process of ridding herself of a selfish, narrow-minded bourgeois monarchy and, with 1848 on the horizon, anything was possible. The writings of Michelet in particular reflect this. Thereafter, historians of the Revolution were motivated by an array of factors: most notably, class loyalty (Tocqueville), France's defeat in 1871 (Taine), support for the infant Third Republic (Aulard), the experience of the Russian Revolution (Mathiez), and anti-Communist zeal (Furet).

On the whole, historians of the Revolution have been male. The only female writer we have examined in any depth is Germaine de Staël, and she was exceptional because of her family links to Necker. That said, we should recognise that in the last few decades, many women historians have come to the fore. Here we should give a special mention to Lynn Hunt, Olwen Hufton and Nora Temple among others. It is also noticeable that whereas in the nineteenth, and for most of the twentieth, century the historiography of the Revolution could be broken down into neat 'schools', reflecting the dominant ideology of the era in question, in the late twentieth and early twenty-first century things became much more diverse and heterogeneous. No one school could claim hegemony; instead, as was demonstrated in Chapter 9, a myriad of differing interpretations emerged. It would also be fair to say that academic interest in the Revolution shows no sign of abating. For many historians, the Bicentenary was a wonderful excuse to produce new interpretations. Since 1989 the market has remained buoyant. The need for new histories has been called into question by some, but they keep on coming. And what is more, new ground is being covered. As Donald Sutherland puts it, the number of writers willing to uphold 'the sacred flame of historical orthodoxy of the French Revolution dwindles each year'.[19]

Our friend, Zhou Enlai, the Chinese revolutionary leader, was right. In all probability it is, *still*, too early to assess the significance and implications of the Revolution.

Notes

1 N. Hampson, 'The French Revolution and its Historians', in G. Best (ed.), *The Permanent Revolution* (London, 1989), p. 211.

2 Published Paris, 2004.

3 The full title of the book is *Human Nature and the French Revolution: From the Enlightenment to the Napoleonic Code* (2004).

4 *La politique de la Terreur: Essai sur la violence révolutionnaire 1789–1794* (2000).

5 P. Gueniffey, *La Politique de la terreur: essai sur la violence révolutionnaire* (2000).

6 See C. Peyrard: *Les Debats sur le droit d'association et de reunion sous le Directoire* (Annales historiques de la Révolution française, 3, 1994, pp. 463–78). Jessenne: *Du Directoire au Consulat* (ed., 2001) and 'Land: Redefinition of the Rural Community' in K. Baker (ed.), *The French Revolution and the Creation of Modern Political Culture* (1994).

7 *The Rise and Fall of the French Revolution* (1996), *The French Revolution, 1789–1799* (2001).

8 S. Desan, 'What's after Political Culture? Recent French Revolutionary Historiography', *French Historical Studies*, Vol. 23, No. 1 (Winter 2000), pp. 163–96.

9 In 1992 and 2000.

10 I. Hampsher-Monk (ed.), *The Impact of the French Revolution* (London, 2005), p. 167.

11 L. Mason, *Singing the French Revolution: Popular Culture and Politics, 1787–1799* (1996) and P. Bourdin & Gérard Loubinoux, *La Scène bâtarde: entre Lumières et romantisme* (2004).

12 'Les provinces vues de Paris: des terres de mission (1793–95)?' in *Annales historiques de la Révolution française* (2002).

13 See *Une autre image de l'Ouest: Les Jacobins de l'Ouest 1789–1799* (1996) – reviewed on *l'Humanité* website, www.humanite.presse.fr.

14 *Contre-Revolution, Revolution et Nation en France, 1789–1799* (1998).

15 See Hampsher-Monk, *Impact*, p. 253.
16 Ibid.
17 Jack R. Censer, 'Revolutionary Historiography since the Bicentennial', *French Historical Studies*, Vol. 22, No. 1 (1999).
18 Ibid, p. 306.
19 See *French Historical Studies*, Vol. 16, No. 4 (Fall 1990), p. 784.

FURTHER READING

This is a short guide to accessible secondary sources that should shed further light on the histories and historians considered.

General

G. Best (ed.), *The Permanent Revolution* (London, 1989)

T. Blanning, *The French Revolution: Aristocrats versus Bourgeois?* (London, 1989)

A. Cobban, *Historians and the Causes of the French Revolution* (London, 1958)

R. Eatwell and N. O'Sullivan (eds), *The Nature of the Right: American and European Politics and Political Thought since 1789* (London, 1989)

A. Forrest, *The French Revolution* (Oxford, Blackwell, 1993)

I. Hampsher-Monk (ed.), *The Impact of the French Revolution* (London, 2005)

G. Kates (ed.), *The French Revolution* (London, Routledge, 1998)

M. Winock, *Histoire de l'extrême droite en France* (Paris, 1994)

D.G. Wright, *Revolution and Terror in France* (Harlow, 1990)

Nineteenth century

A. Cobban, *Aspects of the French Revolution* (London, 1971)

F. Furet, *Interpreting the French Revolution* (Cambridge, 1981)

H. Goldberg, *The Life of Jean Jaurès* (London, 1968)

J. Hayward, *After the French Revolution* (Hemel Hemsptead, 1991)

N. Parker, *Portrayals of Revolution* (Hemel Hempstead, 1990)

G. Rudé, *Interpretations of the French Revolution* (London, 1961)

Twentieth century

K. Baker, *Interpreting the French Revolution* (Cambridge, 1990)

B. Behrens, 'Professor Cobban and his critic', *Historical Journal*, ix (1966)

J. Censer and L. Hunt, *Liberty, Equality, Fraternity: Exploring the French Revolution* (Pennsylvania, 2000)

G. Comninel, *Rethinking the French Revolution* (London, 1990)

W. Doyle, *The Origins of the French Revolution* (Oxford, OUP)

G. Ellis, 'The "Marxist Interpretation" of the French Revolution', *English Historical Review*, xciii, 1978

O. Hufton, 'Women in the French Revolution', *Past & Present* 53 (November, 1971)

P. Jones (ed.), *French Revolution in Social and Political Perspective* (London, 1996)

G. Lewis, *The French Revolution* (London, 1993)

INDEX

1848 Revolution 43, 63, 71, 73, 76–8, 87

Abray, Jane 182
Acton, Lord 48–9
Ado, Snatoli 181
Aftalion, Florin 181
Alembert, Jean le Rond d' 157
anarchism 19, 20, 29
Ancien Régime
  Baker 179
  bicentenary publications 181
  Burke 15–16
  Carlyle 56
  de Maistre 26, 27
  Michelet 62
  Mignet 43–5
  noble privilege 137
  parlements 15–16, 137
  Taylor 143
  Tocqueville 80–1, 82–6, 87
  women 183
Andrew Browning Lectures 172–3
Annales school 65, 112, 121, 155–6, 158, 164
Ardachev, Pavel 142
Aulard, Alphonse
  on Carlyle 64
  causes of revolution 100
  generally 98–105
  Jaurès and 118
  vs Mathiez 104–5, 119
  methodology 101
  republicanism 90–1, 99–100, 102, 104, 114, 196
  Sorbonne Chair 58, 98, 104, 107
  sources 100–2
  vs Taine 90–1, 98, 105
  women in Revolution 103

Baecque, Antoine de 195
Baker, Keith 151, 162–3, 169, 179, 192
Barbier, Louise 184
Barère, Bertrand 45
Barrès, Maurice 97–8
Barruel, Augustin 10, 24, 29, 127
Bastille, fall of 54–5, 95, 103
Behrens, Betty 137
Beik, Paul 25
Benot, Yves 181
Berlin Wall 138, 139, 173
Bertaud, Jean-Pierre 181
Bianchi, Serge 193
Biard, Michel 194
bicentenary re-evaluations
  anti-history 188–9
  celebrations 4, 169–73
  cultural dimension 178–81
  debate 173–8
  economy 181
  end of Revolution 159
  generally 169–89
  Marxist positions 176–8
  military perspective 181
  new general histories 181
  post-bicentenary publications 192–7
  regional studies 185–9
  revisionists 179–81
  women 182–5
Billig, Michael 24
Blanc, Louis 51, 69–70, 73
Blanning, Tim 181, 192–3
Bonald, Louis-Gabriel de 10, 22
Bonaparte, Louis Napoleon 63, 76
Bordereau, Renée 184
Bosher, J.F. 181
Bossenga, Gail 106, 185
Bourdin, Philippe 193
bourgeoisie
  Cobban 141–3
  Comninel 177–8
  Doyle 147
  Furet 158

Hampson 145–6
Marxist orthodoxy 6, 113–16,
  118, 122–5, 128–9, 131,
  149, 156
revisionists 135–6, 149, 156
Brinton, Crane 144
British Museum 171
Brittany 20–1
Burke, Edmund 2, 7, 9, 11–20,
  29, 53, 94, 196

cahiers de doléance 80, 102–3
Calonne, Charles de 157
Cambodia 188
Campbell, P.R. 181
Carlyle, Thomas 51, 52–7, 64, 71,
  130
Carnot, Lazare 129, 174
Carrel, Armand 41
Catholic Church
  anti-clericalism 122, 158
  bicentenary publications
    182
  Bonald 22
  de Maistre 26–7
  de Staël 37
  Hampson 146
  Lamennais 22
  Michelet 62, 69
  Quinet 69
  Rivarol 22
  tithes 125
  Tocqueville 74
causes of revolution
  Aulard 100
  de Maistre 24
  de Staël 37–8
  Furet 157–8
  Marxist orthodoxy 116–17
  Michelet 62–3
  Mignet 43–5
  philosophes 1–2, 24, 28, 81, 94,
    97, 100, 146, 157–8, 164,
    183
  Richet 164
  Taine 94, 97
  Thiers 79
  Tocqueville 79

Cazalès, Jacques Antoine Marie de
  55
Censer, Jack 163, 165–6, 184,
  195
centenary celebrations 170
Cévennes 194
Champ de Mars 183
Chapelier laws 180
La Chapelle-Basse-Mer 188
Charles I 37
Charles X 41, 47, 67
Chartier, Roger 193
Chateaubriand, François-Auguste
  René de 7, 10, 20, 22–4
Chatelet, Achille de 55–6
Chaunu, Pierre 188
China 152, 188
Cholet 184
Chomel, Vital 185
Christian names 193
class
  Jaurès 118
  Marxist orthodoxy 116–17, 131
  Mathiez 120
  Mignet 46–7
  revisionists 135–7, 140–1, 156
  Soboul 128
  Taylor 144
  see also bourgeoisie
Cobb, Richard 148, 181
Cobban, Alfred
  on Aulard 101, 104, 119
  on Carlyle 52, 53
  challenging Great Tradition 42,
    131
  on Funck-Brentano 106
  on Jaurès 118
  legacy 148–9, 156, 158, 166,
    177
  vs Mathiez 119, 143
  on Mignet 35, 43, 52
  myth of French Revolution
    137–8
  nationality issue 154
  non-Marxist social interpreta-
    tion 4
  soft revisionism 3, 4, 42, 104,
    131, 134–43

on Thiers 35, 42, 52
on Tocqueville 73, 87–8
Cochin, Augustin 97, 106, 127
Combourg 20–1
commemorative history 155–6
Committee of Public Safety
    39–40, 45, 46, 49, 97, 121
Communist Party 152, 153
Communist Party Historians'
    Group 129
Comninel, George 91–2, 119,
    159, 176–8
Comte, Auguste 7, 51, 70
Condillac, Etienne Bonot de 180
Condorcet, Marquis de 7, 100,
    183
conservative historians
    early responses 9–10
    meaning 6
conspiracy theorists 4, 24, 97, 127
Constant, Benjamin 35, 151
Consulate 47
contextualisation 162
Corbières 185–6
Cordeliers 183
Cromwell, Oliver 37
Crook, Malcolm 185
culture 162, 164–6, 178–81, 193

Danton, Georges Jacques 45, 106,
    117, 171, 182
Dantonistes 105–6, 119
Darnton, Robert 173
Dauphine 185
Davidson, Denise 185–6
*Declaration of the Rights of Man
    and the Citizen* 2
*Declaration of the Rights of
    Woman* 185
Des Cilleuls, Alfred 142
Desan, S. 181
Descartes, René 157
Després, Françoise 184
destiny theory 4
Dickens, Charles 7, 71
Diderot, Denis 180
Dion, Stéphane 87
Directory 192

Doyle, William 147, 156, 174,
    181, 189

Edmonds, W.D. 185
Egret, Jean 137
Eiffel, Alexandre-Gustave 170
Engels, Friedrich 112, 129
English Jacobins 17
English Revolution 11, 37, 41, 52,
    112, 130, 143
Enlightenment 28, 62, 65, 131,
    144, 146, 157–8, 164
Estates General 53–4
Evrard, Constance 183

Febvre, Lucien 65
Feher, F. 181
Ferry, Jules 170
feudalism
    revisionists 136, 141
    Soboul 125
    Tocqueville 124–5
    see also peasants
Fitzsimmons, M. 185
Fleming, Thomas 94, 97–8
Forrest, Alan 24, 173–4, 181
Forsyth, Murray 179
Franche-Comté 125
Freemasons 24, 146, 157
French Revolution
    competing interpretations 1–7
    complexity 4, 5–6
    divisive event 5, 172–3, 175
    eating itself 40
    end 5–6, 101–2, 159
    live topic in France 7
    periods 5
    uniqueness 147, 192
    watershed 1, 29–30, 83, 137
French revolutions
    1830 41, 48
    1848 43, 63, 71, 73, 76–8, 87
    historiography 4–5
    Paris Commune 1871 43, 94
Funck-Brentano, Frantz 97, 106
Furet, François
    Annales school 155–6, 158
    and bicentenary celebrations 189

bicentenary publications 173, 174, 176, 179, 181
on Cochin 106
collaboration with Richet 151, 164
commemorative history and 155–6
duty of Revolution historians 154
end of Revolution 159
hard revisionism 3, 4, 151–62
legacy 162, 163, 164, 166–7, 193
methodology 158
nationality issue 154
political background 152–3, 196
Russian Revolution and 120
Terror 161–2, 164
Tocqueville and 79, 81, 85–6, 87, 151, 160–1

G7 meeting 170–1
Gaxotte, Pierre 106
genocide 172, 188
Gibson, Ralph 182
Girondins 1, 38, 49, 70, 95, 120, 126
Glorious Revolution 1688 47
Gobry, Ivan 185
Godechot, Jacques 128–9
Godwin, William 19–20, 29
Goldberg, Harvey 118
Gossec, François-Joseph 175
Gottschalk, Louis 121
Gough, Hugh 182
Grande Arche, Paris 169, 170
Great Tradition
challenges 42
and Hampson 86
hijacking 3–4
meaning 2–3, 195
origins 40, 49
revisionism 148–9
Taine and 91, 97
Greifer, E. 26
Grétry, André 175
Griffiths, Robert 181

Gueniffrey, Patrick 192
Guérin, Daniel 129, 164
Guizot, François 51, 52, 63, 65–8, 71, 130, 151

Halévi, Ran 163, 164
Hampson, Norman
bicentenary publications 173, 179
biographies 181–2
Cobb and 148
divisiveness of historiography 5
on Doyle 147
French vs foreign historians 124
on Furet 159
Great Tradition and 86, 98, 147
on Hunt 164
on Mathiez 120
on Michelet 58, 65
on Mignet 40
on Palmer 147
on Soboul 147
soft revisionist 42, 65, 135, 144–6
on Taine 91, 93, 94, 98
on Thiers 40, 42
on Tocqueville 79, 85, 86–7
Hanson, Paul 185
hard revisionists
Baker 151, 162–3, 169, 179, 192
bicentenary publications 179–81
Censer 163, 165–6, 184, 195
Furet see Furet, François
generally 151–67
Hunt 164–6, 182, 196
Lucas 142, 166
meaning 151
Richet 151, 162, 163–4
Sutherland 166, 197
Vovelle 121, 125, 166, 173, 174
Harris, Robert D. 181
Herder, Johann Gottfried 7
Hesse, C. 185
Higonnet, Patrice 151, 179, 193
Hill, Christopher 111
Hincker, F. 181

Hirsch, J.-P. 181
historians
    classification 6–7
    gender 196
    historian politicians 35, 65, 66,
        67–8
    motivations 196
    nationality *see* nationality
    nineteenth-century history
        writing 35–6, 41, 58
    status 6
Hobsbawm, Eric 111, 129, 173
Hufton, Olwen 182, 194–5, 196
Hugo, Victor 7
Hunt, Lynn 164–6, 182, 196

idealism *see* Romantics
Illuminati 24
immediate responses
    Barruel 10, 24, 29, 127
    Bonald 10, 22
    Burke 2, 7, 9, 11–20, 29, 53,
        94, 196
    Chateaubriand 7, 10, 20, 22–4
    de Maistre 2, 7, 9, 22, 24–9, 53,
        196
    de Staël 2, 10, 35, 36–40, 184,
        196
    foreigners 9, 10, 29
    Godwin 19–20, 29
    Lamennais 10, 22
    Mallet du Pan 10, 22
    Paine 10, 17–20, 29, 56, 196
    pre-historiography 2, 9–30
    Rivarol 10, 22
    Wollstonecraft 17–18, 19, 29,
        183
    Young 2, 10, 20–2
international context 129
Ireland 129
Iron Curtain 138, 139

Jacobins
    Barruel 24
    Chateaubriand 23
    contextualisation 188
    de Staël 39–40
    location in National Assembly 1

Marseilles Jacobin Club 186–7
Mathiez 121
Michelet 61
Mignet 45
recent studies 193, 194
Taine 93, 95–7
Jaurès, Jean
    Cobban and 142, 143
    left-wing pioneer 103, 114
    legacy 119
    Marxist orthodoxy 3, 111,
        117–18
    Michelet and 65, 128
Jessenne, Jean-Pierre 192
Jews 24
Johnson, Douglas 105, 119–20
Jones, C. 181
Jones, Peter 181, 182–3
Jourdan, Annie 192
July Monarchy
    Guizot and 65–6, 67, 68
    Michelet 62, 63
    Mignet 41, 46
    Thiers 41, 42–3
July Revolution 41, 48

Kamenka, E. 79
Kates, Gary 119, 134–5, 143, 144,
    147, 154, 156, 158, 162, 179
Kennedy, Emmet 180–1
Kennedy, Michael L. 186–7
Kerensky, Alexander 115
Knights Templar 24
Kovalesky, Maxim 142
Kropotkin, Peter 70

Labrousse, Ernest 127, 129
Lafayette, Marquis de 56
Lamartine, Alphonse de 51, 69–70
Lamennais, Hughes Félicité
    Robert 10, 22
Landes, Joan 183–4
Le Pen, Jean-Marie 1
Lefebvre, Georges
    bourgeois revolution 122–4,
        131
    vs Cobban 137, 138, 139, 143
    legacy 114–15, 123–4, 149

Marxist orthodoxy 3, 103–4, 111, 121–4
  Palmer and 147
  peasants 121, 123, 125, 131
  Tocqueville and 87
Lenin 115
Lesueur, Abbé 74
Levasseur, Pierre Emile 142
Lewis, Gwynne 135, 176, 193
Lewis, Tess 40
liberals
  Acton 48–9
  Carlyle and 52, 56, 57
  Constant 35, 48
  de Staël 2, 10, 35, 36–40, 184, 196
  Furet 166
  generally 35–49
  Guizot and 67
  meaning 6, 35, 49
  Mignet 3, 35, 40–1, 43–8
  pioneers 40–1
  Roederer 35, 48
  rule of law 39
  themes 36, 44
  Thiers 35, 40–3, 52, 65, 79
Liberation 1944 159
liberty
  Acton 49
  Burke 12–13
  Committee of Public Safety 49
  Constant 48
  de Staël 39
  liberal historiography 36
  Mignet 43, 44, 46, 47
  St-Just 46
  Thiers 42
  Tocqueville 82
  Wollstonecraft 18
Liberty Fund 93–4
Lille 185
Limoges 77
Lorraine 98
Loubinoux, Gérard 193
Louis XIV 44
Louis XVI 16, 19, 56, 60, 95, 102–3, 117, 163
Louis XVIII 47, 67

Louis Philippe 42–3, 63, 65, 67
Loutchitsky, J. 142
Louvre Pyramid 170
Lucas, Colin 142, 166
Lyon 45, 185

Macaulay, Thomas Babington 7
McManners, John 137
McPhee, Peter 185–6, 188
Madelin, Louis 105–6
Magna Carta 171
Maillard, Huissier 55
Maistre, Joseph de 2, 7, 9, 22, 24–9, 53, 196
Mallet du Pan, Jacques 10, 22
Malouet, Pierre Victor 181
Marat, Jean-Paul 40
Marie-Antoinette, Queen 36, 182
Marseillaise, La 175
Marseilles 186–7
Martin, Germain 142
Martin, Jean-Clément 194
Martin, Xavier 192
Marx, Karl 65, 85–6, 112–14, 178
Marxist orthodoxy
  Annales school 112
  bicentenary re-evaluations 176–8
  bourgeois revolution 6, 113–16, 118, 122–5, 128–9, 131, 149, 156
  causes of revolution 116–17
  class 116–17, 131
  generally 111–31
  Godechot 128–9
  Great Tradition and 149
  Guérin 129, 164
  hijacking of Great Tradition 3–4, 111
  Jaurès 65, 103, 111, 117–18, 128, 142, 143
  Labrousse 127, 129
  Lefebvre see Lefebvre, Georges
  Mathiez see Mathiez, Albert
  Michelet and 65
  political activists 112
  pseudo-science 135–6, 139
  Reinhard 129

revisionist demolition 134–43
Rudé 129–30, 148, 177, 178, 183
and Russian Revolution 115, 119–20
Soboul *see* Soboul, Albert
see also hard revisionists; soft revisionists
Mason, Laura 193
Mathiez, Albert
vs Aulard 104–5, 119
class struggle 120
vs Cobban 143. 119
influence 121, 128
Jaurès legacy 119
Marxist orthodoxy 104, 111, 118–21
Robespierre 119, 120–1
Russian Revolution and 119–20, 161, 196
Melzer, Sara 194
memoirs 100–1
Michelet, Jules
anti-clericalism 62, 69
Carlyle and 64
Cobban on 73
Great Tradition 58
legacy 65
Middle Ages 51, 67
peuple, le 51, 57, 59–62, 114, 124, 127–8, 130, 186
political context 57, 71, 119, 196
Quinet and 69
republicanism 114
Romantic historian 57–65
Sieyès 64
Middle Ages 51, 52, 57, 67, 70
Mignet, François 3, 35, 40–1, 43–8, 52
Mill, John Stuart 52–3
Mirabeau, Comte de 83
Mitterrand, François 169–71
Montagnards 126
Montauban 21
Montesquieu, Charles de 24, 100, 183
Mornet, Daniel 193

Muret, C. 27
Murray, J. 25, 28

Napoleon I 47–8, 57, 101–2, 162
Napoleon III 63, 76
National Assembly 1, 13–14, 16, 17, 28, 46, 83
National Convention 19, 28
National Workshops 70
nationality
Anglo-Saxon v French historians 7, 124, 131, 135, 137, 145
centrality of French historians 154
early history 9, 10, 29
Furet and 154
National, Le 41
Nazis 24
Necker, Jacques 37, 181
Necker, Suzanne 37
neo-liberalism 164
Newton, Isaac 157
Nivernais 125
Nord Department 121–2, 185
Northcutt, Wayne 65

O'Brien, Conor Cruise 64
Offen, Karen 182
Ozouf, Mona 179, 181

Paine, Thomas 10, 17–20, 29, 56, 196
Palmer, R.R. 65, 73, 124, 129, 147
papacy 26–7
Paris, research on 185, 186, 194
Paris Commune 43, 94
Parker, Noel 6, 25, 43, 69, 128, 148
Past & Present 129
peasants 121, 123, 125, 131, 136–7, 181
Petrey, S. 181
Peyrard, Christine 192, 194
Phillips, C.S. 25
philosophes 1–2, 24, 28, 81, 94, 97, 100, 146, 157–8, 164, 183

Plutarch 65
Pocock, J.G.A. 163
Popkin, J.D. 182
postmodernism 195
pre-historiography *see* immediate
    responses
press 182, 193
Prévost, Abbé 157
Prieur de la Côte d'Or 174
Protestantism 69, 146
provinces 97–8
Prussian War 1870 43, 63, 91, 94
pseudo-science 135–6, 139

Quinet, Edgar 51, 68–9, 71, 151,
    179

Rabine, Leslie 194
Radical Socialist Party 104
radicalism
    1848 63, 68
    Carlyle 56
    meaning 6
    Michelet 63
Reedy, W. Jay 22
Refort, Lucien 57
regional studies 185–9, 193–4
Reinhard, Marcel 129
religion *see* Catholic Church
republicanism
    anti-clericalism 104
    Aulard 90–1, 99–100, 102, 104,
        114, 196
    centenary celebrations 170
    nineteenth-century historians
        114
Restoration 41, 67
revisionism
    compulsion 144
    hard *see* hard revisionists
    meaning 6, 195–6
    post-revisionism 189
    soft revisionism *see* soft revi-
        sionists
    Vovelle on 174
Révolution française 90
Richet, Dennis 151, 162, 163–4
rights of man 1, 170

Rivarol, Antoine 10, 22
Roberts, Andrew 176
Robespierre, Maximilien 40, 45,
    48, 49, 61, 70, 97, 117, 119,
    120–1, 171, 182
Robinet, Jean François 105–6
Roederer, Pierre Louis 35, 48
Romantics
    Blanc 51, 69–70, 73
    Carlyle 51, 52–7, 64, 71, 130
    Comte 7, 51, 70
    generally 51–71
    Guizot 51, 52, 63, 65–8, 71,
        130, 151
    Lamartine 51, 69–70
    Michelet *see* Michelet, Jules
    Middle Ages and 51, 52, 57, 67,
        70
    Quinet 51, 68–9, 71, 151, 179
    Thierry 70
Rose, Barry 182, 194
Rouen 77
Rouget de Lisle, Claude Joseph
    174–5
Rousseau, Jean-Jacques 24, 146,
    157, 183
Roustan, Marius 97
Rudé, George 129–30, 148, 177,
    178, 183
Russian Revolution 95–6, 115,
    119–20, 161, 196

Saint-Aubin monastery 146
St-Just, Louis de 45–6, 181
St-Simon, Claude Henri de 7, 56
sans-culottes 116, 117, 124,
    126–7, 148, 179, 186
Savoy 25
Schama, Simon 164–5, 174–6,
    179
Scott, Walter 7
Secher, Reynald 188–9
Second Republic 63, 76
Sédillot, René 181
Sieyès, Abbé 2, 47, 64–5, 100,
    163, 179
singing 193
Slavin, Morris 155

Soboul, Albert
  Annales editor 121
  Atlantic revolution and 147
  bourgeois revolution 124–5,
    128
  vs Cobban 139, 140–1, 142, 143
  Lefebvre and 123
  legacy 128, 148
  Marxist orthodoxy 111, 124–8
  peasants 125, 131
  sans-culottes 126–7, 148, 186
  Terror, the 164
  on Tocqueville 124–5, 128
Socialist Party 1, 170
Société de L'Histoire de la
    Révolution 90
Société des Études
    Robespierristes 121
Society for the Friends of Unity
    and Equality 103
socio-cultural history 164
soft revisionists
  Behrens 137
  Cobb 148, 181
  Cobban see Cobban, Alfred
  Doyle 147, 156, 174, 181, 189
  Egret 137
  generally 134–49
  Hampson see Hampson,
    Norman
  McManners 137
  meaning 134
  Palmer 65, 73, 124, 129, 147
  political context 138–9
  significance 148–9
  Taylor 135, 143–4, 154, 156,
    158, 165
  tenets 135–7
  Thompson 135, 146–7
Soltau, Roger 25, 29
Soviet Union 138, 152, 164, 188
Spreckelsen, Johan Otto von 169
Staël, Germaine de 2, 10, 36–40,
    69, 184, 196
  liberal perspective 35
Starkey, David 176
Steiner, G. 27, 28
Sutherland, Donald 166, 197

Symcox, Geoffrey 123–4, 128

Tackett, Timothy 193
Taine, Hyppolite 193
  anti-revolutionary perspective 3,
    91–2, 103, 107, 127
  vs Aulard 90–1, 98, 105
  on Carlyle 64
  causes of revolution 94, 97
  generally 90–8
  glorification of provinces 97–8
  Great Tradition and 91
  influences 94
  Liberty Fund and 93–4
  methods 93
  Prussian War and 119, 196
  Tocqueville and 87
Tarcov, Nathan 166
Tarle, Eugene 142
Taylor, G.V. 135, 143–4, 154,
    156, 158, 165
Temple, Nora 196
Tennis Court Oath 122, 195
Terror, the
  Aulard 102
  Blanc 70
  Burke 12
  Carlyle 56–7
  contextualisation 188
  de Maistre 26
  de Staël 37–40
  debate 192
  Furet 161–2, 164
  liberal historians 49
  Marxist historians 117
  Mathiez 120, 120–1
  Michelet 59, 61
  Mignet 43, 45, 46
  Quinet 69
  Roederer 48
  Schama 175
  Soboul 164
  Taine 97
  Thiers 42
  Tocqueville 80
Thatcher, Margaret 171
theatre 193
Thierry, Augustin 70

Thiers, Auguste
  causes of Revolution 79
  Cobban on 52
  historian politician 35, 36, 41,
    42–3, 65
  liberal perspective 3, 35
  origin of Great Tradition 40–3
Third Estate 13, 26, 46, 54, 59,
  64
Third Republic historians
  Aulard see Aulard, Alphonse
  Funck-Brentano 97, 106
  Gaxotte 106
  generally 3, 90–107
  Madelin 105–6
  Robinet 105–6
  Taine see Taine, Hyppolite
Thompson, E.P. 111
Thompson, J.M. 135, 146–7
Tilly, Charles 187–8
Tocqueville, Alexis de
  1848 Revolution 71, 73, 76–8,
    87
  ambiguous position 3
  America 75
  Ancien Régime 80–1, 87
  background 74, 161, 196
  centralised government 83–4
  destruction of feudalism 124–5
  Furet and 79, 81, 85–6, 87,
    151, 160–1
  generally 73–88
  historian politician 75–6
  historical method 78
  legacy 74, 86–8, 128, 165
  liberalism 82
  lines of enquiry 81–2
  Marx and 85–6, 114
  perspective 79–80
  philosophical history 79
  religion 74
  revolutionary continuity 82–6,
    147, 160
  Soboul and 124–5, 128

  style 79
  Taine and 94
Toulon 185
Tracy, Destutt de 7
Tubeuf, Pierre-François 194

Ultras 25
United States 75

Vallon, Madame 184
Varennes flight 55–6
Vendée 1, 172, 184, 187–9,
  194
Vergniaud, Pierre 120, 175
Vichy government 122, 159
Vico, Giambattista 58
Voltaire 24, 100, 146, 157
Vovelle, Michel 121, 125, 166,
  173, 174

Weber, Max 65
Winock, Michel 24, 29
Wollstonecraft, Mary 17–18, 19,
  29, 183
women
  Aulard 103
  bicentenary publications on
    182–5
  de Staël 40
  historians 196
  recent studies 194–5
Woodcock, George 19
working class
  Godechot 129
  Lefebvre 123
  Marxist historians 116
  Michelet see Michelet, Jules
  Soboul 126–7
  see also sans culottes

Yalom, Marilyn 183, 184–5
Young, Arthur 2, 10, 20–2

Zhou Enlai 1, 197